Human–Computer Interaction Series

Editors-in-Chief

Desney Tan
Microsoft Research, Redmond, WA, USA

Jean Vanderdonckt
Louvain School of Management, Université catholique de Louvain,
Louvain-La-Neuve, Belgium

The Human–Computer Interaction Series, launched in 2004, publishes books that advance the science and technology of developing systems which are effective and satisfying for people in a wide variety of contexts. Titles focus on theoretical perspectives (such as formal approaches drawn from a variety of behavioural sciences), practical approaches (such as techniques for effectively integrating user needs in system development), and social issues (such as the determinants of utility, usability and acceptability).

HCI is a multidisciplinary field and focuses on the human aspects in the development of computer technology. As technology becomes increasingly more pervasive the need to take a human-centred approach in the design and development of computer-based systems becomes ever more important.

Titles published within the Human–Computer Interaction Series are included in Thomson Reuters' Book Citation Index, The DBLP Computer Science Bibliography and The HCI Bibliography.

More information about this series at http://www.springer.com/series/6033

Alia El Bolock · Yomna Abdelrahman ·
Slim Abdennadher
Editors

Character Computing

Editors
Alia El Bolock
German University in Cairo
Cairo, Egypt

Ulm University
Ulm, Germany

Slim Abdennadher
German University in Cairo
Cairo, Egypt

Yomna Abdelrahman
Bundeswehr University Munich
Neubiberg, Germany

ISSN 1571-5035   ISSN 2524-4477   (electronic)
Human–Computer Interaction Series
ISBN 978-3-030-15956-6   ISBN 978-3-030-15954-2   (eBook)
https://doi.org/10.1007/978-3-030-15954-2

This Springer imprint is published by the registered company Springer Nature Switzerland AG
The registered company address is: Gewerbestrasse 11, 6330 Cham, Switzerland

To anyone who ever taught us anything.

Preface

Character Computing is defined as any computing that incorporates the human character within its context. The character is the individual person with all of his/her defining or describing features. This includes stable personality traits, variable affective, cognitive and motivational states as well as history, morals, beliefs, skills, appearance, and sociocultural embeddings, to name a few. In practical terms, depending on the application context, Character Computing is a branch of research that deals with the design of systems and interfaces that can observe, sense, predict, adapt to, affect, understand, or simulate the following: character based on behavior and situation, behavior based on character and situation, or situation based on character and behavior. Character Computing can be divided into three main research modules: character sensing and profiling, character-aware adaptive systems, and artificial characters.

Since the introduction of the term "Character Computing" by El Bolock et al., it captured the attention of researchers from diverse research fields ranging from HCI, character modeling, to Psychology. Character Computing is envisioned to be a rapidly growing field, as technologies and computer systems are becoming ubiquitously integrated into our daily lives. This raised the need for a seamless, natural user interface to support daily users. This is reflected in the vast amount of research conducted in the context of user-aware and adaptive interfaces over the past years. Character Computing will exhibit similar importance to that of the well-established Affective Computing field. Affective Computing aims to allow the machine to understand the users' nonverbal communications. For instance, use implicit facial expressions, body postures, gaze, and voice tones to infer the emotional state, as well as, responding accordingly or even exhibiting affects through the interaction modalities. The greater goal would be more seamless natural human–computer interaction. This will provide users a better personalized experience. Further, this will influence the performance of the user, where they will have the support of the machines to achieve their tasks in the most efficient way.

This book is the first of a kind in introducing Character Computing. It provides an overview of the character dimensions and how state-of-the-art technologies would accommodate such a research field. It presents a novel representation of character from various perspectives. Further, this book presents the initial original results as well as the potential deployment of this emerging research field.

The book consists of nine chapters. Since Character Computing is a reasonably novel term, the first part of this book (Chaps. 1–4) presents the background and means of defining characters using different approaches. Chapter 1 defines the term "Character" and focuses on the Character–Behavior–Situation triad and the different modules of Character Computing. While Chap. 2 tackles it from an experimental-psychological approach, and Chap. 3 depicts the psychologically driven, user-aware approach for character modeling. Chapter 4 presents possible applications, challenges, and opportunities within the scope of Character Computing. Chapters 5–9 present the deployment potential of Character Computing and how it would merge into existing fields, to fulfill the vision of Character Computing.

In the following, a brief introduction to the book chapters is presented. Chapter 1 presents a detailed explanation and definition of Character Computing, its components, scope, modules, and implication of the introduced field. Chapter 2 covers the experimental-psychological approach for character modeling. The first part of this chapter discusses how psychological theories of human behavior have inspired the fields of Cognitive Computing, Affective Computing, and Personality Computing. Next, a holistic psychological definition of human behavior is provided to describe human behavior in the context of the Character–Behavior–Situation triad. Additionally, this chapter discusses how psychological understanding of human behavior can guide and improve future research in the domain of Character Computing. Finally, an experimental-psychological framework for Character Computing is discussed considering Character Computing from an interdisciplinary perspective. Chapter 3 extends the modeling of character by presenting a psychologically driven, user-aware approach modeling. This chapter describes how Character Computing can be empirically realized and validated. The psychologically driven interdisciplinary framework for Character Computing is outlined and how it is realized empirically as Character Computing platform. Particular focus in this chapter is laid on experimental validation of the Character Computing approach, including concrete laboratory experiments. This chapter adds to Chap. 2 which discussed the different steps of the Character Computing framework more broadly with respect to specific use cases and applications in the wild. Chapter 4 presents possible applications and state-of-the-art extensions for each of the three Character Computing modules, as well as the challenges and opportunities presented by each module.

Chapter 5 proposes the link between Character Computing and the well-established field of Human–Computer Interaction (HCI), and how HCI could benefit from the emerging field of Character Computing. This chapter presents possible indicators of users' character from the HCI literature, discussing possibilities of recognizing and expressing character. Additionally, this chapter gives insights about potential application domains that might benefit from Character Computing as an emerging field. Lastly, this chapter discusses potential concerns, being as any fields, while Character Computing might open up novel interaction opportunities, it raises concerns from the various perspective from interaction concerns to privacy and ethical concerns. In Chap. 6, the role of emotion and personality is described from several aspects reflecting the current state of the art. First, a general idea of emotion, mood, and personality with their basic theories as well as psychological and computational aspects is discussed. Furthermore, human interaction with an emotional machine is described. This chapter reflects the aspect of affective systems that deals with the assessment of human emotion by a computer system. Apart from computer vision, wearable computing, social media, and virtual reality provide data that is used to learn about the emotional state and personality of an interaction partner. This leads to the model of a complete character rather than a system which just reflects short-term affective reactions to events and perceptions. Part of this character is the personality, but also the personal interaction history, which in turn contributes to habits and environment knowledge, which all in all explain the behavior. It further describes other aspects that deal with emotion and autonomy. Chapter 7 presents the state-of-the-art trends of affect sensing. In this chapter, the authors discuss the stages of sensing affect based on the facial expression, starting from face localization, registration, feature extraction, and state classification. Since our affect is linked to other modalities. This chapter also gives an overview of how speech is one of the explicit communication channels, yet embeds implicit (paralinguistic) information. The implicit information can be used to infer the users' affect state. Further, this chapter discusses body gesture as an affect indicator. Lastly, it lists the widely used physiological sensors for detecting affect including Electrocardiography (ECG), Electroencephalography (EEG), Galvanic Skin Response (GSR), Photoplethysmography (PPG), Electromyography (EMG), and Piezoelectric Respiration Sensor (PZT). Additionally, this chapter discusses the challenges of using all the modalities mentioned above in Character Computing. The later sections of this chapter present personality computing and its models and platforms. The last section of this chapter delisted the architectural layers of the framework for Character Computing Internet of Things (CIoT). The framework comprises the sensing layer, data collection/processing, support systems, and Character Computing services. Chapter 8 looks into how to build characters for digital agents, with the focus on personalization purposes. This chapter introduces a method to distill use case-specific personality features from user interactions with broadly diverse characters. Further, it identifies personality dimensions for characters of digital agents. In this chapter, the authors present the results from an empirical user study on designing and building agent's characters in the context of in-car voice assistants. Finally, Chap. 9 reviews the aspects of character in logical agents. This chapter presents an algebraic logical language which is expressive enough to facilitate the identification of several dimensions along which characters of logical agents may vary.

We would like to acknowledge the people without whom the book and the emerging field it describes would not have been possible. We thank Springer Nature for the opportunity to be part of the Human–Computer Interaction series. We especially thank Nancy Wade-Jones, James Finlay, Helen Desmond, and Beverley Ford for their continuous support. This book would not have been possible without the valuable and unique contributions of the authors. We sincerely thank them for contributing to this book and emerging field. We would like to thank the team of the Department of Computer Science, Faculty of Media Engineering and Technology, the German University in Cairo. They have provided both technical and moral support and were always there to discuss ideas. The Department of Applied Emotion and Motivation Psychology, Ulm University under the supervision of Prof. Dr. Cornelia Herbert provided major Psychology consultations and insights into the discussed topic. We thank Arwa Ismail for her huge help with the proof-reading of the book, even from a distance. We thank our dear friends and family members for their support and belief in Character Computing from the get-go. Enumerating them would require an extra book, but we believe they know who they are. Sincere thanks to God and everyone who was involved in the process of developing Character Computing and accordingly this book! We owe this to you!

Cairo, Egypt   Alia El Bolock

February 2020   Yomna Abdelrahman

                         Slim Abdennadher

Contents

Contributors

Yomna Abdelrahman Bundeswehr University Munich, Neubiberg, Germany

Slim Abdennadher German University in Cairo, Cairo, Egypt

Florian Alt Bundeswehr University and LMU Munich, Munich, Germany

Michael Braun BMW Group Research, New Technologies, Innovations, LMU Munich, Munich, Germany

Alia El Bolock Department of Computer Science, German University in Cairo, Cario, Egypt;
Department of Emotion and Motivation Psychology, Ulm University, Ulm, Germany

Amr El Mougy German University in Cairo, Cairo, Egypt

Cornelia Herbert Applied Emotion and Motivation Psychology, Institute of Psychology and Education, Faculty of Engineering, Computer Science and Psychology, Ulm University, Ulm, Germany;
German University in Cairo, Cairo, Egypt

Haythem O. Ismail Department of Engineering Mathematics, Cairo University, Cairo, Egypt;
Department of Computer Science, German University in Cairo, Cairo, Egypt

Dirk Reichardt DHBW Stuttgart, Stuttgart, Germany

Chapter 1
What Is Character Computing?

Alia El Bolock

Abstract In this chapter, Character Computing is introduced and defined. To do so, character itself is defined as all components that determine human behavior in a specific situation. It consists of general, stable factors (e.g., personality and socio-cultural embeddings) and current factors (e.g., affect, mood, physical state, appearance, and cognitive state). Accordingly, Character Computing is all research on the Character–Behavior–Situation triad which gives insight into the interaction of the three components and how to model said interactions. Character Computing consists of three research modules: sensing the character, adapting to the character, and developing artificial characters. Most existing research toward any of these modules focuses on one aspect such as affect or personality and only takes the perspective of one discipline such as Psychology or Computer Science. Character Computing proposes addressing these questions from a joint perspective of Computer Science and Psychology while focusing on all relevant aspects making up a human being. The aim is providing an interdisciplinary, application-specific framework of human behavior in a specific situation given the human's character.

1.1 Introduction and Overview

Humans are different! This is the one fact that holds for all humans. No two people have exactly the same constellation of behavior, beliefs, appearance, or presence and thus no two should be described in the same way.

We use descriptive words to represent individuals all the time. When talking about someone specific, we might describe their appearance using adjectives such as "tall", "beautiful", "fat", or "long haired". These descriptions help build a specific picture in our minds, no matter how prejudiced or stereotypical it sounds. Alternately, we might describe them in terms of their current state or their behavior toward a specific

A. El Bolock (✉)
Department of Computer Science, German University in Cairo,
Cario, Egypt

Department of Emotion and Motivation Psychology, Ulm University, Ulm, Germany
e-mail: alia.elbolock@guc.edu.eg

© Springer Nature Switzerland AG 2020
A. El Bolock et al. (eds.), *Character Computing*, Human–Computer Interaction Series,
https://doi.org/10.1007/978-3-030-15954-2_1

situation or person. This is done by using words like "angry", "amused", "caring", "mean", "meticulous", or "shy". But we can also describe them in terms of their status, history, and background, to name a few, i.e., "young", "married", "rich", "European", and "Liberal". The former and the latter representations will form an image of this individual based on the built-in predispositions in our minds. If we combine the adjectives from the different representations, we will have a more complete picture that is still mostly stereotypical but probably closer to the truth.

For millennia, the description of humans and their different "types" have been investigated by Greek philosophers such as Homer (1999) and Theophrastus (1904), psychologists such as Freud and Jung (Pervin and John 1999), as well as literary authors (Mowrer 1950) and even game designers (Zammitto et al. 2008).

Differences in human behavior are the leading motivation for many research fields, starting from arts and ending with technology. Exploring human behavior and its driving forces has become one of the most important scientific fields in human-centered Computer Science and not only Psychology. As described in Chap. 2, psychological research and theories constitute building blocks for Cognitive, Affective, and Personality Computing and are crucial for providing a framework for Character Computing.

Because no two humans are alike, there is no size-fits-all equation for human-centered computer science. This inspired the need for adding computer science directions that put factors of humans at the center of technology as investigated by subfields of human–computer interaction, namely, Affective Computing (Picard 1997) and the newly emerging Personality Computing (Vinciarelli and Mohammadi 2014).

Affective Computing adds human emotions to the equation to provide more personalized user experiences. Picard describes it as "...computing that relates to, arises from, or influences emotions" (Picard 1997, P. 1.). This shows the broad nature of research and applications enabled within Affective Computing. It aims at detecting emotional states from different behavioral cues and adapting to them or sometimes altering them. How and when machines should exhibit emotions is also a field of research within Affective Computing. The need for Affective Computing has long been proven in its more than 25 years of history, highlighting why it is essential to include emotions into computational considerations.

While Affective Computing successfully advocated the need for emotions in technology, Personality Computing has started doing the same for another component of human representation, namely, the personality. Personality Computing can be described as computing that aims at automatically recognizing, perceiving, and synthesizing human personality. For the purposes of Personality Computing, personality is mainly represented using trait theory's most popular model, namely, the Five Factor Model (FFM) (Allport and Odbert 1936; Goldberg 1992). Albeit being a young field, there has already been lots of research into Personality Computing even if not initially done under its umbrella.

However, the individual differences between humans cannot be accounted for using personality or affect alone. This is because, given the same situation, two humans with opposing personality traits could experience different emotions. When forced to give a public presentation, for example, one individual could be beaming with excitement, the other sweating in dread. Also, the same person with the same personality can experience different emotions given the same situation. An easygoing teacher might usually tolerate the class clown, but snap at him/her on a day where something out of the usual strongly provoked the teacher.

This is why representing humans by five discrete traits—even if accounting for their interactions—or by their emotions alone is not enough. The former might account for the individual differences between humans and the latter might account for the differences within one human (e.g., differences in affect at two distinct times). But even if we combine the two, it is still not enough to capture the essence of humans and thus account for their core differences. In order to truly form a coherent image about an individual, we require much more than only the emotions and the personality. Depending on the image we need to form, we can either include or exclude different representation factors.

Consider, for example, the easygoing teacher and what might have triggered him to lose his temper at this instance although he is usually calm even if he is having a bad day. It could be that this teacher is currently explaining cancer to his students, to which he just lost a loved one. This would have a teacher on edge resulting in this unexpected reaction from him. In this instance, the emotions can only be explained by taking the history into consideration.

This requires us to consider the human as a whole, i.e., the character (as first proposed in El Bolock 2018; El Bolock et al. 2018, 2017). The character is the individual person with all his/her defining or describing features. As depicted in Fig. 1.1, this includes stable personality traits, variable affective, cognitive, and motivational states as well as history, morals, beliefs, skills, appearance, and sociocultural embeddings, to name a few (as will be described in more detail in Chap. 2).

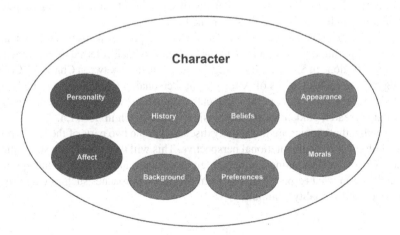

Fig. 1.1 A depiction of some of the components that can be included in a human's character, in addition to the most commonly investigated personality and affect

As most daily interactions now involve technology, we need to have computing that actually relates to, arises from, or influences characters, namely, the whole definition of an individual.

As the next step toward further putting humans at the center of technology, novel interdisciplinary approaches such as Character Computing are developing. Character Computing combines, builds on, and moves past Affective and Personality Computing by adding more than only human affect or five personality factors to the equation. This extension and fusion between the different computing approaches within Character Computing is based on well-controlled empirical and theoretical knowledge from Psychology. This is done by including the whole human character as a central part of any artificial interaction. An artificial interaction is any interaction with technology, be it an adaptive or interactive application, a smart assistant, an agent-based system, or any other computing platform involving human–computer interaction.

Character Computing is any computing that incorporates the human character within its context. In practical terms, depending on the application context, it is computing that senses, predicts, adapts to, affects, or simulates (1) character based on behavior and situation, (2) behavior based on character and situation, or (3) situation based on character and behavior.

Character Computing has three main modules that complement each other but can each also be investigated and leveraged on its own:

- Character sensing and profiling,
- Character-aware adaptive systems, and
- Artificial characters.

The aim of this chapter is to shortly introduce Character Computing and its major components to provide an overview of the field and its far-reaching scope. It presents the various research challenges of Character Computing and suggests different research directions to pursue in the field.

In order to demonstrate the scope of Character Computing and its potential advantages and opportunities, we first need to further define what is referred to as character, which will be done in Sect. 1.2. By doing so, the distinction between Character Computing and the existing fields of Affective and Personality Computing will be highlighted. In Sect. 1.3, the scope of Character Computing will be presented. Finally, the future research guidelines and conclusion will be given in Sect. 1.4.

Crucially, these topics are thoroughly discussed in the two parts of the book from a psychological and computational perspective. This will then lead to the suggestion of how Character Computing can be implemented and realized in basic and applied research and in what respect it differs from previous approaches such as Cognitive, Affective, or Personality Computing.

1.2 What Is Character?

The word "character" originated from the Middle English, Old French word "carac-tere" via Latin from the original Greek word "kharaktēr" which means a stamping tool. This early meaning referred to distinctive marks, i.e., features and traits that can be used as distinguishing qualities.[1]

Over the centuries, the use of the term "character" was enriched with various con-notations depending on the contexts it was used in. The term is used, for example, in psychology, philosophy, linguistics, and computing, however, with different mean-ing. Therefore, the term "character" has many nuances only partly overlapping with and complementing each other. Depending on who you talk to, a specific meaning of character will come to mind:

- In Psychology, the term is used to describe a person's psychological makeup, his/her temperament, mental disposition as well as his/her personality traits which together make up the person's identity (McAdams 2008; Pervin and John 1999).
- Sociologists and philosophers use the term "character" mainly to refer to the moral qualities and thus the virtue of a person (Sherman 1989).
- Writers will think of the literal characters such as the antagonist and protagonist with their identifying roles in the plot of a story (Gerrig and Allbritton 1990).
- From the perspective of movies, TV, and especially games, "character" has a sim-ilar interpretation to that of writers. However, in addition to the mental capacities of the character, the embodiment of the character—i.e., its bodily constitution and appearance—also matters (Cohen 2001; Isbister 2006).

These are only a few of the different interpretations of the term "character" from the perspective of the different domains it is used in. Within the interdisciplinary framework of Character Computing, we consider character from a holistic point of view to represent any and all distinguishing qualities of an individual.

As will be explained in more detail throughout the first part of this book, by the term "character" we consider *all* defining qualities that distinguish individuals from one another. It is all characteristics of a person, including personality as in Personality Computing. However, it also includes the temporary more short-lift and situation-specific factors of a person's character such as affective and motivation state as in Affective Computing. Moreover, it also includes a person's background, his/her social embeddings, morals, beliefs, skills, habits, hopes, dreams, concerns, appearance, presentation, gestures, likes, and dislikes (a similar notion of character, from a moral point of view, is presented in Nucci 2018). Which of those to include into the Character Computing model may depend on the current situation. Of course, the abovementioned components of a human's character are not mutually exclusive and overlap together in many ways and help shape and change each other. For exam-ple, an individual's personality is known to be shaped by their genetics, emotional

---

[1] Character. (n.d.) In Merriam-Webster's collegiate dictionary. Retrieved from http://www.merriam-webster.com/dictionary/character.

states, their cognitive processes, learned behaviors, and many other factors. But still considering each of these components could provide extra identifying information that may predict behavior of a particular person in a specific situation.

1.2.1 The Character–Behavior–Situation Triad

As will be further explained in Chap. 2 and the first part of the book, Character Computing is based on a holistic psychologically driven model of human behavior. Human behavior is modeled and predicted based on the relationships between a situation and a human's character.

The one certain thing is that character is at the center of humans and their relations. For any system to be able to deal with humans as efficiently as possible, it first needs to understand their character. Only in defining what something is and what it is not can we truly understand it.

To further define character in a more formal or holistic manner, we represent it in light of the Character–Behavior–Situation triad. This highlights that character not only determines who we are but how we are, i.e., how we behave. The triad is an extension of the recurring Personality–Behavior–Situation triad of Personality Psychology (Corr and Matthews 2009).

Any member of the Personality–Behavior–Situation triad is a function of the two other members, as shown in Fig. 1.2. In other words, given the situation and personality, the behavior can be predicted, given the behavior and situation, the personality can be predicted, and finally given the behavior and personality, the situation can be predicted.

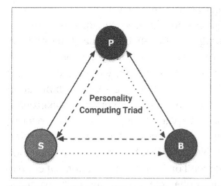 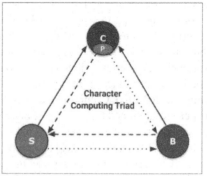

(a) The Personality (P) - Behavior (B) - Situation (S) Triad from Personality Psychology.

(b) The Updated Character (C) - Behavior (B) - Situation (S) Triad from Character Computing with Personality as a subset of Character.

Fig. 1.2 A figure representing the original triad and the updated Character Computing triad, in which Personality is included in character

Of course, as will be shown later, these assumptions are oversimplified as each of the components in the triad can be further decomposed into smaller units and features that may best represent the human's behavior or character in a particular situation.

The triad investigated in Personality Psychology is extended through Character Computing (see Fig. 1.2) to the Character–Behavior–Situation triad. The term character is not just replacing the term personality. Instead, it is rather the personality, cultural, and social predispositions and other stable characteristics as well as temporally less stable characteristics such as affective states.

To further highlight why all character components need to be considered in the triad and not only personality, let us go back to the example of the easygoing teacher who snaps at a student which is out of character for him. We discussed one possible cause which required being familiar with his history, namely, the death of a loved one from cancer. Imagine another scenario where this teacher is an African American history teacher currently explaining Institutionalized Racism. His being African American, i.e., his culture and appearance are the main trigger for his unusual behavior (see Banks 1988).

Character is thus behind a person's behavior in any given situation. While this is a causality relation, the correlation between the three components is often more easily utilized to predict the components that are most difficult to measure from those measured more easily.

Importantly, how can the Character (C)–Behavior (B)–Situation (S) triad be translated into a computational model of Character Computing? The triad can be represented as the triple (C, B, S), where C represents the Character, B the behavior, and S the situation. C is itself a pair of *Traits* and *States*. We define the three main functions relating the three components together as follows:

1. $C = observe(B, S)$,
2. $B = predict(C, S)$, and
3. $S = understand(C, B)$.

One main endeavor of Character Computing is thus to calculate the models representing the three functions: *observe*, *predict*, and *understand*.

As mentioned above and as discussed in the next section, there are infinitely many components to include in the representation of any of C, B, and S. The challenge is always to choose the smallest subset needed for prediction of a person's behavior in a particular situation and the most accurate abstracted representation of *observe*, *predict*, and *understand*.

The ultimate goal is to have a unifying theory of human behavior that can entail and predict how a person behaves—based on his/her character—in a particular situation.

Still, this is a far-reaching goal, requiring collecting a huge amount of information about each individual, which is not scalable or maintainable.

Thus, we approach this from a more application-specific point of view. We narrow down the goal to develop models based on the triad depending on the domain of the current human interaction application in question. Character Computing aims at investigating the most efficient way to collect the minimal amount of needed information to develop a psychologically driven model that can be generalized to human behavior with the least amount of input, for the purposes of the current application or domain of applications.

1.2.2 Components of a Human Character

Given a detailed representation of the building blocks of a person's whole character and the situation they are in, a road map for accurately predicting their behavior given their character and a situation can be developed. Based on the holistic Character–Behavior–Situation triad the same may hold true for detecting the character or certain character components based on the behavior in a specific situation or the situation from the character and behavior, respectively. However, the challenge is that information required for making accurate predictions is not always available and possibly can never be obtained for all people. This necessitates the development of potentially smaller models to be trained to serve as accurate predictors of human behavior in particular situations. These models should find and operate with the smallest needed subset representing character, situation, and behavior. Depending on the use case or data collection medium in question, however, different variables, features, and facets representing markers for the situation (S), the behavior (B), and the character (C) are available and can serve as indicators of C, B, and S.

In the following, we discuss the core C components considered within Character Computing in more detail.

1.2.2.1 Personality Traits

Personality is one of the main components of the character that serves as a trait marker of character. Personality traits are one of the most considered characteristics of individuals in artificial interactions as shown by the following survey of Personality Computing [?], where different papers discussing automatic personality recognition, perception, and synthesis are summarized.

Personality traits are considered temporally stable and have been already considered in previous research on Personality Computing (for an overview, see Vinciarelli and Mohammadi 2014 and Chap. 2).

Psychological models of personality usually rely on validated questionnaires for determining a person's personality traits. People are asked to assess the truth of certain statements describing themselves or others. The main problem with this type of tests is that they are vulnerable to certain intentional or unintentional response biases toward socially favorable answers (Van de Mortel et al. 2008).

The most commonly used trait model is the **Five Factor Model (FFM)** or the Big-Five (BF) (Allport and Odbert 1936; Goldberg 1992). The five traits of the FFM are Extraversion, Agreeableness, Conscientiousness, Neuroticism, and Openness. There are different assessment questionnaires for the FFM with different lengths, items, and corresponding validity. The most commonly used are the NEO Inventories with their different lengths (McCrae et al. 2005). As extensions of the theory, some versions of the FFM questionnaires include also facets for each of the five traits giving more descriptive insight about each individual.

Other noteworthy trait-based personality models that have been used in research on Personality Computing (for an intensive overview refer to Corr and Matthews 2009; Pervin and John 1999) include the Myers–Briggs-Type Indicator (MBTI) (Myers et al. 2003), the Temperament and Character Inventory (Cloninger et al. 1998), the Sixteen Personality Factor Questionnaire (16PF) (Cattell and Mead 2008), Gray's bio-psychological theory of personality, and resulting Reinforcement Sensitivity Theory (RST) (Pickering and Corr 2008) (an extension of the BIS/BAS model Carver and White 1994). Most of these personality models can be mapped to each other (e.g., McCrae and Costa Jr 1989; De Fruyt et al. 2000). But as outlined in detail in Chap. 2, personality measures do not come without limitations.

1.2.2.2 Affective States and Mood

Affective states vary quickly and are not stable. They are easily changed by external factors and do not usually last long. We are intuitively familiar with the physiological presentation of emotions where people sweat or their voices shake in stressful situations or the cheek reddens when feeling shy. There are also some physical cues that are not externally observable but can be sensed such as labored breathing or increased heartbeat. Mood is the more general affective state which one has been in for some time. A person can be happy, in general, and thus has a positive mood but be currently angry because someone, for example, stepped on their foot. While the general mood will not change, the current affective state will have a negative valence and high arousal. However, the duration needed for an affected individual to return to his/her current normal happy mood depends on his/her emotion regulation (John and Gross 2004).

While the mood can be indicated using the same self-report methods as the affective states, but referring to the feeling over the past few weeks or months, it is more prone to errors and participant biases. That is why more research needs to leverage data and other cues for the detection of moods (for more details see Chaps. 5 and 7).

1.2.2.3 Cognitive and Motivational States and Beliefs

Cognition accounts for a big part of how humans process information and thus act on it. It is a systematic way for representing basic human behavior, as a cycle of input of stimuli from the environment, processing through a mediation mental event and thus producing an output as a behavior and/or emotion.

We expect humans to perfectly follow this process of acting in a "rational" way. However, this is seldom the case. Cognitive biases are responsible for affecting an individual's behavior in unexpected ways. They were considered as errors in systematic information processing that could be caused by different factors, such as lack of attention or inaccurate memory (triggered by a specific situation or a specific current state). However, these biases are quite natural and often occur and dictate behavior (Haselton et al. 2015). (For an extensive overview, see Pohl and Pohl 2004.) A few examples of biases that could affect behavior include the following:

- Bandwagon effect: overriding one's own belief to go along with the actions and thoughts of others.
- Hyperbolic discounting: settling for a smaller reward at the moment, instead of waiting for a larger one.
- Status quo bias: making choices that minimize change and maintain the current situation as much as possible.
- Anchoring: relying heavily on one piece of information (usually the most recent one) in decision-making.
- Neglect of probability: discounting actual probabilities based on internal factors and beliefs (such as phobias). An example would be avoiding planes for fear of accidents while normally driving cars.

The motivational state of an individual highly affects their current cognitive state and thus the resulting behavior (Banks 1988). Depending on the stable character traits, the motivational states could highly or mildly affect the current behavior.

Beliefs also dictate behavior, according to the Theory of Planned Behavior (Ajzen 1991). Beliefs are very closely related to cognition and cognitive states (Gilbert and Hixon 1991; Klaczynski 2000). Beliefs are thus highly defined by the current cognitive state and the resulting cognitive biases. If we consider the neglect of probability bias, we can see how one's beliefs are dictated by an individual's cognitive state and own perception.

1.2.2.4 Sociocultural Embeddings

One of the main factors contributing to who we are is where we are and where we have been. The culture someone was born into, their ethnicity, the culture they were raised in, and whether these two are aligned, all contribute in shaping certain characteristic predispositions. The same goes for the religious beliefs or lack thereof. The socioeconomic standard dictates how people perceive certain things and in turn how they react toward them (e.g., Banks 1988; Park 2002). Finally, the languages spoken, when they were acquired and in which context they are used are very telling characteristics. This relationship between language and a person's feelings, beliefs, and personality has been already frequently used in sentiment analysis (see Chap. 2).

Lots of research has been done into whether and why people exhibit different personalities or styles upon speaking different languages or being from different cultures (see Dewaele and Van Oudenhoven 2009; Haritatos and Benet-Martinez 2002).

In case of languages, it usually depends on the context within each language is primarily used and what it is most associated with (e.g., Veltkamp et al. 2013).

Neuroscientific research on affective language and the embodiment of language has provided novel insight into the neural mechanisms underlying this relationship (see Chap. 2). A certain language could be associated with a traumatic period in a person's life, and thus the person's demeanor while speaking in said language could be gloomier than in another language. The effect of different cultures is also the same. People raised with two different cultural backgrounds could have two "different" personalities depending on which culture they are currently operating in.

1.2.2.5 Morals

Morals and ethics are another driving force behind behavior. Ethics dictate morality through distinguishing between and categorizing actions as right or wrong and good or evil. Morals give a value to every behavior. It is thus a set of principles that serve as a guide toward which behavior helps or harms others (Richard and Egger 2011). Accordingly, people with high morals tend to avoid negative behavior and steer closer toward helpful and harmless behavior. Individuals who lack morals, however, are more prone to behave negatively, if it suits them. People like to that believe they live by and act upon their ethical standards. Despite this fact, morals are situation based (Doris 2002). Even the most helpful altruist might help someone when having enough time but rush by them when in a hurry.

1.3 Scope of Character Computing

Character Computing is not limited to one specific field or group of activities. Generally speaking, it is any type of computing where the whole human character is considered. Certainly, this is a very general definition and a very broad goal. In fact, any interaction with technology within the scope of Character Computing can be represented as an instance of the (C, B, S) triad.

A problem in any of the three main modules of Character Computing can easily be mapped to a triad problem. Sensing a specific trait, for example, is merely detecting the correlation between the B of a C in a specific S. Adapting an application can be modeled as predicting the B of a C in the S presented by the app, thus either preventing said B, changing it or simply acknowledging it. Finally, artificial character applications aim at simulating a specific B given an S to be consistent with a specific C.

There are many ways for representing the character, behavior, and situation, each having different components. The tree presented in Fig. 1.3 shows some possible components of each of the three elements of the (C, B, S) triad.

The character consists of a stable, general, and a current state. The general stable factor refers to the person's individual personality and sociocultural embeddings. Though minor changes in personality might occur in it over time, it usually remains the same unless major external or internal factors affect it. The current state of a

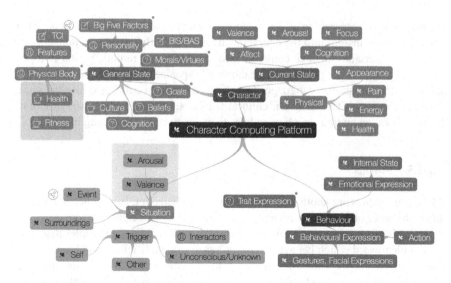

Fig. 1.3 Overview of all the interactions within Character Computing with all the possible components of C, B, and S

person's character consists of the affect during this given time, the mood over the past period, the current physical state of an individual as well as the current appearance and cognitive state.

The behavior is represented by the behavioral, emotional, and trait expression, which each reflects behavior at different levels. The behavior expression is the most externalized and thus the easiest to detect, as it is reflected in actions, gestures, and facial expressions although more subtle behavioral responses could be considered and included. In addition, changes in behavior could be measured via physiological markers.

The situation in which the behavior is displayed can be defined in various ways and different contexts. It can include social interactions with other persons including self-disclosure and emotion expression or empathy. It can be a discrete event or the environmental surroundings. It can include novel and familiar contexts that can directly impact a person's cognitive, motivational, and affective state either in a positive or negative, intense or mild way.

The illustrated interaction tree shows only four levels of depth. The tree can, however, be expanded to show much deeper and wider levels. The presented sample interactions merely serve to show how complex the whole endeavor is but in turn also how far-reaching the scope and its underlying potential.

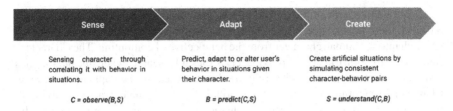

Fig. 1.4 The three main Character Computing modules and their relation to the (C, B, S) triad and its functions

1.3.1 Character Computing Modules

There are different scenarios and aspects to be investigated by Character Computing, in light of all the abovementioned Psychology branches and the wider scope of components to be included when representing the (C, B, S) triad.

Certainly, the holistic model displayed in Fig. 1.3 cannot be used as a starting point and can only be reached in an incremental module-based manner. Not all the variables and features presenting each of the three components of the (C, B, S) triad need to be considered at once, depending on the situations in which a particular behavior should be predicted. As a starting point, some abstractions need to be made.

Figure 1.4 shows an overview of the generic Character Computing framework, where each module can be investigated alone but also serves the bigger picture. The variables/components making up each module can be added and removed as desired.

In summary, these three modules of Character Computing complement each other but can each also be investigated and leveraged on its own:

- Sensing and profiling the character through ubiquitous or invasive sensors, subjective measures, and novel sensing techniques with the help of various technologies and domains such as IoT, Machine Learning, Big Data, Psychology, and Security. Serious privacy and security considerations play an integral part in this module.
- Leveraging characters to build ubiquitous character-aware systems and investigating which use cases would benefit from this adaptation.
- Investigating how to extend artificial intelligence to create artificial characters and when this would be needed.

Each of the modules will be discussed in more detail in Chap. 4, giving guidelines into what can or should be investigated. Important considerations while investigating applications of each module are outlined.

1.4 Conclusion: Theoretical and Practical Implications

This chapter gives an initial definition of Character Computing. This is done by highlighting what is considered as character. Character is all components that define human behavior in a specific situation. It consists of general, stable factors (e.g., personality and sociocultural embeddings), and current factors (e.g., affect, mood, physical state, appearance, and cognitive state). Character Computing focuses on research into the human character from the perspective of computing. The Character–Behavior–Situation triad is one possible basis for said research, where the interactions and components of interest within the triad vary based on the application domain. Character Computing consists of three modules: sensing the character, adapting to the character, and developing artificial characters. Each module is a research realm of its own with diverse challenges and novel opportunities.

Previously, each module has been investigated on its own in different research fields. Research in Affective and Personality Computing aimed at tackling some of the mentioned problems, however, without including all character components. Instead each field relied on one character component, such as affect or personality, respectively, to account for human behavior. Most existing approaches toward understanding and thus adapting to human behavior have always been rooted in one of the two main research fields: Computer Science and Psychology. Character Computing is among the approaches addressing these questions from a joint perspective of Computer Science and Psychology in parallel, leading to a formalized model representing the Character–Behavior–Situation triad and thus enabling all ensuing potential applications. This framework can only be developed if Character Computing is simultaneously developed and investigated from a theoretical, formal and practical, empirical perspective, as will be elaborated in detail in Chaps. 2–4 of this volume.

To define Character Computing in more detail and better understand its far-reaching scope, the following chapters of Part I of the book will explain how the formal representation of the triad discussed in Sect. 1.2.1 can be empirically realized and modeled. Further details about the three modules of Character Computing and their applications will be given throughout the book.

Acknowledgements Huge credit goes to Prof. Dr. Cornelia Herbert for major revisions of this chapter. Special thanks to Prof. Dr. Haythem Ismail for the insightful review of the chapter. Sincere thanks to Prof. Dr. Slim Abdennadher for insights and support.

References

Ajzen I (1991) The theory of planned behavior. Organ Behav Hum Decis Process 50(2):179–211
Allport GW, Odbert HS (1936) Trait-names: a psycho-lexical study. Psychol Monogr 47(1):i
Banks JA (1988) Ethnicity, class, cognitive, and motivational styles: research and teaching implications. J Negro Educ 57(4):452–466
Carver CS, White TL (1994) Behavioral inhibition, behavioral activation, and affective responses to impending reward and punishment: the bis/bas scales. J Pers Soc Psychol 67(2):319
Cattell HE, Mead AD (2008) The sixteen personality factor questionnaire (16pf). In: Boyle GJ, Matthews G, Saklofske DH (eds) The SAGE handbook of personality theory and assessment, vol 2. SAGE, Los Angeles, pp 135–178
Cloninger C, Svrakic D, Przybeck T (1998) A psychobiological model of temperament and character. Dev. Psychiatry Complex 50:1–16

Cohen J (2001) Defining identification: a theoretical look at the identification of audiences with media characters. Mass Commun Soc 4(3):245–264

Corr PJ, Matthews G (2009) The Cambridge handbook of personality psychology. Cambridge University Press, Cambridge

De Fruyt F, Van De Wiele L, Van Heeringen C (2000) Cloninger's psychobiological model of temperament and character and the five-factor model of personality. Pers Individ Differ 29(3):441–452

Dewaele JM, Van Oudenhoven JP (2009) The effect of multilingualism/multiculturalism on personality: no gain without pain for third culture kids? Int J Multiling 6(4):443–459

Doris JM (2002) Lack of character: personality and moral behavior. Cambridge University Press, Cambridge

Edmonds JM, Austen GEV et al (1904) The characters of Theophrastus. Blackie & Son Limited, London

El Bolock A (2018) Defining character computing from the perspective of computer science and psychology. In: Proceedings of the 17th international conference on mobile and ubiquitous multimedia. ACM, New York, pp 567–572

El Bolock A, Salah J, Abdennadher S, Abdelrahman Y (2017) Character computing: challenges and opportunities. In: Proceedings of the 16th international conference on mobile and ubiquitous multimedia. ACM, New York, pp 555–559

El Bolock A, Salah J, Abdelrahman Y, Herbert C, Abdennadher S (2018) Character computing: computer science meets psychology. In: Proceedings of the 17th international conference on mobile and ubiquitous multimedia, ACM, New York, pp 557–562

Gerrig RJ, Allbritton DW (1990) The construction of literary character: a view from cognitive psychology. Style 24:380–391

Gilbert DT, Hixon JG (1991) The trouble of thinking: activation and application of stereotypic beliefs. J Pers Soc Psychol 60(4):509

Goldberg LR (1992) The development of markers for the big-five factor structure. Psychol Assess 4(1):26

Haritatos J, Benet-Martınez V (2002) Bicultural identities: the interface of cultural, personality, and socio-cognitive processes. J Res Pers 36(6):598–606

Haselton MG, Nettle D, Murray DR (2015) The evolution of cognitive bias. In: The handbook of evolutionary psychology. Wiley, Hoboken pp 1–20

Homer-Murray A (1999) Homer, illiad. books 1-12

Isbister K (2006) Better game characters by design: a psychological approach. CRC Press, Boca Raton

John OP, Gross JJ (2004) Healthy and unhealthy emotion regulation: personality processes, individual differences, and life span development. J Pers 72(6):1301–1334

Klaczynski PA (2000) Motivated scientific reasoning biases, epistemological beliefs, and theory polarization: a two-process approach to adolescent cognition. Child Dev 71(5):1347–1366

McAdams DP (2008) The person: an introduction to the science of personality psychology. Wiley, Hoboken

McCrae RR, Costa PT Jr (1989) Reinterpreting the myers-briggs type indicator from the perspective of the five-factor model of personality. J Pers 57(1):17–40

McCrae RR, Costa PT Jr, Martin TA (2005) The neo-pi-3: a more readable revised neo personality inventory. J Pers Assess 84(3):261–270

Van de Mortel TF et al (2008) Faking it: social desirability response bias in self-report research. Aust J Adv Nurs 25(4):40–48

Mowrer O (1950) Learning theory and personality dynamics: selected papers. Ronald Press, New York

Myers IB, McCaulley MH, Quenk NL, Hammer AL (2003) MBTI manual: a guide to the development and use of the Myers-Briggs type indicator, 3rd edn. Consulting Psychologists Press, Palo Alto

Nucci L (2018) Character: a developmental system. Child Dev Perspect 13:73–78

Park CC (2002) Crosscultural differences in learning styles of secondary english learners. Biling Res J 26(2):443–459

Pervin LA, John OP (1999) Handbook of personality: theory and research. Elsevier, Amsterdam

Picard RW (1997) Affective computing, vol 252. MIT Press, Cambridge

Pickering A, Corr PJ (2008) Ja gray's reinforcement sensitivity theory (rst) of personality. In: The SAGE handbook of personality theory and assessment, vol 1. Sage, Thousand Oaks, pp 239–257

Pohl R, Pohl RF (2004) Cognitive illusions: a handbook on fallacies and biases in thinking, judgement and memory. Psychology Press, Hove

Richard R, Egger Y (2011) The miniature guide to understanding the foundations of ethical reasoning. Foundation for critical thinking free press, United States, pp np

Sherman N (1989) The fabric of character: aristotle's theory of virtue. Clarendon Press, Oxford

Veltkamp GM, Recio G, Jacobs AM, Conrad M (2013) Is personality modulated by language? Int J Biling 17(4):496–504

Vinciarelli A, Mohammadi G (2014) A survey of personality computing. IEEE Trans Affect Comput 5(3):273–291

Zammitto V, DiPaola S, Arya A (2008) A methodology for incorporating personality modeling in believable game characters. Arya 1(613.520):2600

Chapter 2
An Experimental-Psychological Approach for the Development of Character Computing

Cornelia Herbert

Abstract Progress in the field of computer science is paving ways for collecting and analyzing huge amounts of data from people from all over the globe almost in any situation be it at home or at work. Data collection and analysis may include the overt behavior of the user but may also explore the hidden affective, motivational and cognitive human factors. Making reliable predictions about human behavior thus means to take overt behavior as well as implicit human factors into consideration. Psychologically speaking, this means to explore the user's whole character—his/her personality traits, his/her current cognitive, affective, and motivational states as well as the user's cultural and social embedding—to best predict behavior in accordance with the user's individual needs, preferences, and subjective well-being. This raises questions of how Character Computing as a novel and holistic approach of human behavior computing can be achieved without violating ethical standards and the user's privacy. This introductory chapter will provide answers to these questions. In the first part of the chapter, it will be discussed how psychological theories of human behavior have inspired the fields of Cognitive Computing, Affective Computing, and Personality Computing. Next, a holistic psychological definition of human behavior will be provided that describes human behavior in the context of the Character–Behavior–Situation triad. It will be discussed how psychological understanding of human behavior can guide and improve future research in the domain of Character Computing. Finally, an experimental-psychological framework for Character Computing will be discussed that considers Character Computing from an interdisciplinary perspective.

C. Herbert (✉)
Applied Emotion and Motivation Psychology, Institute of Psychology and Education,
Faculty of Engineering, Computer Science and Psychology, Ulm University,
Ulm, Germany
e-mail: cornelia.herbert@uni-ulm.de

© Springer Nature Switzerland AG 2020
A. El Bolock et al. (eds.), *Character Computing*, Human–Computer Interaction Series,
https://doi.org/10.1007/978-3-030-15954-2_2

2.1 Introduction and Overview

What drives human behavior? Never before in scientific history has this question attracted as much attention and interest as today. Progress in the field of computer science and Human–Computer Interaction (HCI) has contributed to this interest by paving ways for collecting and statistically analyzing huge amounts of digital data from users from all over the globe. Web-based and computer-assisted communication has become the norm rather than the exception in our global society. HCI-applications (including those based on artificial intelligence and machine learning) are implemented in smartphones, cars, planes as well as in commercially available medical-, office-, and leisure-time devices, making it possible to track and monitor human behavior practically in any situation—be it at home or at work. Despite rapidly growing scientific progress, HCI-algorithms still have problems in accurately predicting human behavior. Especially when there is little data available or when predictions about the behavior of one single user or many users are required for novel situations, predictions made by computer algorithms often still not reach acceptable accuracy. An example may illustrate the problem: imagine a smart affective computing application for ambulatory mood- and stress-regulation developed for use by different users including, for example, college students, elite athletes, shift workers on the one hand or on the other hand, physically and mentally disabled people who—due to their disorder—cannot respond overtly by voice, gestures or hand commands. The task of the computer system is to recognize the user's mood and stress level and then switch to a mode designed to assist the user to up- or down-regulate his/her mood and stress level accordingly. However, people do not always self-regulate their affective states in the same way. Moreover, users may differ in the way they experience, process, and cognitively regulate their emotions, stress, and mood states. Likewise, a single person may routinely use different behavioral strategies. In addition, there may be hidden affective, motivational, and cognitive human factors that significantly contribute to changes in the user's behavior (e.g., stress- and mood-induced changes in bodily, physiological responses). Indeed, humans often make decisions not on rational grounds. Instead, they decide quite intuitively and spontaneously based on their gut feelings, their individual and implicit preferences and personality traits. Remarkably, these hidden and implicit factors drive human behavior without the user being fully aware of them. Thus, predicting human behavior in a user-centered, context-sensitive, and situation-specific manner needs to take into consideration overt and explicit as well as tacit and implicit human factors. Psychologically speaking, this means to explore the user's whole character—his/her personality traits, his/her current cognitive, affective and motivational states as well as the user's cultural and social embedding—to best predict behavior in accord with the user's individual needs, preferences, and subjective well-being. This raises the question of how Character Computing as a novel and holistic computational approach of modeling human behavior can be achieved without violating ethical standards and the user's privacy concerns.

This **introductory chapter** attempts to provide answers to these questions by providing a theoretical and experimental-psychological framework for Character Computing. The first part of this chapter gives a comprehensive overview on psychological theories of human behavior. Different psychological views that have influenced the field of computational modeling of human behavior will be discussed. In particular, it will be shown how these different psychological views influenced our scientific thinking about human behavior and how they have inspired the fields of Cognitive Computing, Affective Computing, and Personality Computing. Each of the existing psychological views and computational approaches has advantages, but also comes with limitations, while some psychological models and theories such as theories of embodied language and embodied cognition may extend existing cognitive computational models of human behavior. Finally, in the second part of this chapter, a holistic psychological definition of human behavior will be provided. The definition will consider overt (explicit) and tacit (implicit) human factors in an attempt to appropriately describe and recognize the factors that underlie and determine human behavior across contexts and situations. It will be discussed how this definition and psychological understanding of human behavior can guide and improve future research in the domain of Character Computing as a novel interdisciplinary and psychologically driven approach that attempts to model, simulate, recognize, and predict human behavior by considering the Behavior–Character–Situation Triad.

2.2 Psychological Theories of Human Behavior: Implications for Computational Modeling of Human Behavior

2.2.1 Human Behavior as Seen from the View of Behaviorism

From a psychological perspective, answering the questions of what drives human behavior and how the factors that determine human behavior can be identified and predicted by computer algorithms is not trivial. No single unifying psychological definition exists that would allow an easy answer to this question. Instead, psychology has developed at least as many theories of behavior as there are psychological disciplines. For example, from the classical view of Behaviorism (which was dominant in 1950 and 1960), human behavior can be explained entirely by stimulus–response relationships and reinforcement, reward and punishment are considered the big driving forces of human learning and behavioral modification. Until today, many effective therapeutic techniques for the treatment of e.g., anxiety disorders, addictive or obsessive–compulsive disorders are rooted in behaviorism. In particular, maladaptive behaviors associated with these disorders can be successfully treated by behavioral interventions based on behaviorist learning principles. Moreover, many of today's maladaptive behaviors such as obsessive smartphone use or Internet addiction can in part be explained by behaviorist learning principles. Therefore, adopting a behaviorist view can be very successful in modifying unwanted behavior and unwanted behavioral habits by means of applying simple rules of classical and operant conditioning. Nevertheless, as a theory, Behaviorism has been heavily criticized for its strict denial of subjective and internal individual factors. Internal factors such as one's own mood, one's own thoughts, and subjective feelings constitute essential parts of human experience. Thoughts, beliefs, feelings, memories, and needs all significantly influence human behavior and contribute substantially to individual variability in behavior across situations and individuals.

2.2.1.1 Implications for Behavior Computing and Limitations

In its extremes, Behaviorism considers human beings as black boxes (see Fig. 2.1) and changes in behavior are explained solely on the basis of stimulus–stimulus and stimulus–response associations. Accordingly, the behaviorist approach of Behavior Computing concentrates on overt human behavior and temporal contingencies in stimulus–response relations. It will search for statistical regularities between overt behavioral responses and contextual factors. For example, one could monitor a user's smartphone behavior and statistically analyze all situations when he/she is using or not using his/her smartphone for successfully predicting the user's smartphone behavior in future situations. One might also identify situations and habits of the user that could be modified via the rules of reinforcement learning. The concomitant computational rules and architecture would be based on stimulus–stimulus and stimulus–response relationships on the basis of which the user's behavior could be described, modeled, and modified according to a set of S-R-S rules. Remarkably, in Behavior Computing, rule-based systems are very often similar to S-R associations. Nevertheless, Behavior Computing that follows a purely behaviorist approach can give little insight into the understanding of the user's thoughts and cognitive operations, his/her motivations, attitudes, beliefs, feelings, and intentions that drive and motivate behavior above and beyond the classical learning principles. Furthermore, considering the user, his/her cognitive operations and subjective experiences as black box (see Fig. 2.1) cannot tell how behavior is mentally represented and stored in the user's memory and mental self-concept. As a consequence, any answer to the question what constitutes human behavior from a behaviorist approach will fall short of considering internal human factors, the latter being the core focus of Cognitive Psychology.

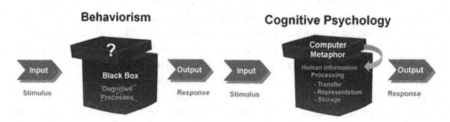

Fig. 2.1 Behavior Computing as seen from the view of Behaviorism versus Cognitive Psychology (see text for detailed explanation)

2.2.2 Human Behavior as Seen from the View of Cognitive Psychology

As a psychological discipline, Cognitive Psychology aimed to shift the focus of human behavior toward information processing. Viewed from the perspective of Cognitive Psychology, understanding human behavior means understanding how humans cognitively process, store and represent information. In its widest definition, cognitive processes involve all processes by which sensory input is processed, transformed, elaborated, stored, represented, and recovered (e.g., for an overview see Neisser 1967 and Neisser 2014). Thus, cognitive models of human behavior are interested in describing the mental processes and mental operations that people use while thinking, remembering, learning, or while interacting with their living and non-living environment. Cognitive theories of perception, attention, memory, decision-making, problem-solving, and language processing are well known across scientific disciplines. Their theoretical assumptions have provided and still provide the major source for well-controlled experimental laboratory investigations to explore and gain insight into the hidden mental processes underlying human behavior.

What all cognitive theories have in common is that they consider humans as information processing systems in analogy to computer systems. The computer metaphor has become very prominent in Cognitive Psychology (see Fig. 2.1). It has influenced much of the terminology in cognitive theorizing. For example, many influential theories of human information processing assume that the cognitive architecture of human information processing consists of modules, processors, operators, buffers, and central memory units for data storage. In analogy to a computer, it is assumed that information that enters the human mind is chunked, transformed, and represented in different formats while it passes through different data processing modules either by sequential or parallel processing prior to data storage. The cognitive operations responsible for information transfer and signal transformation can be described and operationalized by computational rules and algorithms and mathematical equations. Traditional theories of human information processing are based on information processing theory and models of cognitive information processing (IPM), (e.g., Atkinson and Shiffrin 1968). The central assumptions of the IPM are summarized in Fig. 2.2. The IPM assumes that information is processed in a bottom-up and top-down controlled fashion. Regarding bottom-up processing, it is assumed that sensory information received by our senses first enters sensory memory. Next information enters short-term or working memory where information is chunked into parts. Information that is considered significant is then transferred to long-term memory for storage and retrieval. Importantly, it is assumed that human information processing can be controlled top-down by central executive mechanisms. Moreover, it is assumed that the central processing system has limited processing capacities. Furthermore, it is assumed that information transfer from sensory to short-term memory can be significantly influenced by cognitive operations: for instance, attention, rehearsal, and elaboration can influence the availability of information in working memory and its encoding in and retrieval from long-term memory.

Cognitive Information Processing Model

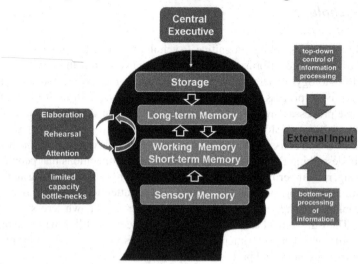

Fig. 2.2 Cognitive Information Processing Model (IPM)

2.2.2.1 Implications for Cognitive Computing and Limitations

Admittedly, one can say that Cognitive Psychology had a significant impact on Computer Science and vice versa. Computational modeling became one of the key methods in Cognitive Psychology to simulate and validate the cognitive predictions about human information processing and behavior. In addition, the common interest of both disciplines in information processing and the common endeavor of developing artificial systems that mimic human "cognitive" functions and human performance have led to significant developments in the field of Artificial Intelligence (AI) and the development of psychologically driven cognitive architectures for the simulation of human behavior in artificial agents. The ACT-R is one of the most frequently explored cognitive architecture in Computer Science and Cognitive Psychology. It is based on cognitive psychological theorizing of Adaptive Control of Thought (ACT)-Theory developed by the Psychologist Paul Anderson (e.g., Anderson 1996; Anderson and Schunn 2000). The ACT-Theory is grounded in empirical research from Cognitive Psychology in the domains of perception, learning, and memory. Its computational implementation provides a unifying psychological framework for building cognitive architectures that allow simulating human information processing (including problem-solving and decision-making). The ACT-R computer model consists of information processing modules and information processing buffers which temporarily represent and store the incoming information (from the perceptual-motor environment) for the execution of a certain goal or for retrieving information from memory systems (see Fig. 2.3). The memory systems comprise a declarative memory system (for the long-term storage of knowledge about facts, e.g., Germany is a

Fig. 2.3 Cognitive architecture (adapted from ACT-Theory, Anderson, 1996)

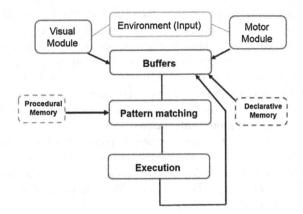

country in Europe) and a procedural memory system that represents "motor" knowledge, e.g., how to walk, drive, etc. Information exchange is monitored by productions consisting of central executive mechanisms and processes. Since its first description, the model's architecture has been extended many times. Furthermore, it developed into a programming language that allows the modeler to include own modules and processes in the architecture—irrespective of whether these modules are based on psychological theory or not (e.g., Bothell 2004).

Although highly promising, as is true for any cognitive psychological approach, assuming behavior to be driven by a set of higher order cognitive processes has limitations and shortcomings. First, a purely cognitive approach may reduce human behavior to cognitive factors. Second, in search of the general principles of cognition, individual differences are often ignored. Third, cognitive models consider cognition often in opposition to emotions and bodily processes. Fourth, information from the sensory and motor organs is thought to be transferred into mental representations that represent knowledge in an abstract, propositional, and disembodied symbolic format in the user's declarative memory system. In particular, it is assumed that information is stored symbolically in a manner that it may no longer bear any relation to its physical referents. Thus, cognitive operations are considered to be stored in an encapsulated fashion, i.e., the rules and operations of the central cognitive processors work independent from the perceptual or motor modules.

2.2.2.2 Challenges for Cognitive Architectures: Embodied Language and Embodied Cognition

In recent years, cognitive and affective neuroscience investigated the relationship between language, perception, emotion, and behavior in the human brain. The studies accumulated empirical evidence against the purely cognitive foundation of behavior. Crucially, the vast majority of studies support the notion that in the human brain, cognitive processing also activates perceptual, affective, and sensorimotor brain areas. The results promote the idea of shared representations and no independence of cognition from perception, action, and emotions. In particular, cognition is considered to be grounded in action, perception and emotion and it is assumed that knowledge representations are based on situated conceptualization and multimodal simulations (for an overview see Barsalou 2008). For example, consider human language which has long been considered the most cognitive ability of mankind: neuroscientific studies on reading and written word processing have shown that processing of action words such as "kick" or "lick" activate the same neural system in the brain that is activated when the particular action is executed (e.g., Pulvermüller 2013). Similarly, reading emotional words influences perception and directs attention (Herbert et al. 2008); it primes motor behavior and activates emotion structures in the brain (e.g., Herbert et al. 2009; Herbert and Kissler 2010; for an overview, see Herbert et al. 2018).

Moreover, it has been suggested that cognitive operations are constraint and dependent upon the characteristics of the physical body of the agent (user), including perception, emotion, and action. Therefore, it cannot be assumed that cognition and knowledge representations are stored independently from the user's bodily and subjective experiences (for an overview, see Wilson 2002). This embodied view of cognition and behavior provided an important framework and building block for robotics. It inspired the development of novel computational architectures that investigate how perception and action modules can interact via symbolic representations and via direct interactions.

2.2.3 Human Behavior as Seen from the View of Affective Psychology and Neuroscience

The embodied view of human behavior outlined above also takes into consideration that perceptual and motor processing modules are involved in emotion processing. Whether at home or at work, emotions drive our behavior and guide our decision-making. Emotional stimuli provoke strong feelings of pleasure or displeasure and arousal and their perception undeniably changes concomitant behavior (James 1884). Theoretically, emotions constitute the biological heritage of mankind to protect survival. Moreover, emotions serve as the "glue" for social interactions. Although emotions are primarily bodily responses, they do have a cognitive component as well (e.g., Scherer et al. 2001). Crucially, emotions are by no means isolated phenomena: cognitive and affective neuroscientific research has left no doubt that emotion and cognition are intricately intertwined in the human brain. Due to this interaction, emotions can influence any kind of higher order cognitive information processing starting with what the user is paying attention to, to what feelings he/she might experience in anticipation of an event (e.g., Duncan and Barrett 2007). Likewise, clinical neuropsychological case studies left no doubt that damage of certain brain regions involved in emotion processing can impair a person's "rational" decision-making behavior such that these patients are no longer able to generate anticipatory emotional responses prior to their decisions and behavioral choices (for a discussion, e.g., Naqvi et al. 2006). Thus, emotions are multimodal events. However, how can emotions be objectively measured, decoded, and predicted by computer algorithms?

2.2.3.1 Implications for Affective Computing and Limitations

In real life, emotional behavior is expressed largely through bodily signals. These signals can be grouped into two main categories or domains: behavioral signals (e.g., facial expressions, hand and body gestures, speech, or written text) on the one hand and physiological signals (e.g., changes in heart rate, pulse, respiration, eye gaze, pupil size, galvanic skin conductance, skin temperature—to name but a few) on the other hand. Thanks to new technologies in Human–Computer Interaction (HCI) and the development of new sensing devices, it is possible to record, collect, and analyze principally any of these overt behavioral responses or tacit and implicit physiological signals from the user irrespective of situational restrictions (e.g., while holding a speech at work, while sleeping, exercising, or chatting with a friend via the Internet). Nevertheless, the plethora of bodily signals that may indicate emotions, their signal complexity and dynamic nature can pose challenges for computer algorithms: whereas humans are good in recognizing, labeling, and interpreting emotions and feelings, for computers, recognition, interpretation, and prediction of emotions become complicated tasks if the sensory input lacks interpretation. Recognizing emotions from external sources such as speech, text, or physiology requires the extraction of meaningful patterns from the recorded data. However, the interpretation of what patterns carry the emotional message and whether this might be meaningful for the user cannot be done without pre-assumptions taken from experimental-psychological research and concomitant psychological and theoretical considerations.

Consider a device being equipped with wireless wearable sensors that track the user's heart rate and galvanic skin response across the whole day while the user engages in several events such as holding a speech at work, exercising, or chatting with her/his best friend. As illustrated in Fig. 2.4, mean heart rate might show peaks during all three events, once because the user is extremely stressed by the open speech, once because he/she is physically active, and once because he/she is being highly amused and positively excited because of the partner telling him/her that she/he loves you. In other words, changes in one single physiologic parameter might be emotion unspecific and indicate changes in physiological arousal that may be common to all three events characterized by either pleasure or displeasure. Experimental emotion research found that physiological signals may not only vary from situation to situation but also from content to content and from individual to individual (for a critical discussion, e.g., Cacioppo et al. 2000). Physiological signals may also vary for self- and other-related information (e.g., Weis and Herbert 2017). In some people, they may change while being exposed to supposedly neutral stimuli which do not share affective meaning in all individuals. Therefore, identifying changes in one physiological behavioral response alone may not give certainty about the emotions

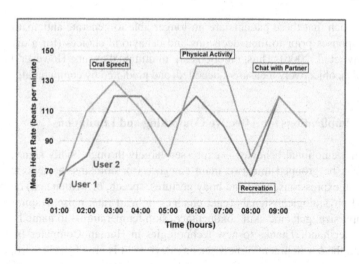

Fig. 2.4 Intra- and interindividual variability of physiological signals as illustrated by changes in heart rate monitored across different situations and users (see text for detailed explanation)

experienced by the user. Moreover, correlations between changes in physiology and subjective experience can be moderate and follow different time courses. Therefore, scientist agree that any model of Affective Computing should be based on multi-modal affect analysis and combine information from various sensors and modalities to detect features and patterns that correspond with high probability to the current underlying emotional state of the user. Hybrid models that combine instructed and uninstructed machine-learning tools with affective databases that are pre-rated by human users and afterwards annotated with emotion labels have therefore become very popular in Affective Computing (for an overview and review e.g., Poria et al. 2017).

2.2.3.2 Challenges for Affective Computing: Linguistic Emotion Expression and Sentiment Analysis

Affective Computing has brought new impetus into the debate on which signals might give best access to the user's affective state. In particular, the focus on emotion recognition from text as approached by sentiment analysis and sentic computing (for an overview e.g., Cambria and Hussain 2015) brings new questions on the relationship between emotion, cognition, and language that traditional definitions of emotions and traditional theories of language have long been neglecting but which recently have been highlighted by embodiment theories (see also Sect. 2.2.2 in this chapter). In daily life, the signals that matter most to humans are linguistic. We text, blog, tweet, and like or dislike others for their posted comments. Today, written language is one of the primary and most natural modes of emotion expression in human–

computer-mediated human–human interaction for conveying emotions from sender to receiver even when no direct face-to-face communication is possible. Scientifically, however, the question of whether language, specifically written language in terms of single words, is able to elicit "real" emotions and feelings has long been under debate. Traditionally, language has been considered a purely cognitive function that evolved for the purpose of representing individual experiences in an abstract way, independent from sensory and motor experience and independent from bodily sensations including emotions (for an overview see, e.g., Herbert et al. 2018). Reading or expressing one's own emotion verbally may activate the semantic meaning of the word including its emotional meaning; nonetheless, in traditional cognitive architectures (see Sect. 2.2), this knowledge would be stored symbolically in semantic networks in which the meaning conveyed by words would have restricted access to the bodily processes characterizing emotions. Thus, any message that we post would not be accompanied by physiological bodily changes or by affective experiences or by changes in motivational behavior of approach or avoidance—neither in the sender nor in the receiver of the message. A disembodied subjective experience would be all that remains and all what we could grasp from the content of the words. Therefore, in this view, any computational approach that seeks to explore the user's subjective feelings by decoding emotion expression solely from words and written text would have little chance to decode real emotions.

In the past decade, systematic psychological research investigating the neural and bodily correlates of language processing found evidence against this disembodied view of language. Akin to other cognitive processes and human abilities such as reasoning and decision-making, language processing can be considered as embodied and grounded in perception, action, and emotion (e.g., Glenberg et al. 2009; Niedenthal et al. 2009). There is experimental evidence that during reading, single words of emotional content (in the absence of any additional sensory input) can evoke physiological changes in the body (e.g., changes in facial muscle activity, sympathetic arousal). As summarized in Fig. 2.5, affective word processing studies (for an overview, see Herbert et al. 2018) show that in laboratory experiments, the presentation of written words can lead to neurophysiological changes in brain regions involved in the detection of emotions (e.g., amygdala, ventral visual processing stream) and in the processing of feelings of emotional ownership (see Fig. 2.5).

The insight gained from these neuroscientific psychological studies can lead to the development of novel computational architectures that take assumptions from embodiment theories into account.

2.2.4 Human Behavior as Seen from the View of Personality Psychology

Whereas models of human behavior from Cognitive and Affective Psychology are dynamic models in as much as they are interested in the mental and bodily processes that determine and modulate human behavior, models from Personality

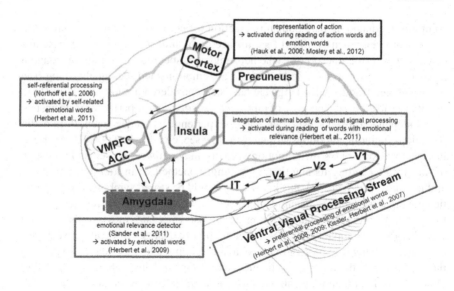

Fig. 2.5 Neural interfaces as derived from affective word processing studies (see text above for a detailed description)

Psychology claim that human behavior is driven by individual trait-like characteristics that influence behavior in a stable and situation-independent manner. Personality traits are considered to be genetically determined, but many psychologists believe that there exist certain critical periods in which environmental factors can influence the development of personality traits. After these critical periods, personality traits are considered stable over time and relatively "resistant" to change across age. Latest since the observation of the patient Phineas Gage (who showed massive changes in his personality after head injury), scientists have found evidence that personality has a neurobiological basis through which it may influence behavior. In line with this, recent brain imaging studies showed that personality is related to brain maturation (Riccelli et al. 2017). Likewise, many psychological theorists assume that individual differences in personality are associated with individual differences in brain functions. Moreover, some theoretical models and self-report scales for the measurement of personality are entirely based on biopsychological assumptions such as, for example, the BIS/BAS scales (Carver and White 1994) that are based on Gray's Reinforcement Sensitivity Theory (Gray 1982). The revised RST (Gray and McNaughton 2000) describes three separate functional brain systems—each being associated with different personality facets and functions that determine how sensitive people are to reward versus punishment and to fight versus flight. Abundant research found correlations between BIS/BAS measures and measures of psychopathological anxiety, depression, or eating disorders. Moreover, BIS/BAS measures seem to correlate with individual differences in work performance and work engagement and with individual differences in physical activity and exercise behavior. Among all existing personality models, the Big Five or OCEAN-Model (McCrae and Costa 1999) is one of the most influential personality models. Notably and in contrast to, e.g., the former RST model, its personality dimensions were derived solely on the basis of statistical factor analysis of verbal descriptors of human behavior. Its five factors, openness, conscientiousness, extraversion, agreeableness, and neuroticism, are considered to capture stable individual personality characteristics that underlie human behavior according to which each individual can be described. As is typical for personality measurement, the different personality dimensions are assessed via self-report in form of questionnaires.

2.2.4.1 Implications for Personality Computing and Limitations

Due to its easy assessment via self-report (e.g., the short version of the Big Five consists of only 10 items) and its many correlations with other self-report measures as well as with cognitive and affective behavior in psychological laboratory studies, personality measures have become quite popular in the field of Behavior Computing. The purpose is to predict the user's behavior and his/her individual preferences on the basis of his personality traits or vice versa. Personality Computing thus works in both directions: first, users from all over the globe can fill in the personality questionnaire and computer algorithms can track the user's behavior (e.g., when during a day he/she is sleeping, eating, exercising, using social media, etc.) to find correlations between personality and behavior outside the laboratory settings. Given that the relationship between personality and behavior is assumed to be stable, one could predict the user's future behavior in various occasions on the basis of his/her personality traits. Moreover, one could try to predict the personality traits of novel users on the basis of his/her behavior. Interestingly, it has been shown that computer algorithms predict the relationship between behavior and personality traits with even higher accuracy than humans do (e.g., see Youyou et al. 2015). Thus, it may come with no surprise (for recent reviews Vinciarelli and Mohammadi 2014) that publications on Personality Computing have increased constantly over the last 5 years. Big Data approaches that analyze web-based computer-assisted communication and behavioral interaction via smartphones and wearable devices have looked into almost every aspect of human life in an attempt to find correlations between a wide variety of human behaviors and stable and easy to measure individual personality characteristics. Most recent approaches aim to determine behavioral patterns that may reliably differentiate users with different personalities. The latter approach is particularly motivated by experimental research from psychology showing that individuals who differ in personality traits also differ in the way they perform certain tasks—including speech and expressive behavior in text. Regarding the latter, research from psychology has identified a number of associations between personality (as measured by self-report), risk for psychiatric disorders, and language use in experiments on expressive writing (e.g., Lepore and Smyth 2002; Mairesse et al. 2007; Herbert et al. 2018).

Although the approach of Personality Computing—and of Automatic Personality Recognition in particular—is appealing, one may not forget that current accounts have their methodological limitations and weaknesses. Moreover, its commercial application may not come without ethical concerns. Methodologically, one restraint is that Personality Computing is based on correlational observations that do not allow causal interpretation. Another restraint is that Personality Psychology has brought up several personality dimensions that may all have their justification. Thus, despite of a clear dominance on the BIG Five personality dimensions, the decision which of any of the existing personality theories and questionnaires one may use in a Big Data Personality Computing Approach still heavily relies on the researcher's decisions. Given that personality traits are theoretical constructs hidden from the observer's view, their detection significantly relies on the validity of the measurement device. Therefore, the reliability and the validity of a personality measurement device play decisive roles. Using self-reports to measure psychological constructs has its strength; however, minor changes in wording, question format, etc. can have significant effects on the validity of self-report methods (Schwarz and Oyserman 2001). Moreover, people often respond desirably to put themselves in a favorable light. As a consequence, the responses given by the participants may not reflect their actual beliefs and behavior ("Socially Desirable Responding"; Paulhus 1989). Although replacing self-assessment with behavioral markers might cure some of these limitations, this does not come without other restraints. Though it is acknowledged that relationships between personality and behavior appear across different cultures, the expression of personality traits in terms of overt behavior can differ across cultures and across situations. For instance, using linguistic markers as proxy for individual differences in personality may depend on situational and contextual factors: according to recent research, extraversion as a personality trait of the Big Five was found to be related to verbal productivity in public but not private language. Similarly, neuroticism was found to be correlated with verbal expression of emotions in private but not in public language. The findings support State–Trait Models of Human Personality and Behavior. According to these models, effects of personality traits on behavior are mediated by state-like variables that often have more direct effect on behavior than traits (Matthews et al. 2003). In fact, regarding language use, besides emotion expression, it is often also cognitive functions words or self-referential pronouns that can tell us how people interpret and regulate emotions during a particular experience Chung and Pennebaker (2007). As shown in recent experiments on expressive writing (e.g., Herbert et al. 2018), use of emotional words (positive words versus negative words), pronouns (referential pronouns, first-person singular versus plural), cognitive function words, and their unique combination differs during the experience of positive, negative, and neutral autobiographical events. This situation-specific use of words may point to the user's motivational states, his/her attitudes, expectations, beliefs, and even to his/her personality (Herbert et al. 2018). Accordingly, behavioral variability is substantially related to interactions between persons and situations.

2.3 Psychological Framework and Definition of Character Computing

As discussed in detail in this chapter, in Psychology, there exist multiple theoretical views that all make basic assumptions about human behavior and its underlying processes and driving forces. Each of these theoretical views has influenced computational models of human behavior significantly. Moreover, each of these theoretical views can contribute to a holistic definition of human behavior and its major driving forces.

2.3.1 Definitions, Aims, and Scope of Character Computing

In essence, a holistic definition of human behavior will include overt (explicit) and covert (implicit) human factors to appropriately recognize the features that drive, underlie, and determine human behavior in a context-sensitive and situation-specific manner. From a psychological point of view, this means to take the user's whole character—i.e., his/her personality traits, his/her affective, cognitive, and motivational state as well as his/her subjective experience, and cultural and social embedding—into consideration to develop truly context-sensitive and user-centered computer systems that allow best fit with the user's overt behavior as well as with the user's individual thoughts, needs, preferences, and his/her well-being.

In the heuristic model of Character Computing, a person's character comprises the user's cognitive, affective and motivational state as well as his/her personality traits. Crucially, these traits can influence the user's current state. Together with the user's current state, his/her traits predict the user's behavior in a particular situation. Critically, the user's behavior (e.g., his/her decision in a particular situation) as well as the affordances of the situation can feed back to the user's cognitive, motivational, and affective state thereby continuously shaping behavior from situation to situation.

Considering human behavior from this holistic perspective paves the way for Character Computing which focuses on the interactions between Behavior, Person (State–Trait), and Situation in order to model, simulate, and predict human behavior (see Fig. 2.6). With this respect, the meaning of term character in Character Computing should be distinguished from the ordinary psychological use of the term character or temperament referring to individual differences that are thought to be biologically based (temperament) and akin to personality traits defined to describe latent person variables. The term character in Character Computing is also not meant as a synonym for personality, the latter referring to those characteristics of a person that are considered to be individually stable and thought to contribute to consistent patterns of behavior over situations and time (e.g., Pervin 2001). As shown in Fig. 2.6, the definition of character in Character Computing is based on an interactionist psychological view. In this view, behavioral variability is considered as a product of interactions between person and situation. Moreover, behavioral reactions are

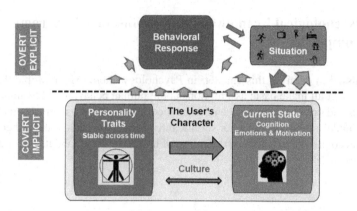

Fig. 2.6 Character Computing: The Character(Trait/State)–Behavior–Situation Triad

thought to feed back to the user's current state. Accordingly, the user's behavior needs to be dynamically modeled on the basis of this mutual triad.

Character Computing may build on existing computational models and architectures. However, the challenge will be to extend these architectures to allow simulation, prediction and evaluation of human behavior on the basis of computing algorithms that identify the user's affective, motivational, and cognitive state and that account for individual differences in personality characteristics. This cannot be done without use cases that are guided by psychological experiments. Obviously, modeling and simulating interactions between the variables "person, situation, and behavior" as well as the interpretation of these interactions need to rely on psychological theories and experimental-psychological findings. Computational approaches that include psychological experiments at the stage of the development and at the stage of the evaluation of the computational architecture are still scarce. Nevertheless, an experimentally driven psychological approach to Character Computing can work best to increase the detection of reliable features and patterns in the data that will predict human behavior. Moreover, an experimentally driven psychological approach to Character Computing will reduce the computing load without losing reliability and validity across situations and applications. Following the premise that a user's character comprises state and trait components that dynamically interact situation-wise requires assessment of the user's behavior with different methods in different situations. Again, methods and situation might be chosen on the basis of psychological experiments and transferred to IoT scenarios for the detection of situation-specific and situation-unspecific patterns of the user's affective, motivational, and cognitive state and traits in situations mimicking real-life scenarios. Psychological studies have repeatedly proven that changes in human behavior do not consist of changes in observable behavior only. In contrast, in humans, thinking, feeling, and acting as an embodied agent are accompanied by changes in psychophysiological and neurophysiological states, and subjectively experienced as well. Signal recording and behavioral markers could therefore include the user's overt behavior (keyboard responses, typing speed, or key response pressure), his/her voice, or semantic text responses as well as the user's subjective and psychophysiological responses. The latter can be monitored in IoT scenarios via contactless wireless sensors and mobile devices connected to smartphones and tablets or smart watches. Contactless wireless sensors are meanwhile available in most if not all smartphone technologies; they can be augmented by corresponding scientific software, low-cost mobile devices, and sensor consumables. Examples of biosignals that can be tracked via smart biosensors include the recording of heart rate and heart rate variability patterns, event-related brain potentials, galvanic skin response, video-based analysis of facial expressions, skin temperature, or electrooculography to name but a few. Although wireless and mobile recording of biosignals has its problems (including treatment of lost data packages, removal of physiological and physical artifacts caused by movement, talking, or sweating, etc.), these problems can be treated by signal preprocessing routines and algorithms for artifact detection, temporal alignment and merging of biosignals and overt behavior.

In Character Computing, alignment of biosignals and overt behavior can also include semantic text responses. As reviewed in this chapter, systematic experimental research on the embodiment of language (see Sect. 2.3 in this chapter) has investigated the interactions between brain, body, and language and provided interesting and novel insights into how our brain construes emotions, feelings, and meaning during verbal interaction with self and others. Therefore, it will be particularly interesting to further exploit the interaction between a user's character as unraveled by sentiment analysis (e.g., while posting tweets, chatting with a friend) and his/her bodily physiological responses as unraveled by, e.g., changes in heart rate or skin conductance (e.g., see Salamon and Mouček 2017; Weis and Herbert 2017). Certainly, this will help to model and simulate human behavior in computational architectures based on the assumptions of embodied cognition.

As outlined above, up to now, a large number of partly complementary computational models have been developed for the purpose of describing and simulating human behavior in artificial agents and computer-mediated applications. The main differences between these computational models lie in the complexity of their architecture, the psychological theories they rely on, and the practical goals the models were designed for (i.e., to predict aspects of human behavior in artificial agents or in real humans). However, most computational models so far have a cognitive design architecture built on cognitive theories of human behavior and are using symbolic representations (e.g., ACT-R Anderson 1996; SOAR Laird et al. 1987; CLARION Sun 2006). Although highly influential, these cognitive architectures focus on cognitive processes and rational human decision-making. Earlier versions lacked the most prominent human factors like emotions and personality traits that significantly drive human thinking and behavior during most if not all daily situations and that determine individual well-being to large extents. Many endeavors have been undertaken in augmenting existing cognitive architectures with these factors. Also, new architectures have been developed for computational modeling of emotions including FLAME, ALMA, EMA, to name but a few. Along these lines, computational models of personality such as PIACT (Karimi and Kangavari 2012) have been developed to recognize personality traits for the creation of authentic human-like artificial personalities.

Despite the plethora of models, architectures for Character Computing are still missing. Here, computational models of human behavior will be confronted with the fact that there exists no single unifying psychological theory that would explain human experience and human behavior in all its facets across situations. Instead, several psychological theories have been put forward, often with ambiguous and contrasting definitions (see in this chapter). Despite this ambiguity in psychological theories, the relations between behavior, situation, and character (including traits and states) are empirically well proven in psychological studies at various levels of behavioral responding (including brain, physiological bodily, behavioral, and self-report). Moreover, considering the relations between behavior, situation, and character and considering that the user's behavior (e.g., his/her actions, responses, and decisions in a particular situation) can feed back to the situation and to the user's current cognitive, motivational, and affective state is in line with the embodiment view that cognitive operations are not independent from characteristics of the physical body of an agent, including perception and action. It is also in account with recent data collection approaches such as the Situated Assessment Method (Barsalou 2019) that samples, models and predicts human behavior in a situated manner within and across situations at the group level and the individual level.

As outlined above and as also discussed in Chap. 1, the architecture enabling Character Computing needs to extend existing cognitive architectures. Psychological models of embodied cognition and embodied language and related experimental-psychological research in this field could be extremely helpful to make decisions about the interactions between the modules in the architecture. Akin to perception–action links, internal bodily states have been suggested to play a key role in higher order cognitive information processing, in emotion processing as well as in the generation of anticipatory feelings, planning, and decision-making. Internal bodily states and physiological bodily changes as well as the perceptions of those changes are also fundamental for the experience of emotions. Moreover, they may guide information processing, reasoning, and language processing. Character Computing needs to account for these various interactions and relationships between cognition, emotion, and behavior. Thus, Character Computing is very much aligned with embodied proposals in the field of robotics and AI and aimed at combining innovations from Cognitive and Affective and Personality Computing.

2.3.2 Applications of Character Computing

Despite its complexity, the advantage of Character Computing for various applications is obvious. Considering human behavior as being driven by dynamic interactions between behavior, character, and situational affordances while at the same time being sensitive to intra- and interindividual differences, language, and culture specificities seems to be a necessary prerequisite for applications that seek to provide human–computer-assisted technologies for health care and health prevention. For instance, consider treatment of affective disorders such as depression whose symptoms produce the largest health burden across the globe. Worldwide, millions of people suffer from depression and prevalence rates are still increasing. According to psychological models, depression is caused by multiple factors including personality, cognitive, and affective processes that all may contribute to the severity of the disorder. Thus, any technological approach for the automatic detection of depressive symptoms and the computer-assisted treatment of this disorder needs to take the interactions between Behavior, Character, and Situation into account. A Character Computing model of depression will consider the dynamic changes in mood, self-esteem, thinking (rumination), and in autonomous-nervous system activity prior, during, and after depression treatment. Character Computing is aimed at "character" and "context" aware modeling and simulation of human behavior in an attempt to validate, enrich, and possibly revise our current understanding of human behavior in a diversity of contexts such as education, health, data science, or social interaction between virtual and human agents.

2.3.3   Ethical and Privacy Concerns

Finally, collecting "character" data from users and taking their behavior from various online sources as probes for Character Computing may raise ethical and privacy concerns if the users cannot be debriefed about the purpose of the data collection and if oral and written consent from the user is not accomplished. Laboratory research has shown that self-disclosure of participants is related to individual worries about privacy and personal trust in the research environment (e.g., Herbert et al. 2018). Thus, any study in which participants self-disclose and indirectly provide "signs", "traces", or implicit "markers" of their personality, about their health, or their feelings and individual preferences, needs to adhere to ethical standards, in particular, also when children or patients with mental diseases are examined. Furthermore, Big Data approaches assessing data outside the safe laboratory environment may take extra effort to ensure that sensitive data of the user cannot be unofficially accessed, shared, or replicated. What follows from this is that Character, Situation, and Behavior assessment need to be transparent to the user to allow the user to consent to or withhold consent for the collection, use, and/or disclosure of information.

2.4   Conclusion

In this chapter, the field of Character Computing was introduced as an innovation complementing already existing fields of Behavior Computing including cognitive, affective, and personality computing. As such, Character Computing is aimed at considering all aspects of human behavior, comprising the user's current cognitive, affective, and motivational state and the user's personality traits as well as the dynamic interaction between person, situation and behavior. This will promote the development of human–computer systems that adapt to the user's behavior in a character- and context-sensitive manner on the basis of psychological theorizing and empirical psychological evidence. Therefore, a discipline such as Character Computing that aims toward cross-cultural, multilingual, and psychologically driven computational approaches will benefit the most from mutual exchange and joint collaboration from Psychology, Computer Science, and Engineering.

References

Anderson JR (1996) ACT: A simple theory of complex cognition. Am Psychol 51(4):355

Anderson JR, Schunn C (2000) Implications of the ACT-R learning theory: No magic bullets. Advances in instructional psychology, Educational Design and Cognitive Science, pp 1–33

Atkinson R, Shiffrin R (1968) Human memory: a proposed system and its control processes. In: Spence K, Spence J (eds) The psychology of learning and motivation: advances in research and theory, vol 2. Academic Press, New York

Barsalou LW (1999) Perceptions of perceptual symbols. Behav Brain Sci 22(4):637–660

Barsalou LW (2003) Abstraction in perceptual symbol systems. Philos Trans R Soc Lond B: Biol Sci 358(1435):1177–1187

Barsalou LW (2008) Situating concepts. Cambridge Handbook of situated cognition, pp 236–263

Barsalou LW (2019) Establishing Generalizable Mechanisms

Bothell D (2004) Act-r 6.0 reference manual. Working Draft. Brooks, R. A. (1991). Intelligence without reason. Artif Intell: Crit Concepts 3:107–63

Bradley MM, Lang PJ (2000) Measuring emotion: behavior, feeling, and physiology. Cognit Neurosci Emotion 25:49–59

Brunetti M, Sepede G, Mingoia G, Catani C, Ferretti A, Merla A, ... Babiloni C (2010) Elevated response of human amygdala to neutral stimuli in mild post traumatic stress disorder: neural correlates of generalized emotional response. Neuroscience 168(3):670–679

Glenberg AM, Webster BJ, Mouilso E, Lindeman LM (2009) Gender, emotion, and the embodiment of language comprehension. Emotion Rev 1:151G–161

Cacioppo JT, Berntson GG, Larsen JT, Poehlmann KM, Ito TA (2000) The psychophysiology of emotion. Handb Emotions 2:173–191

Carver CS, White TL (1994) Behavioral inhibition, behavioral activation, and affective responses to impending reward and punishment: the BIS/BAS scales. J Pers Soc Psychol 67(2):319

Cambria E, Hussain A (2015) Sentic computing: a common-sense-based framework for concept-level sentiment analysis, vol 1. Springer, Berlin

Chung C, Pennebaker JW (2007) The psychological functions of function words. Soc Commun 1:343–359

Darwin C, Prodger P (1998) The expression of the emotions in man and animals. Oxford University Press, Oxford

Duncan S, Barrett LF (2007) Affect is a form of cognition: a neurobiological analysis. Cognit Emotion 21(6):1184–1211

Gray JA (1982) Neuropsychological theory of anxiety: an investigation of the septal-hippocampal system. Cambridge University Press, Cambridge

Gray JA, McNaughton N (2000) The neuropsychology of anxiety: an enquiry into the functions of the septo-hippocampal system, 2nd edn. Oxford University Press, Oxford

James W (1884) What is an emotion? Mind 9(34):188–205

Hauk O, Johnsrude I, Pulvermüller F (2004) Somatotopic representation of action words in human motor and premotor cortex. Neuron 41(2):301–307

Herbert C, Bendig E, Rojas R (2018) My sadness-our happiness: writing about positive, negative, and neutral autobiographical life events reveals linguistic markers of self-positivity and individual well-being. Front Psychol 9. https://doi.org/10.3389/fpsyg.2018.02522

Herbert C, Ethofer T, Fallgatter AJ, Walla P, Northoff G (2018) Editorial: The janus face of language: where are the emotions in words and where are the words in emotions? Front Psychol 9. https://doi.org/10.3389/fpsyg.2018.00650

Herbert C, Sfarlea A, Blumenthal T (2013) Your emotion or mine: labeling feelings alters emotional face perception-an ERP study on automatic and intentional affect labeling. Front Hum Neurosci 7:378. https://doi.org/10.3389/fnhum.2013.00378

Herbert C, Kubler A, Vogele C (2013) Risk for eating disorders modulates startle-responses to body words. PLoS One 8(1):e53667. https://doi.org/10.1371/journal.pone.0053667

Herbert C, Herbert BM, Ethofer T, Pauli P (2011) His or mine? The time course of self-other discrimination in emotion processing. Soc Neurosci 6(3):277–288

Herbert C, Herbert BM, Pauli P (2011) Emotional self-reference: brain structures involved in the processing of words describing one's own emotions. Neuropsychologia 49(10):2947–2956

Herbert C, Pauli P, Herbert BM (2011) Self-reference modulates the processing of emotional stimuli in the absence of explicit self-referential appraisal instructions. Soc Cognit Affect Neurosci 6(5):653–661. https://doi.org/10.1093/scan/nsq082

Herbert C, Deutsch R, Sutterlin S, Kubler A, Pauli P (2011) Negation as a means for emotion regulation? Startle reflex modulation during processing of negated emotional words. Cognit Affect Behav Neurosci 11(2):199–206. https://doi.org/10.3758/s13415-011-0026-1

Herbert C, Kissler J (2010) Motivational priming and processing interrupt: startle reflex modulation during shallow and deep processing of emotional words. Int J Psychophysiol 76(2):64–71

Herbert C, Ethofer T, Anders S, Junghofer M, Wildgruber D, Grodd W, Kissler J (2009) Amygdala activation during reading of emotional adjectives-an advantage for pleasant content. Soc Cognit Affect Neurosci 4(1):35–49. https://doi.org/10.1093/scan/nsn027

Herbert C, Junghofer M, Kissler J (2008) Event related potentials to emotional adjectives during reading. Psychophysiology 45(3):487–498. https://doi.org/10.1111/j.1469-8986.2007.00638.x

Laird JE, Newell A, Rosenbloom PS (1987) Soar: an architecture for general intelligence. Artif Intell 33(1):1–64

Lang PJ, Greenwald MK, Bradley MM, Hamm AO (1993) Looking at pictures: affective, facial, visceral, and behavioral reactions. Psychophysiology 30(3):261–273

Lindquist KA, MacCormack JK, Shablack H (2015) The role of language in emotion: predictions from psychological constructionism. Front Psychol 6:444

Lepore SJ, Smyth JM (2002) The writing cure: an overview. The writing cure: how expressive writing promotes health and emotional well-being 1:3–14

Lang PJ, Bradley MM, Cuthbert BN (1998) Emotion, motivation, and anxiety: brain mechanisms and psychophysiology. Biol Psych 44(12):1248–1263

Karimi S, Kangavari MR (2012) A computational model of personality. Proc-Soc Behav Sci 32:184–196

McCrae RR, Costa PT Jr (1999) A five-factor theory of personality. Handb Personal: Theory Res 2(1999):139–153

Mairesse F, Walker MA, Mehl MR, Moore RK (2007) Using linguistic cues for the automatic recognition of personality in conversation and text. J Artif Intell Res 30:457–500

Matthews G, Deary IJ, Whiteman MC (2003) Personality traits. Cambridge University Press, Cambridge

Naqvi N, Shiv B, Bechara A (2006) The role of emotion in decision making: a cognitive neuroscience perspective. Current Dir Psychol Sci 15(5):260–264

Neisser U (1967) Cognitive Psychology. Prentice-Hall, Englewood Cliffs

Neisser U (2014) Cognitive Psychology: Classic edition. Psychology Press

Niedenthal PM, Winkielman P, Mondillon L, Vermeulen N (2009) Embodiment of emotion concepts. J Personal Soc Psychol 96(6):1120

Paulhus DL (1989) Socially desirable responding: some new solutions to old problems. In: Personality psychology. Springer, New York, pp 201–209

Pervin LA (2001) A dynamic systems approach to personality. Eur Psychol 6(3):172

Poria S, Cambria E, Bajpai R, Hussain A (2017) A review of affective computing: from unimodal analysis to multimodal fusion. Inf Fusion 37:98–125

Pulvermüller F (2013) How neurons make meaning: brain mechanisms for embodied and abstract-symbolic semantics. Trends Cognit Sci 17(9):458–470

Riccelli R, Toschi N, Nigro S, Terracciano A, Passamonti L (2017) Surface-based morphometry reveals the neuroanatomical basis of the five-factor model of personality. Soc Cognit Affect Neurosci 12(4):671–684

Salamon J, Mouček R (2017) Heart rate and sentiment experimental data with common timeline. Data brief 15:851–861

Scherer, K. R., Schorr, A., and Johnstone, T. (Eds.). (2001). Appraisal processes in emotion: Theory, methods, research. Oxford University Press

Schwarz N, Oyserman D (2001) Asking questions about behavior: cognition, communication, and questionnaire construction. Am J Eval 22(2):127–160

Sun R (2006) The CLARION cognitive architecture: extending cognitive modeling to social simulation. Cognit Multi-agent Interact 79–99

Trafton JG, Hiatt LM, Harrison AM, Tamborello FP II, Khemlani SS, Schultz AC (2013) Act-r/e: an embodied cognitive architecture for human-robot interaction. J Hum-Robot Interact 2(1):30–55

Vinciarelli A, Mohammadi G (2014) A survey of personality computing. IEEE Trans Affect Comput 5(3):273–291

Weis P, Herbert C (2017) Bodily reactions to emotional words referring to own versus other people's emotions. Front Psychol 8:1277. *shared first authorship

Wilson M (2002) Six views of embodied cognition. Psych Bull Rev 9(4):625–636

Winkielman P, Niedenthal PM, Oberman LM (2008) Embodied perspective on emotion-cognition interactions. In: Mirror neuron systems. Humana Press, pp 235-257

Youyou W, Kosinski M, Stillwell D (2015) Computer-based personality judgments are more accurate than those made by humans. Proc Natl Acad Sci 112(4):1036–1040

Chapter 3
A Psychologically Driven, User-Centered Approach to Character Modeling

Cornelia Herbert, Alia El Bolock and Slim Abdennadher

Abstract Character Computing is a novel and interdisciplinary field of research based on interactive research between Computer Science and Psychology. To allow appropriate recognition and prediction of human behavior, Character Computing needs to be grounded on psychological definitions of human behavior that consider explicit as well as implicit human factors. The framework that guides Character Computing therefore needs to be of considerable complexity in order to capture the human user's behavior in its entirety. The question to answer in this chapter is how Character Computing can be empirically realized and validated. The psychologically driven interdisciplinary framework for Character Computing will be outlined and how it is realized empirically as Character Computing platform. Special focus in this chapter is laid on experimental validation of the Character Computing approach including concrete laboratory experiments. The chapter adds to the former chapter which discussed the different steps of the Character Computing framework more broadly with respect to current theories and trends in Psychology and Behavior Computing.

3.1 Introduction

As outlined in detail in the previous chapters, Character Computing is a novel and interdisciplinary field of research. The major aim of Character Computing is to provide a scientific framework for the development of computer systems that are user aware and user adaptive and consequently take the human user into the center of their observation. With this major aim in mind, it is clear that Character Computing cannot

C. Herbert (✉) · A. El Bolock
Ulm University, Ulm, Germany
e-mail: cornelia.herbert@uni-ulm.de

A. El Bolock
e-mail: alia.elbolock@guc.edu.eg

A. El Bolock · S. Abdennadher
German University in Cairo, Cairo, Egypt
e-mail: slim.Abdennadher@guc.edu.eg

© Springer Nature Switzerland AG 2020
A. El Bolock et al. (eds.), *Character Computing*, Human–Computer Interaction Series,
https://doi.org/10.1007/978-3-030-15954-2_3

be achieved without integrating psychological theories and psychological research on human behavior into its computational models. With respect to disciplines, this means that Character Computing needs to be based on truly interdisciplinary and interactive research between Computer Science and Psychology. With respect to the framework that guides Character Computing this means that computational models of Character Computing will be of considerable complexity in order to capture the human user's behavior in its entirety. Moreover, to "understand" and interpret human behavior, character computing models will need to integrate as much information as possible about the potential psychological factors that motivate human behavior from situation to situation and across situations. Only then may Character Computing systems best learn from and adapt to its human users in situations as diverse as daily life. Therefore, appropriate recognition, modeling, and prediction of human behavior in a context-sensitive and situation-specific manner means to ground Character Computing on psychological definitions of human behavior that consider overt and explicit as well as covert and implicit human factors and which explain the interaction between these factors and behavior.

3.2 How Can Character Computing Be Empirically Realized?

In Chaps. 1 and 2, a holistic and heuristic psychological definition and conception of a framework for Character Computing was introduced. The proposed definition clearly defines the term character and outlines how human factors (state and trait variables) relate to a human user's character. It also describes how the user's character interacts with the situation and with the user's behavior. The definition takes account of the complexity of human behavior and the fact that building character-aware computer systems means to take into consideration that these systems need to be aware of the user's current state and the user's personality (trait variables) and the situation in which the behavior is shown or elicited. Character Computing may integrate cognitive architectures and signal processing methods from Cognitive, Affective, and Personality Computing (for an overview and critical discussion, see Chap. 2).

The question to answer next is how an interdisciplinary field of research such as Character Computing can be empirically realized. The authors of this chapter have recently started joint research projects (e.g., Herbert and Abdennhader 2019; Herbert et al. 2018; El Bolock et al. 2018; Bolock et al. 2017) that bring together psychologists and computer scientist to join German Egyptian Research Projects. One of the major aims is to set up the psychologically driven interdisciplinary framework for Character Computing and its empirical realization as Character Computing platform. The platform that integrates the computational system architecture is designed such that it allows recording, simulating, modeling, predicting, and evaluating human behavior based on computational and psychological reasoning. As shown in Fig. 3.1 and as further outlined below as well as in Chap. 4, the empirical realization of Character

Fig. 3.1 Scientific framework of character computing and experimental validation (see text for a detailed explanation)

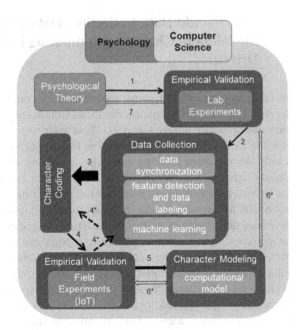

Computing comprises a number of essential steps that are empirically linked and intertwined.

The first step (1) is to have a psychological theory or model. The psychological theory or model provides hypothesis and assumptions about human behavior. These assumptions can be empirically tested in psychological experiments (2). Theory and experiments guide automatic data collection and data labeling for character coding (3) and the construction of the computational model's architecture (5). As illustrated in Fig. 3.1, these steps interact reciprocally and can be iteratively pursued (4*, 6*). Hence, in Character Computing, human behavior can be experimentally tested based on psychological theories. Next, the results are labeled for character coding and translated into a computational model based on which behavior can be simulated. The simulation can again be empirically tested and validated in psychological field and lab experiments (4*, 6*). Accordingly, experimental testing can lead to the acceptance but also to the rejection of the character coding and computing model. To assess human behavior and its underlying human factors (state and trait variables) in a context- and situation- sensitive manner and empirically validate it, the user's behavior needs to be recorded. This requires automated data collection as well as the implementation of data algorithms that automatically record, label, and analyze the human user's behavior according to predefined rules and guidelines for data processing and feature detection (for more details, see Chap. 4). The rules and guidelines that lead to data labeling should be based on knowledge from psychological research derived from experimentally well-defined studies and empirically proven psychological scenarios.

3.3 Why Should Data Collection, Data Labeling, and Data Modeling in Character Computing Be Experimentally Driven?

So far, a large number of partly complementary computational models have been developed for the purpose of describing and simulating human behavior in computer-mediated applications (see Chap. 2). These systems use a cognitive architecture but lack the most prominent human factors like emotions and personality that significantly drive human thinking and behavior during most if not all occasions. As already stated by William James (1890) more than 100 years ago, thinking, acting, and behaving are hardly very neutral or rationally grounded but enriched by emotions and bodily feelings of pleasure and displeasure to large extents. Scientific endeavors have been undertaken in augmenting existing computational models with emotional factors (see Chaps. 1, 4, 2 for overviews). Along these lines, computational models of personality have been developed to recognize personality traits. However, empirical validation from well-controlled psychological experiments is often missing. This lack of empirical validation in terms of psychological experiments with human users can be seen as a major methodological drawback especially in computational approaches that want to be user aware and user adaptive. Methodologically, causal relationships between variables can only be drawn with significant reliability and validity from experiments. Thus, regarding Character Computing, modeling of human behavior may benefit from psychological experimental testing. Psychological experiments aim to be well defined and empirically proven; they assess human behavior under well-controlled and standardized conditions and can be designed to consider the state and trait factors of the user's character. On the basis of these experiments, computing algorithms will be able to identify the user's affective, motivational, and cognitive state and personality traits on the basis of psychological theorizing and empirical psychological evidence.

Of course, well-controlled laboratory experiments may take their toll. Due to the laboratory setting, they may suffer from ecological validity. Thus, the challenge is to transfer the laboratory experimental design to big data approaches that still allow causal inferences akin to experimental laboratory designs. Moreover, human behavior is complex. It may include overt behavior (e.g., key presses such as likes or dislikes on social media platforms or short text messages with semantic and contextual meaning), and thus responses that the user is more or less committed and willing to communicate and share with others. However, behavior may also include covert behavioral responses, i.e., behavior that is hidden from the observer's view and that even the user may not be consciously aware of. Examples are bodily changes such as changes in heart rate, respiration, mimicry (i.e., very small facial muscle contractions) or modulation of muscle tensions, eye blinks signaling approach and avoidance behavior (Lang et al. 1997). Also, the way people write and type and which words they implicitly choose can contain information about the most private parts of our self (e.g., Herbert et al. 2011a, b; Weis and Herbert 2017; Meixner and Herbert 2018). As shown in several psychological experiments, these more or less implicit and covert behavioral responses can provide rich information about the user's character, his/her internal cognitive, motivational, and affective experience (references). Therefore, character-aware systems need to be able to collect behavioral probes on different levels of responding (self-report, overt, and covert behavior including psychophysiological changes). Crucially, to increase the significance and the contextual sensitivity of the behavioral probes, they should be sampled according to the standards defined by experimental psychology.

Regarding multimodal recording of overt and covert behavior, wireless sensors and plug-ins for wearable devices are available in most if not all computer and smartphone technologies. They can be augmented by corresponding scientific software, low-cost mobile devices, and sensor consumables. Examples include biosensors for the recording of heart rate variability patterns, event-related brain potentials (EEG-ERPs), galvanic skin response, facial electromyography and video-based analysis of facial movements, skin temperature, or electrooculography (see Chaps. 2 and 5). However, as outlined in these chapters, analysis of these signals can be time-consuming: the analysis of the data needs to include semi- and fully automated preprocessing of the raw data for feature detection and extraction and these steps as well as signal analysis are recommended to follow guidelines to increase reliability, generalizability, and scientific replication across studies and research groups. Moreover, data recording should be standardized and piloted. This is necessary to avoid favoring physiologically invalid models over physiological valid models during automated data analysis approaches.

All in all, this means that for automated character coding, the collected data recorded via different sensors and devices needs to be integrated into a coherently labeled template. Ideally, the character coding template will comprise the full behavioral profile of each user collected from different sources (experiments). Next, the so developed and empirically proven computing algorithms could be transferred and tested in field experiments to make predictions about many users on the basis of their experimentally well-controlled behavior, however in more realistic IoT settings (see Fig. 3.1, step 4). The mutual exchange between the controlled laboratory driven experimental testing and its transfer to web-based scenarios and real-life communication may improve validation of the character coding procedure and the construction of the computational architectures for the prediction of human behavior.

3.4 Character Coding: An Example of Experimentally Driven Data Collection and Data Labeling

An example of how experimentally driven data collection and signal processing may inform character coding and computational modeling of behavior in Character Computing can be illustrated by the following pilot project conducted in our laboratory at Ulm University. The questions under investigation in this pilot study aimed to answer two important questions of relevance for Character Computing.

(1) Can peripheral-physiological data that comprises different biosignals (e.g., heart rate, startle eyeblink responses) and that is collected during reading under controlled laboratory conditions via wireless devices be integrated into a coherently labeled template for automated character coding? (2) Can we predict from these signals the covert emotional response elicited by a discrete event on the basis of (supervised) machine learning algorithms? To answer these two questions, a total of 60 datasets from healthy participants (all women, aged >18 years) were included in the pilot project. Participants were screened for mental health. Screening included questions asking for certain personality traits (e.g., anxiety) and strict exclusion and inclusion criteria were used to ensure homogeneous group recording with little between-subject variability in personality, mood, and sociodemographic data. The data was taken from a laboratory experiment (conceptualized, designed, and programmed by the first author of this chapter and that is part of a larger current study of the first author; see also Herbert et al. 2006; Herbert and Kissler 2010; Herbert et al. 2013). In this laboratory experiment, a series of words are presented centered on a computer screen (see Fig. 3.2). The visually presented words, for instance, include personality traits and words describing subjective feeling states of positive, negative, or neutral connotation. Word categories (positive, negative, and neutral), preselection of words, and their assignment to the emotional categories are based on normative ratings from previous studies and normative word databases (e.g., Herbert et al. 2006; Herbert and Kissler 2010; Herbert et al. 2013). The words are presented individually on a computer screen while participants are sitting in a comfortable chair and asked to read each word silently. In real life, this laboratory situation would come closest to a situation in which participants watch a consumer advertisement or a health campaign on their tablet, PC, or TV, in which character trait and character state words are used to elicit positive or negative attitudes and approach or withdrawal behavior in the reader to either facilitate or stop a certain behavior.

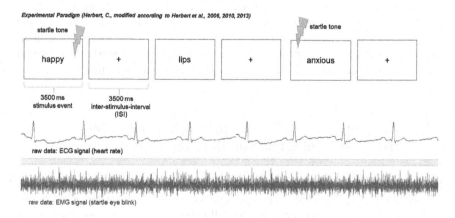

Fig. 3.2 Experimental design for the detection of implicit behavioral reactions elicited during reading of words of positive, negative, or neutral content. Word presentation was kept constant across trials. ISI included jitters to avoid predictability of trial duration. Startle probes were presented in different time windows during word presentation focusing on long intervals

As in the real-life scenario, participants in the laboratory got no task other than to passively view and read each word as long as it was present on the screen. Hence, there was no overt behavioral response (e.g., such as reaction time from key presses, verbal or nonverbal yes–no responses) from the participant. The intent of the study was to investigate how participant implicitly respond to words that relate to the most private aspects of their self (their personality and feelings) and that have a positive, negative, or neutral connotation. To this end, participants' peripheral-physiological responses, including heart rate and startle eyeblink data, were recorded during word exposure from each participant. The startle eye blink response was elicited by a startle tone that was occasionally presented in random order during the presentation of some of the stimulus events. The reflexive eye blink response was recorded in line with current guidelines (e.g., Blumenthal et al. 2005) via sensors attached to the participant's eye. The sensors sense the contractility of the orbicularis oculi muscle which is responsible for the eye blink. As shown in several experiments, the startle eye blink response can be used to determine the participant's implicit approach and avoidance behavior (e.g., Lang 1995). In addition, heart rate was continuously recorded via sensors attached to the participant's left and right wrists to determine changes in physiological arousal and attention focus (for methodological details, see, e.g., Herbert and Kissler 2010; Herbert et al. 2013; Blumenthal et al. 2005). The experimental task used is robust and was empirically validated in previous studies (Herbert et al. 2006; Herbert and Kissler 2010; Herbert et al. 2013). Knowing from several psychological experiments and psychological theories (Lang 1995; Robinson and Vrana 2000; Herbert and Kissler 2010) how the startle eye blink response and changes in heart rate should hypothetically behave in this experiment depending on whether a stimulus of positive, negative, or neutral content is presented (see Table 3.1), we can test if supervised learning methods will be equally successful to detect these patterns with sufficient accuracy and if we can from these methods for each signal draw firm conclusions about the participant's covert behavioral response when exposed to certain events of emotional, motivational, and personal relevance.

Moreover, we can test whether it is possible to label the data for automated character coding. Regarding the latter, the necessary data mining and data preprocessing steps are shown in Fig. 3.3. As illustrated, to construe the template for automated character coding, the data needs to be synchronized and segmented according to the events of interest. Event markers contain the coding knowledge and timing information when an event/stimulus (e.g., here: word or startle tones) was presented on the computer screen and which stimulus category it belongs to.

Table 3.1 Hypotheses regarding changes in startle eyeblink and heart rate when exposed to positive and negative compared to neutral stimuli or baseline

Stimulus valence	Positive	Negative
Startle eye blink	Inhibition	Potentiation
Heart rate (phasic changes)	Acceleration	Deceleration

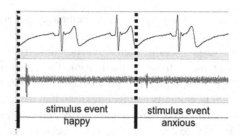

Fig. 3.3 Automatic data labeling according to event files containing the events of interest

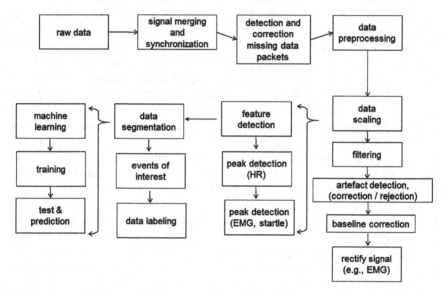

Fig. 3.4 Data collection modules for automatic signal processing (see description in the text)

During wireless data recording, data packets can be lost due to unstable Bluetooth connections between sender (the recording device) and receiver (the recording software). Thus, dropped data packets need to be documented and trials with missing data need to be either rejected from further data analysis or corrected (data interpolation). The same holds true for artifacts that can occur during the recording. Which option is chosen (rejection or correction of lost data packages and artifacts) should be documented as it can significantly affect the results especially with smaller amounts of data.

As illustrated in Fig. 3.4, each of the recorded biosignals needs to be preprocessed following guidelines for psychophysiological research (e.g., Blumenthal et al. 2005) to detect and extract the signal features of interest. Regarding the startle eye blink response, the most prominent and valid feature to detect and extract for later classification is the peak of the startle amplitude extracted from the filtered and rectified

Fig. 3.5 Heart rate and feature detection (R-peak)

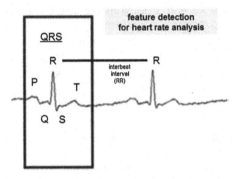

EMG signal and elicited within the first 200 ms after the startle tone was presented. It can be automatically detected by peak detection algorithms that include additional inclusion and exclusion criteria about the latency of the response (20–120 ms) and the magnitude of the peak amplitude (e.g., exclusion of amplitudes smaller than an empirically derived cutoff score).

Regarding heart rate analysis, feature detection is based on a number of preprocessing steps that demodulate signal complexity. As shown in Fig. 3.5, the human heart period or heart cycle is characterized by changes in the recording signal, with the R-peak being the most prominent signal change which is observable by eye from the raw signal. To detect it reliably and validly from the raw signal, certain algorithms have been developed that allow automatic R-peak detection and beat-to-beat (RR or interbeat interval) detection on which heart rate analysis is most frequently based on (e.g., Andersen 2017). Most algorithms include the following steps: data filtering and nonlinear derivation to enhance the QRS complex and enhance medium amplitudes to reduce false positives and false negatives in the signal recording. Next, peaks can be detected, for instance, by using the first Gaussian differentiator to identify the location of the peaks (e.g., Kathirvel et al. 2011).

Next, the preprocessed and labeled data can be used for machine learning. To this end, the data was divided into two datasets: one set was used for training (containing 80%) and the other set (20%) was used for testing. In addition, each biosignal was tested separately. Three different machine learning algorithms were tested to train and predict the data. The models included the LSTM model and neural networks with one or two hidden layers (Chauhan et al. 2018; Faust et al. 2018).

For the startle eye blink responses, the average accuracy to correctly classify responses of the test data into positive, negative, and neutral events ranged from 79 to 81.2% across models (see Table 3.2). For heart rate, accuracy was below 50% irrespective of the model used (see Table 3.3).

The low accuracy of the ECG signal suggests that for single events such as words that elicit little changes in physiological arousal, it may be difficult to draw clear inferences about the user's internal affective state. The same result may be obtained when transferred to more realistic scenarios. Thus, although in affective computing recording of biosignals has already become a valuable means of recognizing hidden human

Table 3.2 EMG signal: startle eye blink: average precision (%), recall (%), F1 score (%), accuracy (%)

Model	Average precision	Average recall	Average F1	Accuracy
LSTM	85.3	84.3	84.2	81.2
1 Layer NN	84.6	84.2	84.1	81.17
2 Layer NN	82.0	81.7	81.9	78.9

Table 3.3 ECG signal: heart rate: R-peaks average precision (%), recall (%), F1 score (%), accuracy (%)

Model	Average precision	Average recall	Average F1	Accuracy
LSTM	43.8	31.0	34.7	42.1
1 Layer NN	35.9	36.1	37.3	37.4
2 Layer NN	37.3	33.2	35.7	41.3

factors such as emotions, the above-described results—although preliminary—show that single modality systems (i.e., systems that record just one biosignal) can fail in emotion recognition, and therefore their application may be restricted to a few daily scenarios. Given that data collection of various biosignals can be costly (e.g., in terms of computing time required for online and real-time signal processing), the development of hybrid systems that can switch between different biosignal inputs might provide a valuable solution, in particular, also for Character Computing approaches that obviously need to collect a huge amount of data. However, as is obvious from the pilot project described above, that experimental testing with psychological tasks and paradigms may help to decide which signals to choose. This can give high computational flexibility while at the same time avoiding useless multiple testing, inflation of alpha errors, and high false positive rates unless multiple comparisons adjustments are made. Thus, in Character Computing, experimental testing may assist in both, i.e., in the decision which signals to choose and which events/situations to monitor to predict behavior.

3.5   Character Modeling

Finally, we will discuss how based on these results Character Modeling could be realized. As shown from the pilot study described above, certain behavioral responses can be estimated from certain biosignals. However, not every biosignal is well suited for each stimulus. By using character coding and thus modeling the character this can be overcome. Character models can be trained to predict which character components to activate, which situation markers to include, and which behavioral cue to monitor.

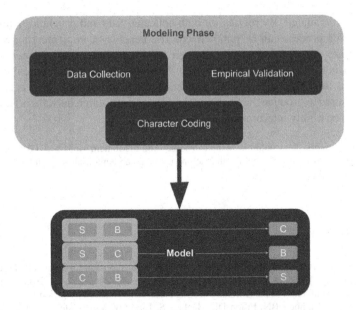

Fig. 3.6 Architecture of the iterative modeling phase

This will be realized through the process proposed in Fig. 3.1. The Character Coding module is the main part responsible for iterating over the modeling phase. As shown in Fig. 3.6, the coding module relies on the multi-modally collected and labeled data. Any extracted character codes, mapping one of the three (C, S, B) triad components to the other two, are then validated. After multiple iterations in the data collection, coding, and validation cycle, the produced character code is added to the global character model.

The architecture of the character coding module itself is set up as follows. One of the two main modeling techniques is rule-based or machine learning models. The former is practical in its quick speed of execution and interpretability. The latter, while lacking speed of execution, gains interpretability, accuracy, and ease of maintenance. However, machine learning relies more heavily on having large data amounts. If we go to other deep learning methods, the required data is even bigger and the process looses interpretability and ease of maintenance. While each technique has its benefits and drawbacks, one current trend is hybrid approached combining the two (e.g., Frias-Martinez et al. 2006; Stuart 2013). Our vision is that this is the way that character coding can be realized. By applying techniques like ensemble learning (Dieterich 2002), rule-based machine learning (e.g., Ray and Chakrabarti 2019), and neuro-fuzzy inference systems (Walia et al. 2015), we aim at further adapting machine learning techniques to the adaption of patterns in human behavior.

Using a hybrid approach will enable speeding up the execution by leveraging results from psychology to compensate for incomplete data. This would thus allow for the reverse engineering for some of the code through rule-based approaches, which can then be validated. By relying on both collected data and psychology research, the modeling process can be parallelized. The benefits of implementing a hybrid approach are thus quicker results through reusing already existing ones without compromising accuracy or interpretability. To be noted is that interpretability is one of the most important outcomes of the character coding phase. While accuracy is highly required to produce the final model codes, early research into character coding requires to be highly interpretable to give more insights.

Acknowledgements We would like to thank Youssef Abd El Moniem Mohamed (GUC) and Nizar El Hawat (Ulm University) for help with machine learning and Nina Blahak (Ulm University) for help with data collection.

References

Andersen RS, Poulsen ES, Puthusserypady S (2017) A novel approach for automatic detection of atrial fibrillation based on inter beat intervals and support vector machine. In: 2017 39th annual international conference of the IEEE engineering in medicine and biology society (EMBC). IEEE

Blumenthal TD, Cuthbert BN, Filion DL, Hackley S, Lipp OV, Van Boxtel A (2005) Committee report: guidelines for human startle eyeblink electromyographic studies. Psychophysiology 42(1):1–15

Bolock AE et al (2017) Character computing: challenges and opportunities. In: Proceedings of the 16th international conference on mobile and ubiquitous multimedia. ACM

Chauhan NK, Singh K (2018) A review on conventional machine learning vs deep learning. In: International conference on computing, power and communication technologies (GUCON). IEEE, p 2018

Dietterich TG (2002) Ensemble learning. The handbook of brain theory and neural networks, vol 2, pp 110–125

El Bolock A et al (2018) Character computing: computer science meets psychology. In: Proceedings of the 17th international conference on mobile and ubiquitous multimedia. ACM

Faust O et al (2018) Deep learning for healthcare applications based on physiological signals: a review. Comput Methods Programs Biomed 161:1–13

Frias-Martinez E, Chen SY, Liu X (2006) Survey of data mining approaches to user modeling for adaptive hypermedia. IEEE Trans Syst, Man, Cybern, Part C (Appl Rev) 36(6):734–749

Herbert C, Abdennhader S (2019) Cross-cultural, multilingual and psychologically-driven computational approaches to character computing - computer science meets psychology. DAAD-BMBF funding project

Herbert C, Kissler J (2010) Motivational priming and processing interrupt: startle reflex modulation during shallow and deep processing of emotional words. Int J Psychophysiol 76(2):64–71

Herbert C, Herbert BM, Pauli P (2011a) Emotional self-reference: brain structures involved in the processing of words describing one's own emotions. Neuropsychologia 49(10):2947–2956

Herbert C, Herbert BM, Ethofer T, Pauli P (2011b) His or mine? the time course of self-other discrimination in emotion processing. Soc Neurosci 6(3):277–288

Herbert C, Kissler J, Junghöfer M, Peyk P, Rockstroh B (2006) Processing of emotional adjectives: evidence from startle EMG and ERPs. Psychophysiology 43(2):197–206

Herbert C, Kübler A, Vögele C (2013) Risk for eating disorders modulates startle-responses to body words. PloS one 8(1):e53667

Herbert C, Abdennadher S, Kargl F, Elmoughy A, Abdelrammahn Y (2018) Character computing for negative behavior intervention and psychological health prevention. Application for GERF-STDF funding project. https://www.daad.eg/de/foerderung-finden/gerf/, http://stdf.eg:8080/

Herbert C, Bendig E, Rojas R (2018) My sadness-our happiness: writing about positive, negative, and neutral autobiographical life events reveals linguistic markers of self-positivity and individual well-being. Front Psychol 9. https://doi.org/10.3389/fpsyg.2018.02522

James W, Burkhardt F, Bowers F, Skrupskelis IK (1890) The principles of psychology, vol 1, no 2. Macmillan, London

Kathirvel P, Manikandan MS, Prasanna SRM, Soman KP (2011) An efficient R-peak detection based on new nonlinear transformation and first-order Gaussian differentiator. Cardiovasc Eng Technol 2(4):408–425

Lang PJ (1995) The emotion probe: studies of motivation and attention. Am Psychol 50(5):372

Lang PJ, Bradley MM, Cuthbert BN (1997) Motivated attention: affect, activation, and action. Attention and orienting: sensory and motivational processes, vol 97, p 135

Meixner F, Herbert C (2018). Whose emotion is it? measuring self-other discrimination in romantic relationships during an emotional evaluation paradigm. PloS one 13(9):e0204106

Ray P, Chakrabarti A (2019) A mixed approach of deep learning method and rule-based method to improve aspect level sentiment Analysis. Appl Comput Inform

Robinson JD, Vrana SR (2000) The time course of emotional and attentional modulation of the startle eyeblink reflex during imagery. Int J Psychophysiol 37(3):275–289

Stuart LC (2013) User modeling via machine learning and rule-based reasoning to understand and predict errors in survey systems

Walia N, Singh H, Sharma A (2015) ANFIS: adaptive neuro-fuzzy inference system-a survey. Int J Comput Appl 123(13)

Weis P, Herbert C (2017) Bodily reactions to emotional words referring to own versus other people's emotions. Front Psychol 8:1277. *shared first authorship

Chapter 4
Applications of Character Computing From Psychology to Computer Science

Alia El Bolock, Slim Abdennadher and Cornelia Herbert

Abstract The integration of Psychology and Computer Science research is one of the main focus points of research into Character Computing. Each field can help further Character Computing and only together can a usable framework for Character Computing be reached. This is done through combining experimental, computational and data-driven approaches. Research into Character Computing can be clustered into three main research modules. (1) Character sensing and profiling through implicit or explicit means while maintaining privacy and security measures. (2) Developing ubiquitous adaptive systems by leveraging character for specific use cases. (3) investigating artificial characters, how they could be achieved and when they should be implemented. This chapter discusses the challenges, opportunities, and possible applications of each module.

4.1 Psychology and Character Computing

As outlined and discussed in detail in the previous chapters, Psychology can provide models and definitions of human behavior that help construe novel interaction methods in technology and computing. The psychological definitions detail how to measure and observe different individual traits and states, what behavioral changes they indicate, as well as how to best adapt indicators of C (character), S (situation), and B (behavior) for computational modeling. Research in the field of psychology will help advance Character Computing by providing the needed framework and guidelines for character modeling and computing. Moreover, research in Character Computing can help to revise existing theories and models of human behavior and work toward their unification. This can be done both through computational modeling and analysis as well as using data-driven approaches and providing scalable data collection solutions. This will render Character Computing a truly transdisciplinary field, helping to tackle the research gaps and challenges of each of the fields through

A. El Bolock (✉) · S. Abdennadher · C. Herbert
German University in Cairo, Cairo, Egypt
e-mail: alia.elbolock@guc.edu.eg

A. El Bolock · C. Herbert
Ulm University, Ulm, Germany

© Springer Nature Switzerland AG 2020
A. El Bolock et al. (eds.), *Character Computing*, Human–Computer Interaction Series,
https://doi.org/10.1007/978-3-030-15954-2_4

the other. Being the interdisciplinary field it is, Character Computing needs to rely on a strong Psychology foundation to reach its full potential. Personality factors as stable traits play a very important role in Character Computing, but measuring personality traits alone is not enough to realize Character Computing. As outlined in Chaps. 1 and 2, Character Computing follows a user-centered approach that focuses on the human user and his/her character. Given that per definition (see Chap. 1), character consists of more facets than personality, and Character Computing therefore needs to go beyond personality computing. This is done by investigating including other character components, alongside personality, and affect, depending on the use case.

Character Computing aims at integrating research from different branches of Psychology, starting with Personality, Cognitive, Affective, and Behavioral Psychology (see Chap. 2). Following this holistic approach requires investigating how to best unify psychological theories and research findings to complete and complement each other, while removing existing redundancies between theories and research findings. This would take us one step closer to accounting for the (C, B, S) triad and its interactions. As a consequence, Character Computing can also help in providing solutions to Psychology by combining computational modeling and data-driven approaches and providing scalable data collection solutions. This would make Character Computing a truly transdisciplinary field tackling the research gaps and challenges of each field through knowledge from the other.

However, how can Character Computing be realized from the interdisciplinary perspective of computer science and psychology? And how can it be empirically realized?

The first fundamental answers to these questions have already been provided by German-Egyptian Research teams consisting of psychologists and computer scientists (e.g., El Bolock 2018; El Bolock et al. 2018b, 2017). As explained in detail in Chaps. 1–3, to realize Character Computing empirically, we introduce a novel framework and architecture for Character Computing that consists of different components or modules with different functions. Chapter 3 also explains how the developed framework and its modules allow us to combine psychological and computational approaches in a way that goes well beyond previous approaches. In particular, as shown in Fig. 4.1 and illustrated in Chap. 3 (e.g., see Fig. 3.1), we combine Psychology-driven experimental approaches (in-lab) experiments with experimental big data approaches (outside the lab). This is done to sense and analyze the character in a theory-driven and ecologically valid way. The collected data is then also used for character modeling. For a detailed discussion and example of the experimental approach and the modules required to implement it into our proposed Character Computing platform, the interested reader is referred to Chap. 3.

Based on the foundation of Character Computing, outlined in Chaps. 1–3, this chapter discusses possible applications of the field. This is done separately for each of the three Character Computing modules given below:

- Character sensing and profiling,
- Character-aware adaptive systems, and
- Artificial characters.

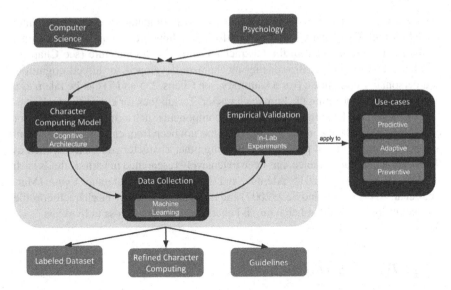

Fig. 4.1 Character Computing framework developed by our team (El Bolock, Abdennadher, and Herbert) and its implementation into the Character Computing platform developed by El Bolock and Herbert to realize character computing empirically

4.2   Sensing the Character

Following an experimental and psychologically driven approach, an important component of Character Computing is to investigate means for detecting or sensing the user's/the individual's character. If we were to draw analogies to Personality and Affective Computing, we would find that one of its core research directions is assessing personality and sensing a person's affect and mood state through various means as shown in Picard (2003) and as discussed and summarized in Chap. 2. This combination of personality and affective assessment is of interest to Character Computing for many reasons. First of all, affect and mood are factors influencing behavior in daily life. Affective responses can occur as a result of a specific situation, as shown in Chaps. 1 and 6. Thus, by sensing a person's affective state given a specific situation and by assessing his/her personality profile as indicators of a person's character, we aim to use this information to set up the observe and predict functions in the computational model. The techniques used in Affective Computing to sense affective states could be extended to Character Computing to sense affect as well as cognitive and motivational states (ElKomy et al. 2017; Cowie et al. 2001; Abdelrahman et al. 2017). Affective and Cognitive Psychology have provided numerous examples of how a person's affective, motivational, and cognitive state can be reliably and validly assessed in well-controlled experimental settings and paradigms. In the previous chapter, we gave a concrete example of how psychological experimental research can be integrated into our Character Computing platform and how it can guide computational modeling and be included in the Character Computing architecture (see Chap. 3). In Character Computing, the sensing mechanism developed for affect, cognition, and personality computing (for a summary, see Chaps. 2, 5 and 7) can be taken as a starting point for profiling the human character. Techniques for efficiently and accurately sensing and detecting other character components such as morals or beliefs, for example, still need to be investigated as this has not been frequently researched from a scalable computational perspective. Sensing other character components, such as the health state or appearance, has been extensively researched in various fields such as Medicine (Islam et al. 2015; Alemdar and Ersoy 2010) and Computer Vision (Martinez et al. 2017; Jaimes and Sebe 2007) and thus can be added to the character profile to account for the fact that behavior and character can vary across individuals.

4.2.1   Data Collection

Any Character Computing investigation, especially that of sensing characteristics requires a large amount of data. If we think about the abovementioned (C, B, S) triple, we need to collect data about every instance of a specific behavior given all character combinations for every situation. Thus, we need to consider the following human factors:

1. general characteristics of the individual, such as personality traits, social and cultural background, beliefs, morals, etc.
2. observe, collect, or induce as many different and similar situations as possible.
3. behavior and state data for every situation or instance thereof.
4. multiple readings of behavior and state pairs for the same situation to check whether the behavior is consistent or variable.
5. multiple readings of the general characteristics to check their stability over time.

The aim is to collect the minimal amount of detailed data needed to be able to fine-tune the three Character Computing functions *observe*, *predict*, and *understand* until they present an accurate model of the (C, B, S) triple and thus of human behavior.

As outlined in detail in Chap. 3, the usual approach in Psychology is to conduct experiments that collect data from certain participants based on specific theoretical assumptions and within well-controlled and standardized designs and situations. In Big Data research and in the wild (e.g., HCI-related field experiments), data is collected from a large number of participants in a less constrained environment than in psychological laboratory experiments but probably in less detail and with less causality (Lazar et al. 2017; Tan et al. 2016). While sensing certain characteristics of C and potentially also B within a given S, consistency needs to be maintained. In our Character Computing platform, this is realized by following the approach presented in Fig. 4.2 which is enabled by applications similar to Alaa et al. 2020.

Fig. 4.2 Given a specific S, the B and C are observed through experiments, correlated through collected data, and modeled computationally to reach a verified accurate model mapping the (C, B, S) triple and its functions

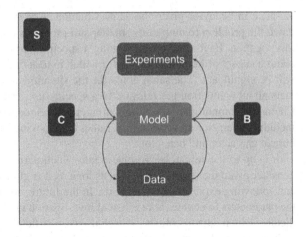

Any correlation between a subset of C and B within a specific S should simultaneously be investigated through (1) constrained in-lab experiments, (2) Big Data approaches by collecting as much data as possible, and (3) setting up a corresponding computational model.

When talking about data collection, especially of such magnitude there are various well-known challenges and obstacles. For instance, there is the trade-off of having little data from a large number of individuals versus lots of data from a smaller number of individuals. Starting with a small experiment, for example, requiring many details and information from a relatively small number of participants will not be easily scalable to a larger number of participants but it can inform which human factors and which indicators should be given preference to (see Chap. 3). The maintainability of any multimodal data collection is a big challenge. As shown by various experiments on life-logging, which can be considered an extreme case of detailed data collection, collecting continuous streams of data is not maintainable in the long run (see, for example, Dang-Nguyen et al. 2017). Another big problem in the maintainability of data collection is the data storage. Even nowadays where the zettabytes of data can be stored, it is still not realistic that detailed accounts of a large number of individuals will be stored in the long run. Psychologically, ethically, and methodologically, it should be known what the data is needed for and the collection should be tailored to that account. Also, the data should periodically be analyzed and discarded after the needed information is extracted and abstracted.

Still big data about every aspect of a person's life, like that resulting from life-logging, is crucial if we are to achieve the full vision of Character Computing that gives a full account of an individual. However, this is not realistic for the time being and is not achievable on a large scale as was discussed. We could have a complete account of a few individuals and predict their behavior through a model tailored specifically to them. But for the time being, it is not possible to create a model that automatically and accurately represents a large number of individuals with all their special features, different behaviors given specific situations and account for variance in behavior given the same situation. Accordingly, we propose breaking down the problem to numerous smaller sub-problems depending on the use case or investigation. Each application serving a specific purpose will require information about a subset of human behavior for which in turn only a subset of characteristics will be significant. The same holds for the situations, as only certain situations or facts about a situation are relevant to a specific use case. Thus, in practical terms, Character Computing consists of continuous incremental research into all aspects of including character into computing, rather than looking for one unifying formula for human character and behavior.

It is up to the researcher to investigate which parameters of the C, B, and S to consider given the specific use case, as long as it is guided by psychological theory and following experimental standards. In the future, we aim to have guidelines for the parameters to enable more efficient investigation in Character Computing which dictates which data to collect for each use case or field.

Thus, depending on the application and research question, some approaches in data collection may be more favorable than others. All these considerations need should be investigated further in future Character Computing applications, to reach the best decisions suited for the current investigation at hand.

The aim of sensing the character components is to generate character profiles for individuals. The profiles detailing the different character components are then used to feedback into the character computing model and update it according to the observed empirical results and the collected data (recall Figs. 4.1 and 4.2. The data needs to be processed, post-collection, to generate (C, B, S) mappings. How information about each of the three components will be represented is dictated by both the current use case and the Character Computing model itself. These mappings are then translated into logic rules representing the interactions between character, behavior, and situation. The rules will have to be enhanced using soft-computing techniques such as fuzzy logic to compensate for the varying and complex nature of the (C, B, S) triple. The resulting model can then be combined with the machine learning models resulting from analyzing the collected data. Such hybrid models (e.g., rule-based machine learning and neuro-fuzzy inference systems) are best suited for modeling complex adaptive systems with a high nature of variation, such as human behavior (see Chap. 3).

4.2.2 Implicit Versus Explicit Sensing

Being able to sense character components is essential for collecting data about the characteristics and behavior of individuals. This data is then needed to correlate character and behavior together in order to generate an accurate model of Character Computing (e.g., the *observe* and *predict* functions discussed in Chap. 1).

Data collection for character detection can be done in an explicit or an implicit manner (see Olson and Kellogg 2014 and Chap. 2) for an overview) and can either be large scale resulting in big data or in a constrained lab environment on a smaller sample size resulting in a smaller amount of data. Each of the approaches and their combinations has their strengths and weaknesses (e.g., see Zeng et al. 2008 for a survey of sensing affective states).

4.2.2.1 Implicit Data Collection

Implicit data collection refers to collecting data unobtrusively with no or little deliberate interaction with the user.

Examples are (1) collecting already existing data such as from social media (Stieglitz et al. 2018; Casler et al. 2013; Paul et al. 2017) and smart home devices (Nelson and Allen 2018; Kaushik and Prakash 2018), (2) collecting information in the background while normally using technology like smartphones do for usage data (El Bolock et al. 2018a; Cao and Lin 2017; Wang et al. 2014) or behavior in games (El Bolock et al. 2020b; Worth and Book 2014), (3) applications that collect the needed data automatically (Apple's Health application; Alaa et al. 2020), (4) collecting information from non-wearable sensors such as stationary eyetrackers (Kassem et al. 2017; Abdrabou et al. 2018) and thermal camera within an experiment (Abdelrahman et al. 2017), or (5) inferring extra information from the already requested data (for overviews see Jaimes and Sebe 2007; Flick 2017).

The advantages of implicit big data collection are obvious. Its main strength lies in requiring minimal or no interaction from the user, thus making it more appealing for users and more sustainable. This means smaller dropout rate; once you get one person involved in an implicit data collection study, you are most likely to keep them till the end. This is because after sometime they might forget about the application running in the background and do not feel a burden of providing the needed data. It is also easier to collect larger amounts of data per individual over longer time intervals, which is usually needed for giving significant insights about character components, as already shown for personality traits (Kosinski et al. 2013). As is true for all empirical studies, making long-term prediction about a specific person requires longitudinal collection of data across situations. Another advantage is making use of readily available data of which there is an abundance nowadays. Huge amounts of data can be collected from social media about virtually everything. Data can also be collected from smartphones, ubiquitous sensors, and smart devices which are now used by a large number of people (Malhi et al. 2017). This existing data opens up a large window of research opportunities. It ensures that the collected data is as accurate as possible. This avoids one of the disadvantages of explicit data collection techniques, namely, biases toward socially favorable images (discussed in more detail below). However, this comes at the cost of not always having all the needed information, as the collected data features are dictated by the already existing used medium.

While implicit data collection has the same general advantages and disadvantages when done large scale or on a smaller scale, there are some notable differences.

If we consider in-lab data collection, there is the advantage of having options to record more data than in the wild, as many sensors can be set up without intruding on the user. By utilizing unobtrusive sensors such as stationary eyetrackers or cameras with different modalities (e.g., RGB or thermal), we can record different nonverbal cues indicating the current state (affective, physical, or cognitive as already shown).

When comparing implicit to explicit sensing in a lab setting, there is also the advantage of reducing the experiment effect. Participants are usually a bit on edge in an experiment, making assumptions about what the researcher is trying to measure or what is the "correct" answer in order to look good. This external effect could be aggravated by being hooked to many sensors, cables, and big devices. Thus, using unobtrusive sensors could help participants be more at ease and reduce the external emotional stimuli.

The main disadvantage of the abovementioned data collection techniques is the privacy concerns it comes with. Given the Facebook-Cambridge Analytica scandal[1] (which is one of many similar ones), one could imagine how reluctant people would be to allow access to their personal information, implicitly or explicitly. They might even be more reluctant to allow implicit access as they would not be aware of everything they are collecting. Nowadays, people are haunted by conspiracy theories where governments and people would steal their personal information and use it for dubious purposes. As will be discussed in Sect. 4.2.3, there are many safety measures that can be applied to minimize this problem and the concerns of people. However, more intensive research needs to be done in this direction, specifically tailored to Character Computing due to the sensitivity of the data giving insight about some of the character components such as the user's preferences, mental health, beliefs, attitudes, etc.

Another disadvantage is that with minimizing the interaction with the user, the type of data to be collected is limited and unlabeled. Instead of asking for missing information, prompting the user to indicate certain facts about their state, models for inferring the missing info and for categorizing and clustering the data are utilized. Relying on such unlabeled data requires more analysis and assumptions and thus leaves room for inaccuracy and loss of precision. Also, the collected data will be more abstracted and have more noise, thus it will be harder to analyze. Without having validation from the user, the accuracy could also be reduced as the baseline of each individual will be affected by external and internal effects.

In Chap. 3, it is described how the abovementioned problems can be avoided by setting up well-controlled psychological experiments that use robust implicit measures of human behavior to determine and predict the direction of behavior (approach or avoidance) from the participant and how data labeling can be achieved and tested by supervised machine learning algorithms.

4.2.2.2   Explicit Data Collection

Explicit data collection refers to collecting data by asking the user to directly provide certain information.

Examples are (1) self-report questionnaires and psychological tests, (2) interviews and diary reports, (3) life-logging, (4) multiple prompts for response and input,

---

[1]https://www.theguardian.com/us-news/2015/dec/11/senator-ted-cruz-president-campaign-facebook-user-data.

wearable devices, and sensors (e.g., Berkovsky et al. 2019), or (5) asking users to perform certain tasks. (Refer to Swan 2013 for an overview and Hong et al. 2018; Can et al. 2019 for examples from the healthcare domain).

One of the main advantages when collecting explicit big data is that we have the direct response of the user. Another problem for any explicit data collection technique is the participant bias. Whether intentionally or unintentionally, people might respond or provide information aligned with social desirability and acceptance. In self-report questionnaires, one might give a less accurate answer to avoid looking or feeling like a negative person. No one would want to say that they are lazy or do not help others in need. Sometimes people are even not aware of their current state and thus cannot accurately report it; they might be confusing anger with stress or blaming other factors for their current feelings. How to validate self-report information and overcome the problem is already a trending topic of investigation. When considering character components, however, one needs to be more careful as some of the components are ambivalent in nature and thus can be used to pass judgement on the "quality" of a person and is prone to misuse. Security and privacy considerations play another vital role here.

When comparing between implicit and explicit data collection techniques, we believe that in most cases a combination of both approaches is needed to get representative data. The challenge there is finding the golden ratio between implicit and explicit data. We need a balance of how much self-report measures to include (accounting for response biases and intentional or unintentional "dishonesty" in self-reporting Van de Mortel et al. 2008) with respect to the validity of the automatically sensed data (considering the resulting sensor biases, noise, and estimation errors e.g., Gundry and Deterding 2018).

Researchers should leverage the (C, B, S) triad to develop models that automatically assign behavioral cues to states by adding more information about the person's character. This endeavor still requires lots of research and validation to reach robust generic usable models.

After discussing the potential advantages and disadvantages of each data collection approach, it is clear that there is not one approach that can be exclusively used. The decision of going toward big data or in-lab experiments can be decided based on the specific use case, needed data type, and scope of the experiment (proof of concept or model generation).

4.2.3 Privacy and Security

Naturally, there are many ethical concerns when considering collecting data about human behavior and characteristics and extracting information therefrom.

All the considered characteristics and behavior metrics are very personal in nature and can be used to evaluate humans. Thus, protecting the privacy of individuals and accordingly their identity is a major concern and important field of investigation when sensing the character (e.g., Gerber et al. 2018). The minimal amount of data needed for extracting the necessary information should be determined for each use case.

Existing measures for protecting the individuals and maintaining their privacy should be applied. No one would want to use an application that, for example, provides a personalized learning experience to achieve the best results at the expense of other people knowing one's weaknesses.

From the practical perspective, if privacy is not guaranteed to individuals then it is very unlikely that many participants would be willing to take part in any experiment. Thus, we need to guarantee full anonymity and data privacy maintenance to encourage individuals to provide us with the needed data. One possibility is to analyze the data in the client side of applications and thus storing as little information as possible about the individuals in global databases (King and Raja 2012). Depending on the applications and the accuracy of the models representing it, the amount of data to be processed at the client side can be determined.

While there are privacy concerns associated with collecting personal data, in general, additional measures need to be investigated for Character Computing. Existing solutions can be employed, but should be extended given the needs of the current use case.

One main privacy measure for Character Computing is fully anonymizing the collected data by not gathering any identifying information such as name and email. We also need to ensure that any collected data (such as IP address) cannot be used to reversely identify the users (Al Ameen et al. 2012). Accordingly, such data should either be skipped or the necessary measures should be applied. For generating the models of the three functions, it is often the case that anonymous data will be more than sufficient, as the (C, B, S) triple is always that of interest and nothing else. Each individual could have an ID with all the collected information mapped to it but no personal information such as name and email address. By employing this measure we aim at increasing the number of interested individuals and thus the amount of collected data and also its accuracy. If individuals are assured that their information will remain private, they are more likely to provide accurate data.

Any system dealing with sensitive data about individuals should have a robust security making it immune to any penetration attempts. A system, containing information about characteristics and behaviors of humans in certain situations cannot be prone to leakage, hacking, or worse data alteration. Security measures for Character Computing do not differ from those of other similar fields and thus existing solutions can be employed (see Roman et al. 2018; King and Raja 2012).

4.3 Adapting to the Character

One main need for considering the whole character[2] in computational models of human behavior is driven by the attempt to build human user-aware computer systems that treat the human user as a whole. As such, Character Computing is thought to not

---

[2]The human character is all stable and temporally varying factors identifying an individual, such as personality, sociocultural embeddings, affective and motivational states, morals, beliefs, skills, habits, hopes, dreams, concerns, appearance, presentation, gestures, likes, and dislikes. (see Chap. 1)

only detect and sense the human user's character but to also serve the human user to change and modify his/her behavior in a particular situation. As the interaction between humans and machines is currently one of the most investigated domains of Computer Science, Character Computing also deals with solutions that allow altering human behavior in an ethical and morally acceptable way. As technology becomes embedded in our daily lives, new methods are derived to try and make the human–computer interaction as seamless as possible, where machines adapt to the user's needs and current preferences with as little interaction from the user as possible. This required machines and applications to acquire a notion of intelligence allowing them to know how to best serve their current users at their current states. Only by including all facets of the human character can this truly be achieved. Most existing adaptive and recommender systems adapt to noncharacter-based cues such as the user's performance (Bunt et al. 2004) or only one character components, namely, affect or personality is considered (Kim et al. 2013).

Hence, adapting HCI systems to the human user's character maybe the logical next step in HCI (e.g. El Bolock et al. 2020a). Thus, next, we will consider a number of situations from daily life in which Character Computing will play a significant role and potentially overcome the limitations of existing computational approaches that so far do not fully consider the whole Character–Situation–Behavior relationship of their users.

4.3.1 Education Use Cases

Imagine a futuristic classroom where the teacher is aided by a smart system capable of adapting to each student's needs. It knows that student A needs reassuring that he's on the right track every step of the way, while student B works independently but competitively to solve the problems before everyone else in class, and student C skips the basic questions to feel satisfied by solving the hardest problem and then slacking for the rest of the class. This is usually true of dedicated human teachers who know each of their students, their strengths and weaknesses. This process is however very time-consuming and only feasible for a sensible number of students and given enough time to adapt the lesson to the style of each student. Imagine an assistive educational tool that knows the character of its users and can simulate the teaching character they would best respond to (e.g., Lopez and Tucker 2018; Kok and Meyer 2018). This would help to adapt the teaching style as needed to the learning style and all other factors affecting learning (e.g., Klein and Keller 1990).

In the trend-setting introductory paper of Affective Computing (Picard and Picard 1997), Picard gives the example of an artificial piano teacher that can perceive the user's affective state alongside their performance. The teacher might thus give the students more challenging problems in case they are pleased or slow things down and encourage the student in case of frustration and too many errors. Picard's idea however needs to be extended to account for different individual characters and corresponding behaviors. In case of frustration, the piano teacher does not necessarily need to slow down, if the student is the type that performs better under pressure, aspiring to prove him-/herself (Elnashar et al. 2019; Waterhouse and Child 1953; Lazarus and Eriksen 1952). While too many errors could indicate the student's type, it could be that the frustration needs to increase more until the challenge within the student is sparked and he/she pulls him-/herself together and overcomes the own frustration and transforms it into the driving force to perform. Other students might give up at the first sight of challenge or frustration and thus the piano teacher needs to clearly monitor those and slow down at the first sign of frustration, sometimes even before the first errors appear.

The examples where knowing more about the student than their current affective state or general personality are numerous (e.g., Borg and Stranahan 2002; Klein and Keller 1990; Banks 1988). Think about the sleep-deprived student who needs more prompting to stay awake and will need a repetition tomorrow or the athlete who has a sports game after the class, so is already elsewhere in thought and will only pay attention to the content of the class after the match is over. Another glaring example is students with special needs and thus needing special attention. This could be students suffering from a permanent learning disability such as dyslexia and Attention-Deficit Hyperactivity Disorder (ADHD), or a temporary special case that requires special treatment for a specific period of time such as stress or insomnia. Lots of researches have already been done into some of these aspects, such as learning types and teaching styles (Entwistle 2013; Romanelli et al. 2009; Charkins et al. 1985), including regular technology-based (Hendrix et al. 2018; Grasha and Yangarber-Hicks 2000) and avatar-based education systems (Gulz and Haake 2006; Cheng 2014; Schroeder et al. 2017).

All these different approaches can benefit from extensions through including other character components alongside the already considered personality and affect.

4.3.2 Smart Cities and Homes Use Cases

We all admired the "Star Trek's" robot "Data" or the artificially intelligent virtual assistant "Samantha" from "Her". Despite their plot-relevant funny failures, they seem to know what to do without being told. They connect with their primary users and they give them what they need, when they need it (until all havoc wreaks, that is!). Still it's an appealing idea to have an artificial companion that knows its owner as well as his/her loved ones or, even better, actually becomes the loved one.

The ultimate *smart assistant* can only be realized if it is character aware.

Imagine, individual A is angry today and has an appointment with his friends, both facts of which the artificial assistant is aware of. Knowing individual A's character, it should know he/she will forget the appointment given the current state and would not want to go. Thus, it should cancel and notify the friends. In case of individual B, whose character experiences short-lived anger which usually subsides in a while, the smart assistant should remind him/her with the appointment in a few hours.

For individual C, it should suggest a visit to the gym to blow off steam, instead of canceling the appointment as prompted in the heat of the anger.

All these scenarios require a mutual interaction between the user and the assistant until it is able to learn and extract the user's behavioral patterns according to their character. Having Character Computing models predicting certain aspects of the (C, B, S) triad would help improve this learning process.

Another example would be a smart alarm that takes into consideration, general sleeping style, the sleep quality of the previous night, current health, the reason of waking up, traffic as well as getting ready conditions to set up the alarm. While this is similar to other smart alarms, the difference would be in including more character components.

The smart home assistant can also be applied to cars, where the *smart car* assistant will have a more crucial role, given the safety-oriented nature of car driving. One example is having an angry driver. Knowing that this driver is not capable of controlling his/her temper, likely resulting in speeding or irrational driving, the car should implement countermeasures (Nasoz et al. 2002). These could range from notifying the driver to pay attention or preventing the driver from operating the car in the current state in extreme cases. The same could be said about temporarily incapacitated drivers. Who would not want the car to prevent drunk drivers from driving until they are fully sober.

4.3.3   Healthcare Use Cases

In the domain of healthcare applications, adaptation is currently a trending topic of investigation (for an overview, see Alam et al. 2018 and Blandford 2019). There are many applications ranging from generic applications for maintaining individual health (Cimler et al. 2014) to specific applications for special groups of people such as elderly individuals (Ahmad and Mozelius 2019), or people suffering from mental illnesses (Søgaard Neilsen and Wilson 2019).

One range of applications requires adaptation similar to that discussed in education, namely, the method of delivery and interaction with the patients. Examples of such applications are automated physiotherapy or rehabilitation. In these applications, the considerations of individual differences need to be seriously taken into account (Rajanna et al. 2016).

The same can be said for a smart personal trainer that needs to push the trainees just the correct amount to help them reach their desired effect without having them dropout. Automated diet plans need the same balance which can only be achieved by knowing the user's behavior profile alongside their health needs (Möller et al. 2012).

There are numerous other opportunities for providing smart assistance to users by having their full character profiles, which should be investigated further. The abovementioned examples are just a small sample of the potentials of Character Computing.

4.3.4 When to Adapt

All the above-discussed use cases are just the tip of the iceberg of opportunities to be realized through Character Computing. But do we always need technology to adapt? Why are there still not enough widely used adaptive systems but countless mainstream applications that behave in the same way for everyone?

This is an integral part of research in this domain. While investigating how to have technology and applications adapt to the user's needs, anticipate, refine, and alter them, we also need to stop and ask ourselves: do they need this? Depending on the use case and type of users (also their characters) having an adaptive technology could either be the big break that simplifies their life or the breaking point.

For example, a GPS application might not need to visually adapt to the user, as they would probably find it too troublesome to provide it with the needed information, for the little gain of presenting the map in a different way, while they could manually adapt it. It might need to adapt other features to the user's character, by personalizing notifications, for example, as discussed above.

On the other hand, a visualization application for education could benefit from adapting to the users, as they themselves might not be aware of their better responsiveness to a different representation methods (e.g., Shiban et al. 2015). Adaptive entertainment applications, such as movie and music recommendation and selection (Kumar et al. 2018), are another very popular example of applications benefiting from personalization (Amato et al. 2019). However, recent guidelines highlight ensuring responsibility and ethical considerations in such applications (Gray and Chivukula 2019).

Adaptive systems should allow the user to give feedback on the provided adaptations from time to time. This is because some users could be flexible enough to adapt to the system itself instead of it adapting to them. In this case, the user's would unknowingly get used to adaptations not suitable for them. The design of the adaptive applications should also have strong psychological foundations, to help minimize such occurrences.

4.4 Artificial Character

The previous section presented opportunities for developing applications based on the understanding of character. However, once something is truly understood it can be reproduced.

Artificial character is one of the already investigated domains of AI. The realization has long been made, that in order to achieve computer systems capable of performing tasks requiring human intelligence, they also sometimes need to have other human factors such as emotions, to go that extra step (Tatai et al. 2003). This is because the human intelligence is not really clean cut or separated from the other makings of the human mind. Intelligence has other character components intertwined with it.

However, it is not always required for the application to adapt to the user, it is not always required for an AI to personify a character of its own. One very popular example of such applications is chatbots. Depending on the application domain, chatbots may need to exhibit character components (Nguyen et al. 2017). Technical support (Subramaniam et al. 2018), customer service (Xu et al. 2017), and e-commerce (Cui et al. 2017) chatbots, for example, do not need to exhibit a character. Chatbot applications for marketing (Dejnaka et al. 2017) or targeted advertisement (Makar and Tindall 2014), for example, could benefit from character components. One important example of chatbot applications requiring a carefully crafted artificial character is those designed for aiding with certain psychological and mental conditions (Lee et al. 2017). In this case, the character of the chatbot is very crucial to the response of the user to the application. Due to the sensitive and high-risk nature of these conditions these applications deal with, lots of caution need to be exercised throughout the development and testing (for more details into a careful iterative process, see Chap. 3).

Artificial agents with character are one of the three modules of Character Computing, whose development heavily relies on the results of the other two modules. Research of how to sense character can, for example, be used to regenerate character components. Also, the same approaches used to adapt to character can be used to generate the characters, as it already manipulates the behavior of the application or artificial agent to achieve a specific result.

Creating agents with artificial character will be discussed in more detail by giving detailed examples and laying a foundational framework in Chaps. 8 and 9, respectively.

4.5 Conclusion

This chapter provided insights into the possible applications of Character Computing. This was done by discussing the three modules of Character Computing. The challenges, opportunities, and possible applications of each module are summarized. There are lots of approaches for collecting data to profile or sense the character whether implicitly or explicitly. Each of the approaches has their benefits and drawbacks and should thus be chosen according to the use case in question. The collected data can in turn be used to model the character and serve as a predictive or assistive tool. Depending on the use case, interactive applications can adapt to different aspects of the character. A special consideration should be given to when and if an application should adapt to the character and to which extent. Similarly, having artificial agents with characters requires lots of research that should be targeted toward specific use cases. Care should be exercised when deciding when artificial agents require character and which factors of the character to include. Security and privacy considerations should play an integral role in all research onto the three Character Computing modules. This chapter only scratches the surface of each of the three modules. The rest of this book will tackle each of the modules separately. Research into each module is one of the main future interests of Character Computing. The highlight therein is the integration of Psychology and Computer Science research to provide a usable framework for all Character Computing endeavors. This is done through combining experimental, computational, and data-driven approaches.

References

Abdelrahman Y, Velloso E, Dingler T, Schmidt A, Vetere F (2017) Cognitive heat: exploring the usage of thermal imaging to unobtrusively estimate cognitive load. Proc ACM Interact Mob Wearable Ubiquitous Technol 1(3):33

Abdrabou Y, Kassem K, Salah J, El-Gendy R, Morsy M, Abdelrahman Y, Abdennadher S (2018) Exploring the usage of EEG and pupil diameter to detect elicited valence. In: International conference on intelligent human systems integration. Springer, pp 287–293

Ahmad A, Mozelius P (2019) Critical factors for human computer interaction of ehealth for older adults. In: ICSLT 2019, vol 5. Association for Computing Machinery (ACM)

Al Ameen M, Liu J, Kwak K (2012) Security and privacy issues in wireless sensor networks for healthcare applications. J Med Syst 36(1):93–101

Alaa M, El Bolock A, Abas M, Abdennadher S, Herbert C (2020) Symposium on Applied Computing. In: A framework for automatic generation of data collection apps. ACM

Alam MM, Malik H, Khan MI, Pardy T, Kuusik A, Le Moullec Y (2018) A survey on the roles of communication technologies in IoT-based personalized healthcare applications. IEEE Access 6:36611–36631

Alemdar H, Ersoy C (2010) Wireless sensor networks for healthcare: a survey. Comput Netw 54(15):2688–2710

Amato G, Behrmann M, Bimbot F, Caramiaux B, Falchi F, Garcia A, Geurts J, Gibert J, Gravier G, Holken H et al (2019) AI in the media and creative industries. arXiv:1905.04175

Banks JA (1988) Ethnicity, class, cognitive, and motivational styles: research and teaching implications. J Negro Educ 57(4):452–466

Berkovsky S, Taib R, Koprinska I, Wang E, Zeng Y, Li J, Kleitman S (2019) Detecting personality traits using eye-tracking data. In: Proceedings of the 2019 CHI conference on human factors in computing systems. ACM, p 221

Blandford A (2019) HCI for health and wellbeing: challenges and opportunities. Int J Hum-Comput Stud

Borg MO, Stranahan HA (2002) Personality type and student performance in upper-level economics courses: the importance of race and gender. J Econ Educ 33(1):3–14

Bunt A, Conati C, McGrenere J (2004) What role can adaptive support play in an adaptable system? In: Proceedings of the 9th international conference on intelligent user interfaces. ACM, pp 117–124

Can YS, Arnrich B, Ersoy C (2019) Stress detection in daily life scenarios using smart phones and wearable sensors: a survey. J Biomed Inform 103139

Cao H, Lin M (2017) Mining smartphone data for app usage prediction and recommendations: a survey. Pervasive Mob Comput 37:1–22

Casler K, Bickel L, Hackett E (2013) Separate but equal? A comparison of participants and data gathered via Amazon's MTurk, social media, and face-to-face behavioral testing. Comput Hum Behav 29(6):2156–2160

Charkins R, O'Toole DM, Wetzel JN (1985) Linking teacher and student learning styles with student achievement and attitudes. J Econ Educ 16(2):111–120

Cheng G (2014) Exploring students' learning styles in relation to their acceptance and attitudes towards using second life in education: a case study in Hong Kong. Comput Educ 70:105–115

Cimler R, Matyska J, Sobeslav V (2014) Cloud based solution for mobile healthcare application. In: Proceedings of the 18th international database engineering and applications symposium. ACM, pp 298–301

Cowie R, Douglas-Cowie E, Tsapatsoulis N, Votsis G, Kollias S, Fellenz W, Taylor JG (2001) Emotion recognition in human-computer interaction. IEEE Signal Process Mag 18(1):32–80

Cui L, Huang S, Wei F, Tan C, Duan C, Zhou M (2017) SuperAgent: a customer service chatbot for e-commerce websites. In: Proceedings of ACL 2017, system demonstrations, pp 97–102

Dang-Nguyen DT, Zhou L, Gupta R, Riegler M, Gurrin C (2017) Building a disclosed lifelog dataset: challenges, principles and processes. In: Proceedings of the 15th international workshop on content-based multimedia indexing. ACM, p 22

Dejnaka A et al (2017) Technologization of marketing communication–new trends. Ann Univ Mariae Curie-Skłodowska Sect H Oecon 51(2):59–68

El Bolock A (2018) Defining character computing from the perspective of computer science and psychology. In: Proceedings of the 17th international conference on mobile and ubiquitous multimedia. ACM, pp 567–572

El Bolock A, Salah J, Abdennadher S, Abdelrahman Y (2017) Character computing: challenges and opportunities. In: Proceedings of the 16th international conference on mobile and ubiquitous multimedia. ACM, pp 555–559

El Bolock A, Amr R, Abdennadher S (2018a) Non-obtrusive sleep detection for character computing profiling. In: International conference on intelligent human systems integration. Springer, pp 249–254

El Bolock A, Salah J, Abdelrahman Y, Herbert C, Abdennadher S (2018b) Character computing: computer science meets psychology. In: Proceedings of the 17th international conference on mobile and ubiquitous multimedia. ACM, pp 557–562

El Bolock A, El Kady A, Herbert C, Abdennadher S (2020a) Towards a Character-based Meta Recommender for Movies. In: Computational science and technology. Springer, pp 627–638

El Bolock A, Ahmed G, Herbert C, Abdennadher S (2020b) International Conference on Intelligent Human Systems Integration. In: Detecting impulsive behavior through agent-based games. Springer

ElKomy M, Abdelrahman Y, Funk M, Dingler T, Schmidt A, Abdennadher S (2017) ABBAS: an adaptive bio-sensors based assistive system. In: Proceedings of the 2017 CHI conference extended abstracts on human factors in computing systems. ACM, pp 2543–2550

Elnashar Z, El Bolock A, Salah J, Cornelia H, Abdennadher S (2019) Effect of Big Five Personality Traits on Quality of Performance under Frustration. In: International conference on games and learning alliance. Springer, pp 595–604

Entwistle NJ (2013) Styles of learning and teaching: an integrated outline of educational psychology for students, teachers and lecturers. David Fulton Publishers, London

Flick U (2017) The SAGE handbook of qualitative data collection. SAGE, Los Angeles

Gerber N, Reinheimer B, Volkamer M (2018) Home sweet home? Investigating users' awareness of smart home privacy threats. In: UNENIX symposium on usable privacy and security (SOUPS), Baltimore, MD

Grasha AF, Yangarber-Hicks N (2000) Integrating teaching styles and learning styles with instructional technology. Coll Teach 48(1):2–10

Gray CM, Chivukula SS (2019) Ethical mediation in UX practice. In: Proceedings of the 2019 CHI conference on human factors in computing systems-CHI, vol 19

Gulz A, Haake M (2006) Design of animated pedagogical agents—a look at their look. Int J Hum-Comput Stud 64(4):322–339

Gundry D, Deterding S (2018) Validity threats in quantitative data collection with games: a narrative survey. Simul Gaming. https://doi.org/10.1177/1046878118805515

Hendrix M, Bellamy-Wood T, McKay S, Bloom V, Dunwell I (2018) Implementing adaptive game difficulty balancing in serious games. IEEE Trans Games

Hong L, Luo M, Wang R, Lu P, Lu W, Lu L (2018) Big data in health care: applications and challenges. Data Inf Manag 2(3):175–197

Islam SR, Kwak D, Kabir MH, Hossain M, Kwak KS (2015) The internet of things for health care: a comprehensive survey. IEEE Access 3:678–708

Jaimes A, Sebe N (2007) Multimodal human-computer interaction: a survey. Comput Vis Image Underst 108(1–2):116–134

Kassem K, Salah J, Abdrabou Y, Morsy M, El-Gendy R, Abdelrahman Y, Abdennadher S (2017) DiVA: exploring the usage of pupil diameter to elicit valence and arousal. In: Proceedings of the 16th international conference on mobile and ubiquitous multimedia. ACM, pp 273–278

Kaushik G, Prakash R (2018) Collection of data through cookies and smart devices–a case study

Kim J, Lee A, Ryu H (2013) Personality and its effects on learning performance: design guidelines for an adaptive e-learning system based on a user model. Int J Ind Ergon 43(5):450–461

King NJ, Raja V (2012) Protecting the privacy and security of sensitive customer data in the cloud. Comput Law Secur Rev 28(3):308–319

Klein JD, Keller JM (1990) Influence of student ability, locus of control, and type of instructional control on performance and confidence. J Educ Res 83(3):140–146

Kok R, Meyer L (2018) Towards an optimal person-environment fit: a baseline study of student teachers' personality traits. S Afr J Educ 38(3)

Kosinski M, Stillwell D, Graepel T (2013) Private traits and attributes are predictable from digital records of human behavior. Proc Natl Acad Sci 110(15):5802–5805

Kumar S et al (2018) Survey on personalized web recommender system. Int J Inf Eng Electron Bus 10(4):33

Lazar J, Feng JH, Hochheiser H (2017) Research methods in human-computer interaction. Morgan Kaufmann, Burlington

Lazarus RS, Eriksen CW (1952) Effects of failure stress upon skilled performance. J Exp Psychol 43(2):100

Lee D, Oh KJ, Choi HJ (2017) The chatbot feels you-a counseling service using emotional response generation. In: 2017 IEEE international conference on big data and smart computing (BigComp). IEEE, pp 437–440

Lopez C, Tucker C (2018) Towards personalized adaptive gamification: a machine learning model for predicting performance. IEEE Trans Games

Makar MG, Tindall TA (2014) Dynamic chatbot (18 September 2014) US Patent App. 14/287,815

Malhi GS, Hamilton A, Morris G, Mannie Z, Das P, Outhred T (2017) The promise of digital mood tracking technologies: are we heading on the right track? Evid-Based Ment Health 20(4):102–107

Martinez B, Valstar MF, Jiang B, Pantic M (2017) Automatic analysis of facial actions: a survey. IEEE Trans Affect Comput

Möller A, Roalter L, Diewald S, Scherr J, Kranz M, Hammerla N, Olivier P, Plötz T (2012) GymSkill: a personal trainer for physical exercises. In: 2012 IEEE international conference on pervasive computing and communications. IEEE, pp 213–220

Nasoz F, Ozyer O, Lisetti CL, Finkelstein N (2002) Multimodal affective driver interfaces for future cars. In: Proceedings of the 10th ACM international conference on multimedia. ACM, pp 319–322

Nelson BW, Allen NB (2018) Extending the passive-sensing toolbox: using smart-home technology in psychological science. Perspect Psychol Sci 13(6):718–733

Nguyen H, Morales D, Chin T (2017) A neural chatbot with personality

Olson JS, Kellogg WA (2014) Ways of knowing in HCI, vol 2. Springer, Berlin

Paul PV, Monica K, Trishanka M (2017) A survey on big data analytics using social media data. In: Innovations in power and advanced computing technologies (i-PACT). IEEE, pp 1–4

Picard RW (2003) Affective computing: challenges. Int J Hum-Comput Stud 59(1):55–64

Picard RW, Picard R (1997) Affective computing, vol 252. MIT Press, Cambridge

Rajanna V, Vo P, Barth J, Mjelde M, Grey T, Oduola C, Hammond T (2016) KinoHaptics: an automated, wearable, haptic assisted, physio-therapeutic system for post-surgery rehabilitation and self-care. J Med Syst 40(3):60

Romanelli F, Bird E, Ryan M (2009) Learning styles: a review of theory, application, and best practices. Am J Pharm Educ 73(1):9

Roman R, Lopez J, Mambo M (2018) Mobile edge computing, Fog et al.: a survey and analysis of security threats and challenges. Futur Gener Comput Syst 78:680–698

Schroeder NL, Romine WL, Craig SD (2017) Measuring pedagogical agent persona and the influence of agent persona on learning. Comput Educ 109:176–186

Shiban Y, Schelhorn I, Jobst V, Hörnlein A, Puppe F, Pauli P, Mühlberger A (2015) The appearance effect: influences of virtual agent features on performance and motivation. Comput Hum Behav 49:5–11

Søgaard Neilsen A, Wilson RL (2019) Combining e-mental health intervention development with human computer interaction (HCI) design to enhance technology-facilitated recovery for people with depression and/or anxiety conditions: an integrative literature review. Int J Ment Health Nurs 28(1):22–39

Stieglitz S, Mirbabaie M, Ross B, Neuberger C (2018) Social media analytics-challenges in topic discovery, data collection, and data preparation. Int J Inf Manag 39:156–168

Subramaniam S, Aggarwal P, Dasgupta GB, Paradkar A (2018) COBOTS-a cognitive multi-bot conversational framework for technical support. In: Proceedings of the 17th international conference on autonomous agents and multiagent systems. International Foundation for Autonomous Agents and Multiagent Systems, pp 597–604

Swan M (2013) The quantified self: fundamental disruption in big data science and biological discovery. Big Data 1(2):85–99

Tan CH, Silva A, Lee R, Wang K, Nah FFH (2016) HCI testing in laboratory or field settings. In: International conference on HCI in business, government, and organizations. Springer, pp 110–116

Tatai G, Csordás A, Kiss Á, Szaló A, Laufer L (2003) Happy chatbot, happy user. In: Rist T, Aylett RS, Ballin D, Rickel J (eds) Intelligent virtual agents. Springer, Berlin, pp 5–12

Van de Mortel TF et al (2008) Faking it: social desirability response bias in self-report research. Aust J Adv Nurs 25(4):40

Wang R, Chen F, Chen Z, Li T, Harari G, Tignor S, Zhou X, Ben-Zeev D, Campbell AT (2014) Studentlife: assessing mental health, academic performance and behavioral trends of college students using smartphones. In: Proceedings of the 2014 ACM international joint conference on pervasive and ubiquitous computing. ACM, pp 3–14

Waterhouse IK, Child IL (1953) Frustration and the quality of performance. J Personal 21(3):298–311

Worth NC, Book AS (2014) Personality and behavior in a massively multiplayer online role-playing game. Comput Hum Behav 38:322–330

Xu A, Liu Z, Guo Y, Sinha V, Akkiraju R (2017) A new chatbot for customer service on social media. In: Proceedings of the 2017 CHI conference on human factors in computing systems. ACM, pp 3506–3510

Zeng Z, Pantic M, Roisman GI, Huang TS (2008) A survey of affect recognition methods: audio, visual, and spontaneous expressions. IEEE Trans Pattern Anal Mach Intell 31(1):39–58

Chapter 5
Character Computing and HCI

Yomna Abdelrahman

Abstract Personalization plays an important role in human–computer interaction. A vast body of work has been directed into establishing research fields aiming to provide adaptive and personalized experience, e.g., Affective Computing and Adaptive Systems. However, current digital systems are largely blind to users' character and traits. Systems that adapt to users' character show great potential for augmenting character and for creating novel user experiences. This chapter presents possible indicators of users' character from the HCI literature, discussing possibilities of recognizing and expressing character. Additionally, this chapter gives insights about potential application domains that might benefit from Character Computing as an emerging field. Lastly, this chapter discusses potential concerns, being as any fields, while Character Computing might open up interaction opportunities, it raises concerns from the various perspective from interaction concerns to privacy and ethical concerns.

5.1 Introduction

Building systems that provide personalized and tailored interaction experiences have been a core theme in human-centered computing since its inception. These aspirations have been carried out on through multiple research programs, including Affective Computing (Rosalind 1997), Physiological Computing (Fairclough 2009), and more recently Symbiotic Interaction (Jacucci et al. 2014) and Human Amplification (Schmidt 2017). These user-aware systems aim to sense users' internal states and to adapt their interface and behavior accordingly. Such systems offer opportunities to tailor different activities, e.g., educational activities in online learning environments, to dynamically optimize workflows for knowledge, to improve performance for assembly line workers (Funk et al. 2015), and to focus users' attention in critical systems. A crucial step in building user-aware systems is capturing different aspects of users' mental states, such as their cognitive load, loci of attention, and

Y. Abdelrahman (✉)
Bundeswehr University Munich, Neubiberg, Germany
e-mail: yomna.abdelrahman@unibw.de

© Springer Nature Switzerland AG 2020

A. El Bolock et al. (eds.), *Character Computing*, Human–Computer Interaction Series,
https://doi.org/10.1007/978-3-030-15954-2_5

affect. Despite over 50 years of work in the area, how to sense users' states in a robust, accurate, timely, and unobtrusive way is still an open challenge. Additionally, most of the conducted research consider the current sensed state rather than considering the full picture, by covering the character of the user and how to adapt to the sensed state based on the users' character. For instance, some characters work better under stress/pressure. Hence, when the system detects high cognitive load, it should not try to reduce the cognitive load. By adding character sensing capabilities to the adaptive systems rather than relying solely on the current state novel adaptive systems will evolve, allowing more tailored interactive experience. Furthermore, novel interaction modalities will be introduced to the human–computer interaction field. The first part of this chapter introduces an overview of the existing methods to sense the users' internal states that have been intensively deployed in various adaptive systems and research projects. The second part discusses how these methods could be potentially used to recognize the character, as well as how these character features could be expressed. The third part discusses the potential application fields that could benefit from the character sensing capabilities. Finally, informed by the literature and previous research, we discuss potential concerns and challenges of deploying Character Computing.

5.2 Recognizing the Character from Users' States

In our daily lives, we as humans are always transmitting information about ourselves, through both verbal, e.g., using a set of words and nonverbal cues, e.g., body language and physiological data. These cues could be interpreted to reflect our internal states. These cues have been utilized to understand the human in both human–human and human–computer interactions. However, most of our attempts to understand the user/human relay on the current temporal response or state. Prior work investigated examining human affective states, with a well-established research area named affective computing. In this field, both subjective and objective mean to sense, analyze, and classify affect states. Where the subjective measures were more accurate, given it is reported by the user, it is not always feasible to use it in real-life scenarios. Objective measures deployed the availability of sensors in our vicinity and its evolving unobtrusive nature to detect different affect states. While there have been advances in this area of research, to complicate manners further, human affect states do not follow "one size fits all" scheme. For instance, the same affect state could be perceived differently by different people. Furthermore, the context, as well as the transient response to different stimuli, is personal dependent. Affective computing was successful in sensing the users' state in a particular window of time, and hence systems based on this concept only response to the temporal state of the user, rather than considering the full picture. On the other hand, personality computing tried to address this by examining the personality traits along with the response. These traits are often captured by questionnaires, as to capture objectively it needs long-term monitoring and annotation of the recorded data. Another aspect of having a complete picture of the user is to incorporate the character of the user to interpret the detected affect states better. For instance, considering the example of adaptive interactive systems in a work environment, typicality, these systems monitor the cognitive load and assume high cognitive correlates to task difficulty. Hence, the systems give more instructions to assist the user through the work process. However, the system does not consider that the cognitive load could have been due to the monotonous nature of the task. However, if the system knows the character of the user and knows their competitiveness would interpret the measured cognitive load differently.

As presented in Chaps. 1 and 2, character is a complex module, and its building blocks could be treated as different states and qualities that distinguish individuals from one another. Accordingly, it should follow the standard procedure of interaction, namely, character information capture and modeling, character understanding, and expression. Users represent their character through a series of reactions to different stimuli and situations. These reactions are expressed via physiological signals such as heart rate, skin temperature, conductance, voice behavior, brain signals, etc. The following section will provide an overview of the most current key technologies in these areas, such as bio-signals and cues extraction, multimodal systems, character understanding, and generating.

In the field of HCI, there has been a vast body of work on how to recognize users' states. In this chapter, we present our vision on how HCI and Character Computing could merge to utilize existing technologies that have been used in HCI to recognize states. We envision that based on the detected states, we can infer and replicate character traits.

The remaining of this chapter is structured as follows: first, we introduce an overview of the common users' states sensing technologies with the focus on unobtrusive technologies. Second, we discuss how these technologies could be utilized in potential applications that use the concept of Character Computing. Lastly, we discuss the accompanying concerns from such emerging field.

Physiological Signals For Users' State Detection

Physiological signals have been measured traditionally in two ways: (1) by subjective self-reporting and (2) by observing user performance in a task. For instance, to measure the cognitive load, the NASA Task Load Index (TLX) is a typical example of the first category, where participants are asked to report their load concerning six different categories. Another example where study participants are asked to report their estimates can be found in Sweller et al. (2011). The drawback of these approaches is that the answers are highly subjective. Furthermore, the self-reporting itself adds to the cognitive load. Measuring cognitive load through the performance in the task itself or a secondary task (e.g., Lane Change Task for Automotive user interface, ISO 26022) only provides a rough estimate and is typically only suitable for laboratory studies and not for creating cognition-aware real-time systems. Likewise, for the Character, the Big Five is a common way to define users' character subjectively.

On the other hand, there has been limited work in defining users' character using nonsubjective measures. However, considering the ability to collect physiological signals in response to different stimuli, this might inform researchers about the users' character. Building upon the fact that different character types would react differently to the stimuli. Hence, in this section, we present a brief overview of existing sensing technologies.

Capturing users' state information is a challenging task—being mostly invisible from the outside of the users' brain, and introspection often fails to reason about them in an unbiased and objective way. Monitoring users with the help of sensors can give us clues about different states. Though specific physiological sensors can be highly specialized, expensive, and therefore only applicable under lab conditions, advances in sensor technology have led to inexpensive solutions that can be easily integrated into personal devices. Such sensors typically fall in one of two categories: invasive versus noninvasive sensing, with invasive methods being mainly found in a medical context and hardly applicable in everyday consumer situations. On the other hand, psychological variables can be monitored in noninvasive ways and have been investigated extensively over the past decades.

Different approaches have been introduced to infer different states, ranging from using facial expressions (Wang et al. 2012), eye movements (Haak et al. 2009) and pupil size (Beatty 1982; Pfleging et al. 2016), skin conductance (Hernandez et al. 2014; Labbé et al. 2007; Shi et al. 2007), brain signals (Crowley et al. 2010; Shirazi et al. 2012, 2014), electrodermal activity (EDA) (Parnandi et al. 2013a, b; Goyal and Fussell 2017), heart, and respiration rate (Labbé et al. 2007). For instance, Petersen et al. (2011) used the EPOC and to distinguish emotional responses when viewing different contents. Parnandi et al. considered real-time adaptive biofeedback games (Parnandi et al. 2013a, b). They monitored players' EDA to infer their arousal states (Parnandi et al. 2013a). Additionally, they used biofeedback sensors (respiration rate sensor and adaptive games) to manipulate their behavior (Parnandi et al. 2013b).

Wang et al. (2012) and ElKomy et al. (2017) explored how to build an adaptive system that helps workers who use computer heavily daily by extracting user's features, such as face pose, eye blinking, yawn frequency, and eye gaze from a recorded video, to monitor the user's state. Healey et al. (2005) and Schneegass et al. (2013) used physiological monitoring for driver stress indication.

Researchers investigated the usage of facial and vocal expressions for affective states modeling. A significant limitation with both voice- and facial-based approaches is that users can be quite skilled at manipulating the parameters being sensed by the system. On the other hand, physiological metrics, such as heart rate, galvanic skin response (GSR), blood volume pulse (BVP), and electromyography (EMG), have the advantage that they are primarily under the control of the autonomic nervous system (ANS) and are therefore less susceptible to conscious manipulation. However, a significant limitation of current physiological approaches is the need for sensors to be in direct contact with the user or to be implanted. As a result, such sensors are impractical for most routine user environments. For instance, the long setup time and contact requirements of Brain–Computer Interfaces (BCI)s, or the drift over time (Levenson 1988) and fluctuations due to arm movements in GSR.

In other words, physiological sensors, such as functional magnetic resonance imaging (fMRI), EEG, and GSR sensors, show potential as possible sensing techniques but are limited in their application in ubiquitous computing environments since they require users to wear obtrusive additional hardware (e.g., electrodes on their skin). On the other hand, recently, researchers have explored and leveraged the potential of adding sensing capabilities to the environment rather than burdening the user. Researchers intensively investigated the usage of integrated RGB cameras in the environment to capture facial expressions to infer affect states. One of the main advantages is the ability to capture users' states continuously in an unobtrusive manner. However, the operating limitations of RGB cameras hinder the capturing process. For instance, is dependent on the light condition, skin color, face exposure, and the limited amount of information observed via the RGB cameras. It's worth mentioning that unobtrusive sensors are not limited to thermal imaging. Its an emerging area of research, where researchers strive to find means to capture the users' affect states. These include eye tracking, behavior tracking, voice assessment, and non-visible imaging.

Currently, technologies are evolving to support sensing users' states in a subtle, real-time, and continuous way, for instance, having thermal imaging as a sample sensor. Originally, thermal imaging was used by special users and applications, e.g., military and medical applications. Recently, the availability of technology made it commercially affordable and deployable in wider use cases. Thermal imaging is a strong candidate for the task of measuring users' affect state. Thermal cameras are both unobtrusive and able to capture information from multiple users at a distance and at the same time. Previous research has shown that thermal patterns reveal different aspects of our internal states, including affect (Ioannou et al. 2014; Stemberger et al. 2010; Abdelrahman et al. 2017), stress (Puri et al. 2005), and deception (Rajoub and Zwiggelaar 2014). Further, advances in miniaturization and mass production have continuously brought down the prices of these devices. With consumer-grade cameras readily available in the market for a few hundred dollars, measuring affect states at a larger scale becomes feasible (Table 5.1).

Thermal imaging is only one example highlighting the feasibility of assessing various users' states unobtrusively. However, technology evolves every day, allowing more opportunities to capture users' states by augmenting the environment rather than the user. This enables the continuous tracking of the user subtly; hence, learn about user behavior and response in various situations. These would be the bases of our vision of mapping the detected responses to diverse triggers to the character and personality traits as depicted in Fig. 5.1.

There has been a vast amount of research conducted in the field of HCI, aiming to enhance user awareness and designing systems using user-centered design. This research direction has paved the way for an emerging field like affective computing and adaptive systems. However, reviewing the literature, researchers highlighted the need for a more vibrant interpretation of the users' state. As different states might be perceived differently by various personalities and characters. In the context of this introduced field Character Computing, we aim to utilize and build upon existing HCI

Table 5.1 Overview of the direction of temperature variation in the considered regions of interest across Emotions (Ioannou et al. 2014)

Emotions								
	Stress	Fear	Startle	Sexual arousal	Anxiety	Joy	Pain	Guilt
Regions								
Nose	↓	↓		↑		↓		↓
Cheeks								
Forehead	↑ ↓	↓		↑	↑			
Maxillary	↓	↓						↓
Periorbital				↑	↑			
Lips/mouth				↑				
Finger/palm		↓						
Supraorbital					↑			
Neck-carotid								

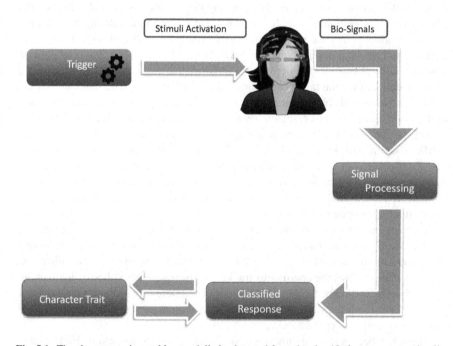

Fig. 5.1 The character traits could potentially be detected from the classified responses to stimuli, as well as the response may be predicted from the character trait

research, namely, users' state sensing to seamlessly create a comprehensive profile of the user that considers the users' character traits accompanied by the current state, rather than solely considering the temporal aspect of the users' state.

5.3 Applications of Character Computing in HCI

Character Computing could serve different application domains in HCI, varying from workplaces and adaptive systems to entertainment. For instance, consider the diverse field that affective computing has been integrated and deployed in, Character Computing is envisioned to outperform and penetrate further domains by providing a comprehensive users' profile. In the following, we will discuss existing HCI research outcomes and how they could potentially benefit from Character Computing.

5.3.1 Adaptive Assistive Systems

One of the ongoing challenges of adaptive and personalized systems is there nature of "One Size DOES NOT fit all." For instance, considering a working setup where an adaptive assistive system to be installed. The system should not be under- or over-challenging. The challenge level is user dependent based on external factors, e.g., task nature, expertise level, etc. Additionally, internal factors (e.g., competitiveness, work behavior) play a significant role, inspired by the progress and performance of currently available adaptive systems (Funk and Schmidt 2015; ElKomy et al. 2017). For instance, considering an adaptive assistive assembly system that takes the cognitive state of the worker in real time into account. Based on four biosensors (see Fig. 5.2), we infer cognitive load in real time and support the worker according to

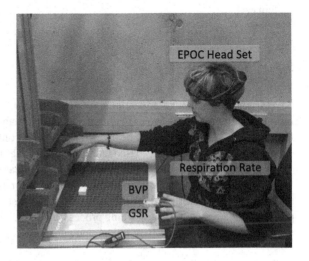

Fig. 5.2 Four different biosensors to assess a worker's state during an assembly task: GSR, BVP, Respiration Rate, and EEG

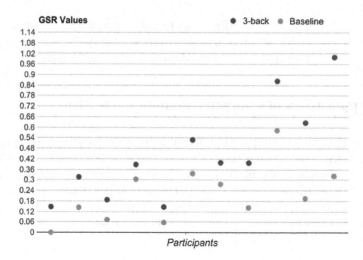

Fig. 5.3 Relation between the baseline and 3-back GSR values

the current workload during assembly tasks. To evaluate our system, we conducted a user study, where we had a cognitive load inducing tasks, e.g., 3-back task. As shown in Fig. 5.3, cognitive load from performing a challenging task is reflected in the GSR readings, as opposed to the relaxed baseline task. Our findings showed that biosensors could reliably detect cognitive workload in workplace settings and allow instructions to be adapted according to these measured workload levels. However, having a more in-depth look into the results, it is evident that it is participant dependent. Moreover, when interviewing the participants for feedback, we detected a cofound between cognitive load and boredom. We envision adding the character layer would further enhance both the performance and the experience of the personalizing process as the system would be able to bypass the cofound limitations of the current adaptive systems.

5.3.2 Education

Several existing adaptive educational systems were developed trying to reach the most convenient methodologies for enhancing the adaptability of educational content. Different key aspects needed to be investigated in this context, namely, emotions that can be triggered during game-based learning. Techniques used to evaluate the current emotional state of the students, which game metrics can be adaptive to the state of the student and what are the changes that should be done to these metrics leading to a better learning experience for them. Where these systems showed significant and potential enhancement in the learning process, again it considers the temporally valid state of the student, rather than being character aware. One of the main challenges reported by teachers and researchers is the diverse characters of students, where some students liked to be challenged to excel, others rather be calmly taught. Character Computing will not only assist in building character-aware systems but will enhance the awareness of the teachers and educators about their students, which in turn will positively impact their performance.

5.3.3 Virtual Reality

Virtual reality (VR) is one of the emerging fields that could benefit from Character Computing and character awareness. VR acquired the attention of HCI researchers, with the focus on factors that influence users' experience, realism, and perception. These factors included the appearance and animation of the avatars. However, there is limited work conducted to explore avatars' behavior and "character" and how they influence the users' experience. Currently, most of the VR systems allow the user to choose and personalize the appearance of their avatars, but not the character. Considering, gaming in VR, if the user can inform the game about their character traits, these would be mapped to the virtual world. For example, the game would adjust the interface, the nonplaying characters, or even the storyline of the game. Recent games are already trying to achieve this by building up the character by monitoring the players' behavior and choices throughout the game. However, the explicit collection of subjective might hinder and influence the experience. Hence, we assume the ability to identify and declare characters might have a positive impact on the VR experience (Fig. 5.4).

Fig. 5.4 Avatars selection in VR

5.3.4 Human–Robot/Agent Interaction

Where the abovementioned exemplary application domains would benefit from Character Computing, one of the main areas that would have a tangible enhancement is Human–Robot/Agent interaction. Adaptive character-aware systems are aimed to better understand users to adapt accordingly while trying to overcome any cofounds from solely using the temporally valid affect state and cognition. Another aspect that could be deploying Character Computing is artificial agents. Currently, robots' and artificial agents' designers and developers are striving to add character and personality to their agents. Character Computing would pave the way for such humanization of agents and robots. As mentioned earlier, from the response and behavior, character traits could be inferred; in this context, it will be the other way around. The user would define and preset the agents/robots character traits, and accordingly the agent would exhibit and respond to different triggers. The user would then be able to set the artificial agent character that either reflects the user character or being compatible with the user character. This would enable users to have humanized agent/robot both in behavior, appearance, and response. These scenarios have been envisioned and materialized in science fiction TV shows, e.g., Black Mirror and movies, e.g., Her. These are not futuristic vision anymore, where the technology is just around the corner (Fig. 5.5).

These examples can merely identify potential benefits of Character Computing in existing fields of HCI. Expansion is expected to be witnessed in the use cases and applications of Character Computing and the evolution of character-aware annotation. However, this would come with a cost. While Character Computing would open

Fig. 5.5 Humanoid Robot interacting with human subject

up opportunities, it will raise concerns and challenges as well. An overview of the possible challenges is discussed in the following section.

5.4 Potential Challenges

Informed by the literature and as discussed earlier in Chap. 2, Character Computing might impose some challenges both in the lab and in the wild. In the context of Character Computing and HCI, challenges could be present in different aspects starting from the technical challenges of realizing such character-aware systems to the ethics of operating these systems in our daily life.

5.4.1 Technical Consideration

The technology advancement and sensing technologies are ubiquitous and well integrated into our vicinity. It's still an open challenge to collect data continuously. Furthermore, the analysis and interpretation of the recorded data in real time without any cofounds is a challenging task. However, researchers might overcome these challenges by design, building, and evaluating different approaches. However, researchers must be aware of potential challenges. For instance, how to design their studies and experiments to control the tested variables, as well as controlling the subjects to avoid and cofounds in the results. Additionally, to have consistent results and reliable character prediction, the studies should be conducted over a long period. Unlike typical lab studies in HCI, this, in turn, would impose some challenges for researchers.

5.4.2 Ethical Consideration

The important factors to be considered while designing character-aware systems are ethics and privacy considerations starting from the consent of data collection from the human subjects during the studies to the deployment and data usage for adaptation. Additionally, governments are imposing new data protection laws, e.g., the EU General Data Protection Regulation (GDPR) that might hinder the releasing, sharing, and usage of datasets across researchers and systems. Researchers must ensure that they design and built transparent character-aware systems and interfaces, where the user has full control over the recorded data, its visibility, and where it is physically stored. Character Computing would serve as a window into our souls and character; hence, the collected and stored data would include sensitive data, e.g., behavioral response toward diverse triggers. This would impose another field of research to address the privacy concerns accompanied by Character Computing.

5.5 Summary

In this chapter, we discussed how Character Computing could potentially complement already existing research in the field of HCI, namely, affective computing and
adaptive systems, where we envision Character Computing as a comprehensive profiling of the user including all aspects of human behavior, comprising the user's
current cognitive, affective, and motivational state and the user's personality traits as
well as the dynamic interaction between situation and behavior, as presented earlier
in Chaps. 1 and 2. This will pave the way for more character-aware and personalized
experiences in various application domains. We envision in the near future with the
emergent of such a field, novel interactive techniques would be designed utilizing the
character-awareness feature. However, unleashing Character Computing would also
raise some challenges, ranging from technical and privacy challenges for data collection and utilization to user experience and empirical studies design that consider
the character in the design space.

Acknowledgements This work is inspired by the work done in the Usable Security and Privacy
Institute in the Bundeswehr University, Munich.

References

Abdelrahman Y, Velloso E, Dingler T, Schmidt A, Vetere F (2017) Cognitive heat: exploring the
usage of thermal imaging to unobtrusively estimate cognitive load. IMWUT 1(3):33:1–33:20
Beatty J (1982) Task-evoked pupillary responses, processing load, and the structure of processing
resources. Psychol Bull 91(2):276
Crowley K, Sliney A, Pitt I, Murphy D (2010) Evaluating a brain-computer interface to categorise
human emotional response. In: ICALT, pp 276–278
ElKomy M, Abdelrahman Y, Funk M, Dingler T, Schmidt A, Abdennadher S (2017) ABBAS: an
adaptive bio-sensors based assistive system. In: Proceedings of the 2017 CHI conference extended
abstracts on human factors in computing systems, pp 2543–2550. ACM
Fairclough SH (2009) Fundamentals of physiological computing. Interact Comput 21(1–2):133–
145
Funk M, Dingler T, Cooper J, Schmidt A (2015) Stop helping me-i'm bored!: why assembly
assistance needs to be adaptive. In: Proceedings of the 2015 ACM international joint conference on
pervasive and ubiquitous computing and proceedings of the 2015 ACM international symposium
on wearable computers, pp 1269–1273. ACM
Funk M, Schmidt A (2015) Cognitive assistance in the workplace. IEEE Pervasive Comput
14(3):53–55
Goyal N, Fussell SR (2017) Intelligent interruption management using electro dermal activity
based physiological sensor on collaborative sensemaking. Proc ACM Interact, Mob, Wearable
Ubiquitous Technol 1(3):16
Haak M, Bos S, Panic S, Rothkrantz LJM (2009) Detecting stress using eye blinks and brain activity
from EEG signals. In: Proceeding of the 1st driver car interaction and interface (DCII 2008), pp
35–60
Healey JA, Picard RW (2005) Detecting stress during real-world driving tasks using physiological
sensors. IEEE Trans Intell Transp Syst 6(2):156–166

Hernandez J, Paredes P, Roseway A, Czerwinski M (2014) Under pressure: sensing stress of computer users. In: Proceedings of the SIGCHI conference on Human factors in computing systems, pp 51–60. ACM

Ioannou S, Gallese V, Merla A (2014) Thermal infrared imaging in psychophysiology: potentialities and limits. Psychophysiology 51(10):951–963

Jacucci G, Spagnolli A, Freeman J, Gamberini L (2014) Symbiotic interaction: a critical definition and comparison to other human-computer paradigms. Springer International Publishing, Cham, pp 3–20

Labbé E, Schmidt N, Babin J, Pharr M (2007) Coping with stress: the effectiveness of different types of music. Appl Psychophysiol Biofeedback 32(3–4):163–168

Levenson RW (1988) Emotion and the autonomic nervous system: a prospectus for research on autonomic specificity

Parnandi A, Ahmed B, Shipp E, Gutierrez-Osuna R (2013a) Chill-out: Relaxation training through respiratory biofeedback in a mobile casual game. In: Mobile computing, applications, and services, pp 252–260. Springer

Parnandi A, Son Y, Gutierrez-Osuna R (2013b) A control-theoretic approach to adaptive physiological games. In: 2013 Humaine association conference on affective computing and intelligent interaction (ACII), pp 7–12. IEEE

Petersen MK, Stahlhut C, Stopczynski A, Larsen JE, Hansen LK (2011) Smartphones get emotional: mind reading images and reconstructing the neural sources. In: International conference on affective computing and intelligent interaction, pp 578–587. Springer

Pfleging B, Fekety DK, Schmidt A, Kun AL (2016) A model relating pupil diameter to mental workload and lighting conditions. In: Proceedings of the SIGCHI conference on human factors in computing systems, CHI '16, New York. ACM

Picard RW (1997) Affective computing. MIT Press, Cambridge

Puri C, Olson L, Pavlidis I, Levine J, Starren J (2005) Stresscam: non-contact measurement of users' emotional states through thermal imaging. In: CHI'05 extended abstracts on human factors in computing systems, pp 1725–1728. ACM

Rajoub BA, Zwiggelaar R (2014) Thermal facial analysis for deception detection. IEEE Trans Inf Forensics Secur 9(6):1015–1023

Schmidt A (2017) Augmenting human intellect and amplifying perception and cognition. IEEE Pervasive Comput 16(1):6–10

Schneegass S, Pfleging B, Broy N, Heinrich F, Schmidt A (2013) A data set of real world driving to assess driver workload. In: Proceedings of the 5th international conference on automotive user interfaces and interactive vehicular applications, pp 150–157. ACM

Shi Y, Ruiz N, Taib R, Choi E, Chen F (2007) Galvanic skin response (GSR) as an index of cognitive load. In: CHI'07 extended abstracts on human factors in computing systems, pp 2651–2656. ACM

Shirazi AS, Funk M, Pfleiderer F, Glück H, Schmidt A (2012) Mediabrain: annotating videos based on brain-computer interaction. In: Mensch & computer, pp 263–272

Shirazi AS, Hassib M, Henze N, Schmidt A, Kunze K (2014) What's on your mind?: mental task awareness using single electrode brain computer interfaces. In: Proceedings of the 5th augmented human international conference, p 45. ACM

Stemberger J, Allison RS, Schnell T (2010) Thermal imaging as a way to classify cognitive workload. In: 2010 Canadian conference on computer and robot vision (CRV), pp 231–238. IEEE

Sweller J, Ayres P, Kalyuga S (2011) Measuring cognitive load. Springer, New York, pp 71–85

Wang Z, Yan J, Aghajan H (2012) A framework of personal assistant for computer users by analyzing video stream. In: Proceedings of the 4th workshop on eye gaze in intelligent human machine interaction, p 14. ACM

Chapter 6
Affective Computing Needs Personalization—And a Character?

Dirk Reichardt

Abstract The role of emotion and personality is described from several aspects reflecting the current state of the art. First, a general idea of emotion, mood, and personality with their basic theories as well as psychological and computational aspects is discussed. Furthermore, the human interaction with an emotional machine is described. In this scenario, the machine shows signs of emotion and augments the communication with the user by that. Another aspect of affective systems deals with the assessment of human emotion by a computer system. Apart from computer vision, wearable computing, social media, and virtual reality provide data that is used to learn about the emotional state and personality of an interaction partner. This leads to the model of a complete character rather than a system, which just reflects short-term affective reactions to events and perceptions. Part of this character is the personality, but also the personal interaction history, which in turn contributes to habits and environment knowledge which all in all explain the behavior. A further aspect deals with emotion and autonomy. In this scenario, emotion is part of a model, which is used to control an autonomous system. Eventually, application scenarios for emotion-based systems are discussed. Every section deals with emotion as well as with the current state of integrating personality models.

6.1 Introduction

The field of Character Computing aims at introducing novel user experiences by extracting the "building blocks" of their character (El Bolock et al. 2017). In this chapter, the role of emotion is discussed in the context of Character Computing. Individual differences in humans are addressed in more and more software applications. Today, products are designed to meet user experience (UX) objectives. Products and the connected user experience models are designed for a specific target group and those are in parts very individual, dynamic, and include affective human–machine interaction. More and more applications include speech and gesture recognition. Due

D. Reichardt (✉)
DHBW Stuttgart, Stuttgart, Germany
e-mail: dirk.reichardt@dhbw-stuttgart.de

to their use in smartphones and tablet computers, people get used to gesture control. A more advanced way is touch-less gesture recognition, not only in the context of virtual and augmented reality. Moreover, wearable devices and cameras provide a large dataset on individual behavior, which leads to potential individualization. When systems adapt to a human user, they usually build a model of the user over time. This involves various applications for machine learning. More and more computer systems integrate concepts of emotion. In the design phase, UX approaches integrate emotional aspects of the users. In UX design, it is essential to know the target user in order to know the right triggers to generate positive emotional responses. Therefore, personas are developed in the design process—archetypical users representing a large group of users of the future product. Those personas also contain a personality. Applications that are even more interesting, adapt to the user's emotional state. In order to do this adequately, the system needs to have a concept of emotion or at least a shallow model of human emotion and its effect. As far as emotion recognition is concerned, the task is much easier for a human in case the observed person is well known. Therefore, the classification of the observed information is user dependent. It is not surprising that individualized classifiers are more accurate than general ones (see also Kim et al. 2009). Obviously, a human does not act and react in the same way all the time, even though the computer-perceived situation seems to be the same. Emotional state and personality contribute to cognitive bias, influence social and memory bias, and induce different behavior. An ideal model of the human user, therefore, includes models of emotion and personality. The following chapters discuss different aspects of emotion and personality. First, building a consistent model of emotion and personality is discussed. Then, the following sections deal with

- interactions between a human and an emotional computer system,
- the assessment of emotion and personality, and
- the importance of emotions for an intelligent autonomous system.

In addition, a couple of affective system examples are given to show their impact and importance for current systems. While this chapter is about affective computing and personalization, the role of Character Computing is addressed as a missing link between the model theory and the situation it is applied to.

6.2   Emotion and Personality—General Thoughts, Basic Theories, and the Big Five

Since the late 90s, with a major impact of the work of Picard (1997), Affective Computing has been a recognized discipline in the intersection set of artificial intelligence, psychology, and other adjacent fields like neuroscience. Many models of emotion have been discussed and implemented since then in various local application scenarios. Implementing psychological models in a computer system is clearly an interdisciplinary task and two very different scientific disciplines join forces to be successful. Whereas psychological models aim at explaining phenomena on a rather general and abstract level, a computer model simulates the model on a very different level of detail, which sometimes calls force changes in the more abstract psychological model as well. Ekman and Friesen published the Facial Affect Scoring Technique (FAST) and later the Facial Action Coding System (FACS) in the 70s (see Ekman et al. 1971; Ekman and Friesen 1978) based on their cross-cultural research. These models assume a set of basic emotions (happiness, sadness, surprise, anger, disgust, and fear) and determine static and dynamic indicators in the face grounded on worldwide empirical research. The models provide a level of detail, which makes it accessible for image processing approaches in computer science. Numerous software systems for emotion classification from faces have been implemented on this basis, whereas FAST and FACS define how to interpret facial expressions in order to recognize human emotions, and other emotion models explain how emotions are elicited. These models are suitable for autonomous systems that integrate emotion in their decision-making as well as for systems that try to explain observed user behavior. The dominant emotion theories nowadays are based on the cognitive appraisal theory. This theory goes back to the 60s with publications by Arnold and Lazarus, as well as Scherer in the twenty-first century (Scherer et al. 2001). The cognitive appraisal model developed and proposed by Orthony, Clore, and Collins in 1988 was intended to be computationally tractable (Ortony et al. 1988). Many implementations take this model as a basis for an emotion engine. The model assumes that emotions are valenced reactions to events and their consequences for oneself and others, actions of agents, and aspects of objects. The model can be adapted to the specific situation by the use of global and local intensity variables. Those variables eventually determine the emergence of an emotion. At this point, a gap between theory and application can be noticed. The model is not covering the way how to use these intensity variables. This is left open and has to be handled outside the model. Any system running in a real-world application needs a situation-dependent additional model to provide information for these intensity variables. Character Computing aims at filling this gap. The so-called "Big Five" model currently is the dominating psychological model of personality. The five traits are extraversion, agreeableness, conscientiousness, neuroticism, and openness. The traits are directly related to the emotional reactions of the individual. The neuroticism scale gives some hint about the person's predisposition to get stressed, to have mood swings, to generally worry, to feel upset, or to be anxious. Agreeableness may tell something about the individual's ability to feel empathy and to feel other's emotions. The conscientiousness shows control and self-discipline which may also result in controlling one's own emotions, such that they are less likely to be perceived by others. A computer scientist and artificial intelligence researcher would prefer a consistent model integrating emotion, mood, and personality in order to predict behavior of an artificial being. How do these components work together? The personality is the most stable of the three components. It hardly changes over time. It has a strong influence on the elicitation and intensity of an emotion of a person. Moreover, the predominant mood and the dynamics of mood changes are determined by the personality. The mood has a much longer duration than an emotion but it has less intensity and usually no direct relation to an action or event. If emotions are elicited, influence goes in both

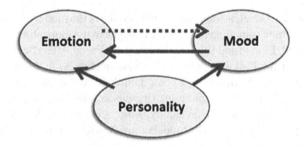

Fig. 6.1 Emotion, mood, and personality

directions. Depending on the mood, the same situation, event, or action may lead to different emotions or emotion intensities for the same individual. On the other hand, the mood can be changed by this as well. This can be depicted in a very generic way as shown in Fig. 6.1. A missing part of this simplified model is the link to the "outside", or in other words, the real world and the current situation.

Mehrabian (1996a,b) introduced a mapping of personality traits to the PAD Model, a dimensional model describing emotional states by the pleasure (or valence), arousal, and dominance scales. The PAD model was introduced by Mehrabian and Russel in 1974 and is widely used (Mehrabian and Russell 1974). It can be seen as an alternative approach to the more symbolic and discrete approaches of modeling emotions mentioned before. A clear functional dependency of the personality traits and the basic or default mood of a character is determined on this basis in the ALMA model proposed by Gebhard at German Research Centre for Artificial Intelligence (DFKI) (Gebhard 2005). There has been done a lot of research in order to assess personality traits via inventories and questionnaires. Vinciarelli and Moham-madi give a good overview of personality, especially on personality computing (Vinciarelli and Mohammadi 2014). They discuss the different aspects of personality recognition and perception by applying the Brunswik lens model (Brunswik 1956), which describes characteristics in human–human and human–machine interactions. According to Vinciarelli and Mohammadi, this basically leads to three personality computing aspects as follows:

- automatic personality recognition,
- automatic personality perception, and
- automatic personality synthesis.

The idea of personality recognition is based on the externalization of the personality by distal cues. The task is to find a covariance of distal cues and the personality. In contrast, the target of personality perception is not to determine the true person-ality, but puts into focus which personality is attributed by others. The cues which are used to infer both personality models (or perceptions) can also be collected in computer-based communication, i.e., social media, wearable devices, etc. Another study addressed the influence of artificial emotions in human–machine interaction using a simplified public goods game scenario (Göttlicher et al. 2009), which is known from game theory. In this experiment, the focus was on the influence of emotional reactions of artificial agents on a human player and his or her decisions. A model of emotion generates the artificial emotions of the agents. The model was adapted to the specific scenario and it integrated a dimensional model (pleasure, arousal, and dominance) with the Orthony, Clore, and Collins model of emotion (Ortony et al. 1988) and a concept of mood and personality. The idea of the ALMA model provided the groundwork for the experiment (Gebhard and Kipp 2006). In the experiment, the reactions of the human player were compared in two scenarios with and without visual emotional feedback of the other agents. As visual feedback, the virtual agent "Greta" (Niewiadomski et al. 2008) was used to embody the emotions generated by the model. As a first step, adequate emotion recognition was proven by an online survey validating the correct valence and intensity perception. The experiment showed a significantly higher amount of investment of the human player when the emotional state of the artificial agent players was shown while playing the public goods game. This was a closed-loop approach to integrate emotion, personality, and autonomous agent interaction but the potential of a personality model was not yet examined in more detail. Nevertheless, the same scenario was used in Reichardt (2007) to sketch the idea of an emotional Turing test. The intention was to automatically produce emotion-based decisions, which are not distinguishable from human decisions in the same context. When looking at this scenario from the point of view of Character Computing, the suitability is more or less hard-coded and well defined. It's much less complex than real-world scenarios. The personality of an opponent (agent) can be concluded from its behavior in the last games and the system (or human player) can adapt to that.

There is enormous ongoing research aiming at robot companions. Already 15 years ago, companion concepts were discussed by Dautenhahn (2004). According to today's findings, research on the emotional effects of human–robot interaction or human–virtual agent interaction is essential for success. Application scenarios include support for elderly as discussed by Lee and Hun Yoo (2017). The concept of emotion and empathy has been pointed out in the context of cooperative interaction by Boukricha et al. (see Boukricha et al. 2011, 2013). In the field of robot companions, the therapeutic robot PARO needs to be mentioned as an example. The robot is used in therapy support and helps elderly people suffering from dementia following a similar idea of pet therapy (Wada et al. 2009). One step further, Character Computing adds a consistent model of the companion by stabilizing its emotional reactions using a model of personality.

6.3 Interacting with an Emotional Machine

One major aspect of affective computing is the interaction with a machine, which adds social and emotional cues to the conversation with a human. Especially in the field of robotics, efforts are made to mimic human emotional cues. Moreover, already more than 20 years ago, Reeves and Nass claimed that people treat computers in many aspects like human beings. They tend to be polite to computers—depending on their interface—and show different reactions depending on the chosen voice of a navigation system and the like (Reeves and Nass 1996). It is not necessary to have a humanoid robot as an interaction partner. In student experiments, it was shown that the movements of a Pleo robot can be used to generate a clearly distinguishable expression of happiness and anger (Baumann 2014), whereas this expression of the robot was intended, other experiments show the emotional reactions of humans to the robot, which are not caused by the robot itself. In an experimental study of Rosental-von der Pütten et al. (2013), the Pleo robot was used to examine the reactions of humans when watching an interaction with the robot. Two scenarios were shown: a friendly video and a torture video. The participants showed increased physiological arousal when they watched the torture video as compared to the normal video. According to the authors, the participants expressed empathic concern for the robot. This can be considered in line with the ideas discussed by Reeves and Nass. In these cases, we have a scenario in which a human observes, rather than interacts in both directions. Again, Character Computing provides the potential to improve the effect these "emotional machines" can have on a human by explicitly adding a situation model into the equation.

6.4 Assessing Emotion and Personality

A lot of research has been done on recognizing the emotional state of a person. Using image processing, facial expressions are interpreted to determine the current emotion of the person. Many systems use the basic emotion model of Paul Ekman as a basis for classification (Ekman 2005). Especially the facial action coding system (FACS) was used as a theoretical background for classifiers before approaches applied deep learning algorithms on labeled training data. Recognizing emotion in the faces of people we know is considered easier than doing the same thing with strangers. There are variations and individual differences, which in turn are important to be part of classification algorithms (Cohn et al. 2002). In addition to direct human–machine interaction, the analysis of YouTube videos has become an application domain which also includes personality aspects as discussed in Teijeiro-Mosquera et al. (2015). In the last years, image processing has been augmented by using the thermal image of the head to add information. Conclusions can be drawn from temperature change in certain regions and the thermal information can be used in order to improve feature and muscle movement detection in the face (Puri 2005; Abd Latif et al. 2015). Of course, interpreting the voice has been a research subject for years. As an example, Sagha, Deng, and Schuller discussed the effect of personality trait, age, and gender on speech valence recognition (Sagha et al. 2017). The issue can be seen from both perspectives: how does a synthetic speech system have to modulate the output in order to achieve a desired personality trait and how can a technical system recognize these cues from a human–machine conversation? With wearable computing and mobile devices, more sources for data collection can be exploited and gestures and posture can be interpreted, especially physiological data can be collected by wearables. The large amount of collectible data provides a good basis for analysis using data science methods. Recently, Cai, Guo, Huang, Yu, and Yang discussed the analysis of correlations between this kind of sensor data and personality traits (Cai et al. 2018). Moreover, some approaches enhance the task to emotion and personality detection. As an example, Craenen, Deshmukh, Foster, and Vinciarelli discuss attributed personality traits and observed gestures (Craenen et al. 2018). Moreover, recently, sensors like EEG were not only used to detect emotional reactions but also to derive hints toward personality (Zhao et al. 2018). Since there are a lot of commercial physiological sensors available, the collection of relevant data has become less complicated. While many approaches aim at the classification of emotional states from a single source like facial features, voice, or gestures, more and more approaches build models, which integrate a multitude of different signals in a multimodal approach (Kim et al. 2009). For scientific experiments, the database ASCERTAIN has been built. This database connects personality traits and emotional states with physiological responses recorded by Electroencephalogram (EEG), Electrocardiogram (ECG), Galvanic Skin Response (GSR), and facial activity data. The experimental results using this database indicate that personality differences can be determined (Subramanian et al. 2018). Without the physical presence of a human, a further area of research is the interpretation of social media data. This field has become more and more popular in the last years. The basis is the analysis of text, especially short text-based utterances for their emotional component (Alm et al. 2005). The analysis can be done on Twitter posts and other social media to make a sentiment analysis for certain topics (Colneriĉ and Demsar 2018; Chatzakou and Vakali 2015; Perikos and Hatzilygeroudis 2018; Akram and Tahir 2018). The text analysis is augmented by adding conclusions to the individual personality drawn from the profile pictures of the users (Bhatti et al. 2017). When interpreting this kind of data, the context of utterances and pictures is highly relevant for the interpretation. The context is comparable to the situation in real-world scenarios, and therefore similar concepts can be used to solve the task. Text understanding and Character Computing might have some common ground here.

6.5 Emotion and Autonomy

Autonomous systems need to have a model in order to make decisions. Designing intelligent autonomous systems is a major discipline of AI. One big issue in this field is to make these agents "believable" by integrating emotional aspects in their decision models. In case these agents are human-like or animal-like, their appearance needs to be adapted to show the emotions as part of the communication with a human. Beyond this perception aspect, the quality of simulations is an issue. As an example, in traffic simulation, the vehicle behavior is generated automatically for a large number of traffic participants to analyze the effects of incidents, regulations, or specific scenarios. In this kind of simulation, driver types and emotional reactions are essential to provide realistic predictions. In Reichardt (2008), an emotion model is combined with a model of risk in order to provide believable and realistic driver behavior in a simulation. After solving safety issues, this could be transferred to autonomous vehicles operating in mixed traffic. An important aspect of autonomous systems is the adaptation to the environment, achieved by learning. For the learning task, emotion systems can be used as an input for a reinforcement learning approach as described in Lu et al. (2016). Looking closely at this, the model of risk needs a situation model which transfers environment information from the sensors into a representation of risk.

6.6   Affective System Applications

Which are application scenarios for a software that includes a model of personality, mood, and emotion? In this section, the idea of learning and virtual reality as a framework for emotional virtual agents with personality is sketched out. Personality aspects get more important in long-term interactions of a human with a virtual agent. In the past, learning mainly took place at schools and universities or seminars in advanced vocational training. The main learning and teaching concepts imply learning and working in groups. Traditional learning concepts consist of a teacher and a group of learners, which have a common lecture with a given content or at least learning objectives and a set method. Therefore, the learning pace is not—or only partially—set by the individual. This is changed by new means of learning, which put the learner into control of learning content and pace. Personalized e-learning has the potential to seriously improve individual learning outcomes. As Canavan already put together in 2004, adaptive learning systems can and should be aware of the learning style of the learner (Canavan 2004). New learning systems, therefore, have to adapt to the learner and do so by understanding the learner's emotional reactions and also his or her personality. The personality of a learner agent, virtual learning scenarios, and adaptive aspects have become a field of research (Liew and Tan 2016). As an example, Shun et al. (2015) discussed the motivational aspect of a learning system which takes the learner's personality into account when orchestrating learning items. As some of the examples already indicate, virtual reality is getting more and more important for teaching interpersonal skills through the use of virtual role-playing. Medical, as well as, military use of virtual training scenarios implementing social interactions has increased with the improvements of the technology. For such purposes, virtual humans have been developed to "live" in simulated environments. These agents have the ability to interact with humans using both verbal and nonverbal cues to express their own emotions and to understand the human participants' emotion (Hart et al. 2013). Approaches to this field have been studied in projects like FearNot! (see Paiva et al. 2004) where children learn how to cope with bullying in school, and E-Circus (education through characters with emotional-intelligence and role-playing capabilities that understand social interaction, see André 2008).

6.7   Conclusion

There is a good scientific foundation for computer systems that recognize and understand human emotion and personality and there are models that can be used and adapted to scenarios in which a computer-based system needs to produce emotional decisions and reactions. Some applications have already left the research domain and work in commercial environments. With new ways to access data—via social media, wearable sensors, voice control systems, and virtual reality—new applications are enabled. A vast amount of data is generated and stored and can be analyzed and scrutinized by data mining and machine learning approaches extracting information on emotion and personality. The theoretical models of emotion and personality need to be augmented by a model that addresses the assessment of the situation. Future applications will contain long-term interaction concepts with a human user and a conversation (or interaction) partner. This provides a basis for adaptive- and personality-based models. The history of interactions and potential experience of the virtual character often play a role in believable interactions. To make them part of the model is one of the main issues for Character Computing and it will be one of the important fields of research in intelligent interactive systems.

References

Abd Latif MH, Yusof HMd, Sidek SN, Rusli N (2015) Thermal imaging based affective state recognition. In: 2015 IEEE international symposium on robotics and intelligent sensors (IRIS). Langkawi, pp 214–219

Akram J, Tahir A (2018) Lexicon and heuristics based approach for identification of emotion in text. In: 2018 international conference on frontiers of information technology (FIT), Islamabad, Pakistan, 2018, pp 293–297

Alm CO, Roth D, Sproat R (2005) Emotions from text: machine learning for text-based emotion prediction. In: Proceedings of human language technology conference and conference on Empirical methods in natural language processing, October. ACL, 2005, pp 579–586

André E (2008) Design and evaluation of embodied conversational agents for educational and advisory software. In: Luppicini R (ed) Handbook of conversation design for instructional applications. Information Science Reference

Baumann R, Höhne J, and Spangenberger J (2014) Untersuchung der Differenzierbar-keit von Emotionen dargestellt durch Bewegungsabläufe des Dinosaurier Roboters Pleo, study thesis, DHBW Stuttgart, 2014

Bhatti SK, Muneer A, Lali M, Gull X, Din SMU (2017) Personality analysis of the USA public using Twitter profile pictures. In: 2017 international conference on information and communication technologies (ICICT), Karachi, 2017, pp 165–172

Boukricha H, Nguyen N, Wachsmuth I (2011) Sharing emotions and space - empathy as a basis for cooperative spatial interaction. In: Kopp S, Marsella S, Thorisson K, Vilhjalmsson HH (eds) LNAI, vol 6895. Proceedings of the 11th international conference on intelligent virtual agents (IVA). Springer. Reykjavik, Iceland, Berlin, Heidelberg, pp 350–362

Boukricha H, Wachsmuth I, Carminati MN, Knoeferle P (2013) A computa-tional model of empathy: Empirical evaluation, Humaine association conference on affective computing and intelligent interaction (ACII) (pp 1–6). Institute of Electrical and Electronics Engineers (IEEE). Geneva, Swizerland

Brunswik E (1956) Perception and the representative design of psychological experiments. University of California Press, Oakland

Cai R, Guo A, Ma J, Huang R, Yu R, Yang C (2018) Correlation analyses between personality traits and personal behaviors under specific emotion states using physiological data from wearable devices. In: 2018 IEEE 16th international conference on dependable, autonomic and secure computing, 16th international conference on pervasive intelligence and computing, 4th international conference on big data intelligence and computing and cyber science and technology congress (DASC/PiCom/DataCom/CyberSciTech). Athens 2018, pp 46–53

Canavan J (2004) Personalised e-learning through learning style aware adaptive systems. Dissertation, University of Dublin, 2004

Chatzakou D, Vakali A (2015) Harvesting opinions and emotions from social media textual resources. IEEE Int Comput 19(4):46–50

Cohn JF, Schmidt K, Gross R, Ekman P (2002) Individual differences in facial expression: stability over time, relation to self-reported emotion, and ability to inform person identification. In: Proceedings of the fourth IEEE international conference on multimodal interfaces, Pittsburgh, PA, USA, 2002, pp 491–496

Colnerîc N, Demsar J (2018) Emotion recognition on twitter: comparative study and training a unison model. In: IEEE transactions on affective computing

Craenen B, Deshmukh A, Foster ME, Vinciarelli A (2018) Shaping gestures to shape personalities: the relationship between gesture parameters, attributed personality traits and godspeed scores. In: 27th IEEE international symposium on robot and human interactive communication (RO-MAN). Nanjing 2018, pp 699–704

Dautenhahn K (2004) Robots we like to live with?! - a developmental perspective on a personalized, life-long robot companion, RO-MAN 2004. In: 13th IEEE international workshop on robot and human interactive communication (IEEE Catalog No.04TH8759). Kurashiki, Okayama, Japan 2004, pp 17–22

Ekman, P. (2005), "What the Face Reveals: Basic and Applied Studies of Spontaneous Ex-pression Using the Facial Action Coding System (FACS)", Series in Affective Science, Ox-ford University Press, 2005

Ekman P, Friesen WV, Tomkins SS (1971) Facial affect scoring technique: a first validity study. Semiotica 1:37–53

Ekman P, Friesen WV (1978) Facial action coding system: a technique for the meas-urement of facial movement. Consulting Psychologists Press, Palo Alto

El Bolock A, Salah J, Abdennadher S, Abdelrahman Y (2017) Character computing: challenges and opportunities. In: Proceedings of the 16th international conference on mobile and ubiquitous multimedia. ACM, New York, USA

Gebhard P (2005) ALMA - a layered model of affect. In: Proceedings of the fourth international joint conference on autonomous agents and multiagent systems (AAMAS'05), 29–36, Utrecht

Gebhard P, Kipp KH (2006) Are computer-generated emotions and moods plausible to humans? In: IVA 2006: intelligent virtual agents, Springer, 2006, pp 343–356

Göttlicher K, Stein S, Reichardt D (2009) Effects of emotional agents on human players in the public goods game. In: 3rd international conference on affective computing and intelligent interaction and workshops, Amsterdam, 2009, pp 1–6

Hart J, Gratch J, Marsella S (2013) How virtual reality training can win friends and influence people. In: Best C, Galanis G, Kerry J, Sottilare R (eds) Fundamental issues in defence training and simulation, Chapter: Fundamental issues in defence training and simulation, Ashgate Publishing

Kim J, André E, Vogt T (2009) Towards user-independent classification of multimodal emotional signals. In: 3rd international conference on affective computing and intelligent interaction and workshops, Amsterdam, 2009, pp 1–7

Lee SB, Hun Yoo S (2017) Design of the companion robot interaction for sup-porting major tasks of the elderly. In: 14th international conference on ubiquitous robots and ambient intelligence (URAI), Jeju, 2017, pp 655–659

Liew TW, Tan S (2016) Virtual agents with personality: adaptation of learner-agent personality in a virtual learning environment. In: 2016 eleventh international conference on digital information management (ICDIM), Porto, 2016, pp 157–162

Lu C, Sun Z, Shi Z, Cao B (2016) Using emotions as intrinsic motivation to accelerate classic reinforcement learning. In: 2016 international conference on information system and artificial intelligence (ISAI), Hong Kong, 2016, pp 332–337

Mehrabian A (1996a) Analysis of the big-five personality factors in terms of the PAD temperament model. Aust J Psychol 48(2):86–92

Mehrabian A (1996b) Pleasure-arousal-dominance: a general framework for describing and measuring individual differences in temperament. Curr Psychol 14(1996):261–292

Mehrabian A, Russell JA (1974) An approach to environmental psychology, 1st edn. MIT Press, Cambridge

Niewiadomski R, Ochs M, Pelachaud C (2008) Expressions of Empathy in ECAs. In: Prendinger H, Lester J, Ishizuka M, 8th international conference on intelligent virtual agents, IVA 2008

Ortony A, Clore GL, Collins A (1988) The cognitive structure of emotions. Cam-bridge University Press, Cambridge

Paiva A, Dias J, Sobral D, Aylett R, Sobre-perez P, Woods S et al (2004) Caring for agents and agents that care: building empathic relations with synthetic agents. In: Proceedings of the third international joint conference on autonomous agents and multiagent systems AAMAS '04 (pp 194–201). IEEE Computer Society, Washington

Perikos I, Hatzilygeroudis I (2018) A framework for analyzing big social data and modelling emotions in social media. In: 2018 IEEE fourth international conference on big data computing service and applications (BigDataService), Bamberg, 2018, pp 80–84

Picard RW (1997) Affective computing. Massachusetts Institute of Technology

Puri C, Olson L, Pavlidis I, Levine J, Starren J (2005) StressCam: non-contact measurement of users' emotional states through thermal imaging. In: CHI'05 ex-tended abstracts on human factors in computing systems, pp 1725–1728, ACM, 2005

Reeves B, Nass C (1996) The media equation: how people treat computers, television, and new media like real people and places. Cambridge University Press, Cambridge

Reichardt D (2007) A definition approach for an emotional turing test. In: Proceedings of the second international conference on affective computing and intelligent interaction, ACII 2007. In: Prada APR, Picard RW (eds) Lisbon, Portugal, September 2007, LNCS 4738, Springer

Reichardt D (2008) Approaching driver models which integrate models of emotion and risk. In: IEEE intelligent vehicles symposium, Eindhoven, 2008, pp 234–239

Rosenthal-von der Pütten A, Krämer NC, Hoffmann L, Sobieraj S, Eimler SC (2013) An experimental study on emotional reactions towards a robot. Int J Soc Robot 5(1):17–34

Sagha H, Deng J, Schuller B (2017) The effect of personality trait, age, and gender on the performance of automatic speech valence recognition. In: Seventh international conference on affective computing and intelligent interaction, ACII. TX, San Antonio, pp 86–91

Scherer KR, Shorr A, Johnstone T (eds) (2001) Appraisal processes in emotion: theory, methods, research. Oxford University Press, Canary, pp 21–22

Shun MCY, Yan MC, Zhiqi S, Bo A (2015) Learning personality modeling for regulating learning Feedback. In: 2015 IEEE 15th international conference on advanced learning technologies, Hualien, 2015, pp 355–357

Subramanian R, Wache J, Abadi MK, Vieriu RL, Winkler S, Sebe N (2018) ASCERTAIN: emotion and personality recognition using commercial sensors. IEEE Trans Affect Comput 9(2):147–160. Accessed 1 April–June 2018

Teijeiro-Mosquera L, Biel J, Alba-Castro JL, Gatica-Perez D (2015) What your face vlogs about: expressions of emotion and big-five traits impressions in YouTube. IEEE Trans Affect Comput 6(2):193–205. Accessed 1 April–June 2015

Vinciarelli A, Mohammadi G (2014) A survey of personality computing. IEEE Trans Affect Comput 5(3):273–291. Accessed 1 July–Sept 2014

Wada K, Shibata T, Kawaguchi Y (2009) Long-term robot therapy in a health ser-vice facility for the aged - A case study for 5 years -. In: IEEE international conference on re-habilitation robotics, Kyoto 2009, pp 930–933

Zhao G, Ge Y, Shen B, Wei X, Wang H (2018) Emotion analysis for personality inference from EEG signals. IEEE transactions on affective computing 9(3):362–371. Accessed 1 July–Sept 2018

Chapter 7
Character-IoT (CIoT): Toward Human-Centered Ubiquitous Computing

Amr El Mougy

Abstract Character Computing envisions systems that can detect, synthesize, and adapt to human character. The development and realization of this field hinge upon the availability of data about human character traits and states. This data must be comprehensive enough to model the embedded causality in the triad of behavior–situation–character that makes up the core of Character Computing. Acquiring this data requires an intelligent and scalable platform for sensing, processing, analysis, and decision support, which we label as Character-IoT (CIoT). This chapter investigates how this CIoT can be realized. A comprehensive study of sensing modalities in the areas of affective and personality computing is presented to identify the technologies that can be adopted in Character Computing. This includes facial expressions, speech, text, gestures, and others. We also highlight artificial intelligence techniques that are most commonly used in areas of affective and personality computing and analyze which ones are suitable for Character Computing. Finally, we propose an architectural framework for CIoT that can be adopted by future researchers in this field.

7.1 Introduction

Computing systems continue to weave themselves into every aspect of our everyday lives. In this ubiquitous computing environment, human users are surrounded with smart devices and systems capable of a wide range of interactions that promote healthy, comfortable, and enjoyable lifestyles. Traditional Human–Computer Interaction (HCI) designs were computer centered, where the goal was to simplify for the human user, as much as possible, the intricate task of using a computing device. Today, computer systems have evolved immeasurably to serve humans in a much easier way. Thus, HCI designs are now evolving to be more human centered. The primary objective of human-centered HCI is to depart from the static, reactive, and socially unaware computer-centered design, where devices simply respond to user

A. El Mougy (✉)
German University in Cairo, Cairo, Egypt
e-mail: amr.elmougy@guc.edu.eg

© Springer Nature Switzerland AG 2020

A. El Bolock et al. (eds.), *Character Computing*, Human–Computer Interaction Series,
https://doi.org/10.1007/978-3-030-15954-2_7

commands, to an anticipatory, emotionally intelligent design. These designs should explore the full range of the naturally occurring multimodal human communications (audio, visual, linguistic, gesture, body, etc.). Human-centered systems should be able to detect and recognize subtle but relevant changes in user behavior, to understand the context behind this behavior, to detect repeating and characterizing patterns of behavior, and to respond in a synthesized human-like form. The last decade has witnessed tremendous activity in the research of human-centered HCI. The area of Affective Computing (AC) has seen significant advancements in detection and recognition of human affective states. In addition, the area of Personality Computing (PC) has ventured into learning distinctive qualities that make up a human's personality, which can be used to explain or predict behavior in certain situations. As we now embark on the new era of Character Computing, we need systems that can detect and recognize the abstract traits of a person and their set of morals and beliefs that define how humans deal with each other. Thus, it can be said that Character Computing is the ultimate step for computing devices to gain a deep understanding of the human psyche. However, the complexity and variability of human psychology implies the need for long-term collection, storage, and processing of human-related information, perhaps also contextually labeled, in order to realize the goal of Character Computing. Accordingly, this chapter focuses on the sensing layer of Character Computing. Particularly, the objective is to understand the requirements and challenges of developing a ubiquitous system of sensing, recognizing, and synthesizing multimodal human communications, which we entitle Character Internet of Things (CIoT). Since this CIoT is still in its infancy, we survey the most relevant state-of-the-art literature in AC and PC to identify solutions that can possibly be adopted in Character Computing. We discuss different types of sensing systems and the human attributes they detect. We also investigate supporting technologies such as context awareness and artificial intelligence that ensure efficient utilization of the collected sensory data. Based on this survey, we propose an architectural framework for CIoT that can be adopted by researchers. Open challenges and future research directions are highlighted as well.

7.2 Trends in Sensing Affect

AC is a multidisciplinary research area that has witnessed vigorous activity in recent years. Research in this area involves fields such as psychology, computer vision, natural language processing, and artificial intelligence (Zeng et al. 2009; Calvo and D'Mello 2010). In fact, the overall progress in the field of AC hinges upon progress in these related fields.

There are two prevalent models of affect detection and recognition in literature: the discrete model (Tomkins 2008) and the dimensional model (Russel and Mehrabian 1977). In the discrete model, affect is categorized into a finite set of basic emotions, typically fear, anger, happiness, sadness, disgust, and surprise. Frustration and stress are often added to this list. This limited categorization simplifies the task of automatic recognition systems, especially if they are aided by machine learning algorithms. This is proven by the high accuracy reported in many research works utilizing this model. However, the discrete model has been often criticized by its limited scope, which may not capture the unlimited range of human emotions. This is addressed by the dimensional model, which assumes there are three psycho-physiological constructs that influence affect: arousal, valence, and motivational intensity (Greene et al. 2016a). Arousal is basically the activation of an emotion by the Autonomic Nervous System (ANS). Measuring this dimension using physiological sensors is usually straightforward, as we will see later in this section. The valence dimension refers to the type of emotion being detected: positive, negative, or neutral. The combination of arousal and valence can be used to estimate the emotion itself. For example, high arousal and positive valence can be interpreted as excitement, while high arousal and negative valence can be interpreted as anger. Finally, the motivational intensity refers to the likelihood of eliciting an action out of this emotion. In this chapter, we will review the trends in AC that are most relevant to Character Computing. A comprehensive survey of affect detection and recognition is out of scope of this chapter. The interested reader can refer to Zeng et al. (2009), Calvo and D'Mello (2010). However, the goal here is to review promising trends and relevant efforts that can be used to create a CIoT platform that can be used in Character Computing research.

7.2.1   Detecting Affect from Facial Expressions

Facial Expressions (FE) are among the strongest emotional cues that human beings convey (Ekman 1982). In fact, evolutionary studies such as the one by Charles Darwin have shown that this fact is true of all humans across cultures and geographical boundaries (Ekman 1971). Moreover, there is a significant degree of universality in FEs. From a biological standpoint, the facial bones and muscles used for FEs are found in all humans. Accordingly, FEs have been thoroughly studied in the context of AC (Corneanu et al. 2016), with significant success. For example, Fig. 7.1 shows the mapping of FEs to the primary emotions used in discrete modeling of affect (See Sect. 7.2). In this section, we discuss the automatic detection of these FEs.

Fig. 7.1 FEs conveying basic emotions. From left to right: disgust, fear, joy, surprise, sadness, and anger

The three main types of media used in affective recognition of FEs are RGB, 3D, and thermal images and video. Generally speaking, the recognition process involves a set of common steps (Corneanu et al. 2016):

- Face localization,
- Registration,
- Feature extraction, and
- Classification.

Algorithms for localizing the face in an image or video can be classified into two categories: detection and segmentation (Zhang and Zhang 2010). Detection algorithms utilize machine learning techniques to identify the boundaries of a face. Occlusions and pose variations often have an impact on the accuracy of some detection algorithms. However, research has shown that probabilistic techniques and convolutional neural networks can overcome these challenges in a variety of scenarios (Jones and Viola 2003). On the other hand, segmentation algorithms assign a binary label to each pixel to specify whether a face is present or not (Sirohey 1998). Most segmentation algorithms make this decision using color and texture information in the image/video. Machine learning techniques can then be used to improve the accuracy of these segmentation decisions. Segmentation approaches have also shown significant accuracy in thermal images, where the decision is made according to the radiant emittance of each pixel (Trujillo et al. 2005). Joint visible/thermal facial expression recognition, where thermal extracted features were used to augment the visible image classifier, has also been explored in Wang et al. (2018) with excellent accuracy. Segmentation can also be applied to 3D images (Colombo et al. 2006). Here, the facial curvatures are used to detect features such as nose tip, ears, etc. Machine learning techniques are also used to label these parts appropriately. For 4D facial expression recognition, the work in Zhen et al. (2016) stressed the importance of analyzing muscle movement for accurate detection. Facial registration follows localization, where key points on the face are identified. Here, the goal is to encode key information about the face that can be later used by recognition algorithms. This information may include geometry, intensity, and labeled parts (Wang et al. 2018). 3D images require a 3D model to map the detected geometric features (Tam et al. 2013). Regression and other machine learning techniques are used to find the closest mapping between the model and the detected features. After key points are registered, a recognition algorithm would have to extract meaningful features to use them for classification in the last step. Feature extraction is typically done using machine learning algorithms. Here, either the algorithms are given a specific set of predefined features that have to be extracted, or are left to explore the features in each face according to the training set. In the first case, the predefined features may include appearance information (intensity, color, etc.) or geometric information (distances between landmarks, curvatures, etc.) Corneanu et al. (2016). In 3D images, feature extraction often involves dividing the face into regions and describing the features in each region separately (Soylemez et al. 2017). Also, geometric approaches are not suitable for thermal images. Here the features involve measuring the differences between facial regions, and algorithms use models to map these differences (Wang et al. 2014; Yoshitomi et al. 2010). After feature extraction, automatic models of FE recognition can operate. Here, the trained algorithm can be given a new image to detect its FE. These recognition algorithms can be classified into static or dynamic. Static algorithms are used to detect a finite set of expressions. For example, the emotions in the discrete affect model described in Sect. 7.2 can be mapped to FEs, and the recognition algorithm would then detect these FEs and specify which emotion is conveyed. Static algorithms typically use a trained classifier for each expression to be detected, and methods for resolving conflicts can be used when the output is not clear (Corneanu et al. 2016). On the other hand, dynamic recognition methods use continuous multidimensional space to map FEs. The advantage here is the ability to detect subtle differences between expressions. In addition, unsupervised learning algorithms (mainly clustering) can be used to evolve the recognition algorithm in order to detect new expressions beyond the initial predefined set. Recurrent Neural Networks (RNNs) have found use in many research efforts on dynamic recognition (Fragopanagos and Taylor 2005), where the techniques use the detected geometric features and clustering data to map the FE in the continuous space.

7.2.1.1 Challenges in Using FEs in Character Computing

As mentioned before, FEs have been used with great success in automatic recognition of emotions. Detecting the affective states is a core component in Character Computing, and a CIoT platform should utilize FE recognition using the above techniques. However, the main challenge to be considered in Character Computing is that most studies in FE have been performed in controlled environments. Studies in the wild have been limited and have shown varying success (one of the biggest databases can be found in Dhall et al. 2011). Data collection for Character Computing is expected to require long durations in order to identify stable patterns of behavior. This has not been attempted in literature yet, according to the best knowledge of the author.

7.2.2 Detecting Affect from Speech

Humans are unique beings in their ability to communicate effectively through speech. In fact, human speech offers explicit (linguistic) information as well as implicit (paralinguistic) information. Automatic recognition of this explicit and implicit information can be used to detect affect. Even though this has been a highly active research area, it is much more challenging than FEs, and often has smaller accuracy (Anagnostopoulos et al. 2015). There are many reasons for this. First, the boundaries of human emotions conveyed through speech are not as clear cut as those in FEs. Also, cultural differences impact how humans speak, which means that a generic model cannot be used on all persons. Additionally, certain human traits such as sarcasm may confuse classifiers and are often difficult to detect. Finally, classifiers may fail to detect speech impediments if they exist.

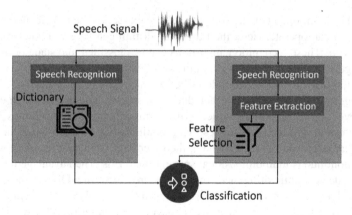

Fig. 7.2 Pipeline for emotion recognition from speech

Nevertheless, speech remains one of the most important sources for detecting affect, which is why this section is dedicated to the discussion of prominent research efforts in this direction. Speech processing provides a variety of powerful tools for assigning quantitative measures to the paralinguistic information in speech. This includes extraction of prosodic and spectral features. This is often aided by speech recognition systems for the detection of linguistic information, which can provide qualitative information about the conveyed emotions. It is worth mentioning that emotion recognition from speech often utilizes the dimensional affect model Zeng et al. (2009) (see Sect. 7.2), as it is suitable for speech processing techniques to detect arousal and valence. Figure 7.2 provides a generic model for the pipeline of emotion recognition from speech, as found in Anagnostopoulos et al. (2015).

In paralinguistic emotion recognition, the key step is the extraction and selection of features, collectively known as the creation of the feature vector. Here, two types of features are typically extracted: segmental and suprasegmental. To extract the segmental features, the speech signal is divided into small windows (25–50 ms) and the features are calculated for every segment. This is mainly to analyze the temporal evolution of the speech signal. On the other hand, suprasegmental features are extracted from the entire speech signal duration. The segmental and suprasegmental features can then be jointly analyzed to detect emotions. Speech features are classified into Low-Level Descriptors (LLD) and statistical features. LLDs are the suprasegmental prosodic features and the segmental spectral features. They include frequency features, pitch, speaking rate, jitter, energy, and voice quality parameters. Quite often, the most important LLDs are the Mel Frequency Cepstral Coefficients (MFCC), which provide a frequency representation of the human speech as close as possible to what the human ear perceives, and Linear Prediction Cepstral Coefficients (LPCC) Mao et al. (2009), where each sample provides a linear combination of past speech samples. On the other hand, statistical features are derived from the LLDs and are also suprasegmental (Giannakopoulos et al. 2009). They include mean, maximum, minimum, zero-crossing rate, etc. Extracting linguistic features follows a different process. This starts with the uttered phrase, which is passed to a speech recognition and word extraction module (Anagnostopoulos et al. 2015). Afterward, an updated dictionary of salient words is used to aid the emotion classification process. Here, the spoken words themselves may provide hints about the valence of the speaker's emotion. Moreover, speech analysis can provide additional information about the affective state. For example, repeated words or phrases may be a hint of frustration or anger. Combining this information with paralinguistic information results in improved accuracy (Wu and Liang 2011). Paralinguistic vocalizations such as outbursts of laughing or crying can also provide important insights into emotion recognition. After feature extraction is done, the classification process can start. Research in human speech classifiers is quite extensive. Several tools have been used for paralinguistic classification such as Hidden Markov Models (HMM), Gaussian Mixture Models (GMM), Support Vector Machines (SVM), and decision trees (Anagnostopoulos et al. 2015). Each classifier offers advantages and suffers drawbacks. For example, it is difficult to define a generic number of states in HMM for all speech signals. Similarly, determining the optimum number of components is difficult in GMM. In SVMs, even though training is typically more optimum, research has shown that overfitting is possible in many cases as a result of not choosing kernel functions properly (Yang 2009). On the other hand, linguistic classification is typically done using a Bag of Words (BoW) and a natural language processing model such as N-Grams. Hybrid classifiers have also been proposed and often show improved accuracy (Anagnostopoulos et al. 2015).

7.2.2.1   Challenges in Using Emotional Speech Recognition in Character Computing

As in FE recognition, speech recognition can be an important tool for detecting the affective states of a user, which is a key component in Character Computing. However, similar to the case of FEs, most studies of emotional speech recognition have been attempted in controlled environments. Character Computing will require capturing natural speech patterns over extensive time periods. These emotions also have to be correlated with context to determine how the person is reacting in different situations. For example, detecting that a person appears to be always tense or nervous in conversations with people in larger groups may imply introversion. An important challenge in speech recognition is the availability of datasets. This will be additionally challenging in Character Computing since it may require the availability of datasets of long-term natural conversations. These conversations will have to be labeled for context and the character types of the speakers, which may be quite challenging. In addition, not all speech can be used to detect core beliefs of users, which is required in Character Computing. This means that the CIoT platform needs to look for certain types of speech for Character Computing. Future researchers may need to develop alternative models that do not require extensive training or may find alternative ways for using speech in Character Computing.

7.2.3 Detecting Affect from Body Gestures

In addition to FEs and speech, humans constantly communicate through gestures and body language. Humans use these expressions in a variety of ways. For example, nodding at a slow or moderate rate can express agreement or interest, while nodding at a fast rate can express boredom or disinterest. Tilting the body posture forward can express courtesy, while tilting it backward and raising the chin upward can express arrogance. There are countless examples of how humans use body gestures for communication. The interested reader can refer to Pease and Pease (2004) for more examples. Even though body gestures are used by virtually all humans, the gestures themselves are not universal. Cultural differences impose different meanings on gestures (Noroozi et al. 2018). For example, patting one's own chest is an Egyptian expression of apology, which is not used by many other cultures. Extending one's arm forward with the fist clenched and facing upward and moving the index finger repeatedly in a circular motion means come here in many countries. In Asia, this gesture is not welcome as it is used only with dogs. However, cultural openness has led to many gestures becoming de facto universal, especially among younger generations. For example, thumbs up is now universally recognized as an expression of agreement, when it was not so before. Cultural differences are not the only challenge in body gesture recognition and interpretation. There are also gender differences in how gestures are used (Noroozi et al. 2018), and some of them even have evolutionary reasons. Generally speaking, women are more expressive of their emotions, while men may frequently hold back. On the other hand, men have higher tendency to show power and dominance, for example, through open and spread postures. Men also have higher tendency to show anger. In many cultures, these gender differences are fading and may not be an issue in the future (Einstein et al. 2013). Nevertheless, these challenges have led to lower detection accuracy in automatic detection systems compared to FEs and speech. Fortunately, technologies for capturing gestures (mainly RGB and depth cameras) have significantly evolved in recent years, thus allowing for better detection and recognition than was permissible in the past. The pipeline for emotion detection from body gestures is shown in Fig. 7.3. This pipeline was proposed in Noroozi et al. (2018). The first step, which is human detection, is done using similar techniques to face localization, which was explained in Sect. 7.2.1. Technologies for this step are quite mature and have high success rates.

Body pose estimation requires a model of the human body. Generally speaking, there are two types of models: part based and kinematic (Noroozi et al. 2018). Part-based models divide the body into parts that are detected independently based on domain knowledge of the human body. These independent detections are then combined to estimate the pose. On the other hand, kinematic models use cyclical graphs for a simplified representation of the human skeleton. Here, nodes of the graph represent the body joints, parameterized by the degrees of freedom. 3D kinematic models are also available. The difference between part-based and kinematic models is shown in Fig. 7.4. The images on the left are for part-based models, while kinematic models are illustrated in the images on the right. Body pose estimation is typically done using

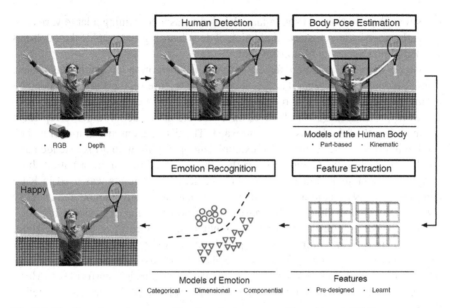

Fig. 7.3 Pipeline of emotion recognition from body gestures (Noroozi et al. 2018)

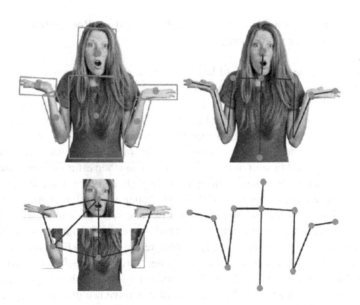

Fig. 7.4 Human body models. On the left is a part-based model and on the right is a kinematic model (Noroozi et al. 2018)

classifiers that are trained using a large labeled dataset containing a large variety of poses. In recent research, the combination of deep learning and graphical models has yielded higher accuracy (Tompson et al. 2014).

After body pose estimation, feature extraction and emotion recognition take place. These two steps are closely related as choosing the feature vector is highly dependent on the set of emotions to be recognized and how they are modeled. For example, the work in Vu et al. (2011) focuses on a discrete set of action units to represent the movements of the hands, legs, and waist. The discrete emotional model is then used to interpret these features. For example, an open pose with arms extended and hands spread can reflect happiness. On the other hand, additional information about body movement such as the velocity and acceleration of joints was used in Kipp and Martin (2009) in combination with the dimensional emotional model to quantify arousal and valence. Other studies have focused on particular expressions and their body language manifestations such as laughter states (Griffin et al. 2013). Here, torso and limb information were compared with different classifiers to identify if the laughter state was fake, awkward, social, or hilarious. In Senecal et al. (2016), the authors studied continuous body movements during a theater performance. Here, neural networks are used to model the body movement as a trajectory on a modeling diagram.

7.2.3.1 Challenges in Using Emotional Body Gesture Recognition in Character Computing

As with speech, the availability of large datasets for training is a major challenge in emotional body gesture recognition. The datasets are even more scarce if a specialized study is required (such as focusing on head movement or particular expressions). Another important challenge is multi-person emotional recognition. This may be important in systems deployed to monitor large crowds. In this case, the system has to determine the number of persons in the frame even if they occlude each other. Some approaches start by detecting persons and then estimate their poses (Cao et al. 2016), while others detect different body parts and then associate each body part to a person Papandreou et al. (2017). The latter approach is more dominant in research, where clustering is often used to associate body parts to persons. As with FEs and speech, detection of habits and patterns over extended durations is critical for Character Computing and has not been attempted in research. Even though gesture recognition can be used to detect affective states, it remains unclear how this can be used in Character Computing. It would be interesting to study how human character affects gestures, and whether the detection of repetitive use of certain gestures can imply certain character traits. Such a study must be done across cultures and must encompass different character types, suggesting that it must be a large-scale study.

7.2.4   Detecting Affect from Physiological Sensors

The automatic recognition systems that we have discussed so far focus on detecting emotions that humans communicate through FEs, speech, or body gestures. Human bodies also experience manifestations of emotions that can be detected using physiological sensors. Elevated heart rate, heavy breathing, and brain activity are all examples of how human bodies react to certain emotions. Some of the physiological sensors that have been explored in AC literature include (Greene et al. 2016b) the following:

- **Electrocardiography (ECG)**: for measuring electrical activity of the heart.
- **Electroencephalography (EEG)**: for measuring electrical activity of the brain.
- **Galvanic Skin Response (GSR)**: measures changes in sweat gland activity.
- **Photoplethysmography (PPG)**: optically measures changes in blood volume in each heartbeat.
- **Electromyography (EMG)**: for measuring electric activity of the muscle tissue.
- **Piezoelectric Respiration Sensor (PZT)**: for measuring respiratory activity.

One of the most investigated sensors in AC is EEG. This is because research on the link between brain activity and emotions has now become quite mature, and EEG sensors can capture this activity clearly. EEG sensors use electrodes attached to the scalp that measure electrical conductivity of the brain. These electrical signals occupy different frequency bands, depending on the brain activity, which can be used to identify emotions. For example, asymmetrical activity of the frontal part of the brain in the alpha band (8–13 Hz) can be used to measure valence. Typically, right frontal activations in the alpha band are associated with negative emotions while left frontal activations are associated with positive emotions. A comprehensive description of the correlation of brain activity and emotions can be found in Alarcao and Fonseca (2018). Detecting emotions using EEG usually follows a standard pipeline (Alarcao and Fonseca 2018):

1. Subjecting users to stimuli.
2. Recording brain activity using EEG.
3. Removing noise and artifacts from the recorded signal.
4. Extracting features.
5. Classification of emotions.

The chosen stimuli depend on the purpose of the study. Generally speaking, subjects are either internally stimulated (for example, asking them to remember a certain memory) or externally stimulated, also known as event-based stimulation (exposing the subject to an event). Since the brain is responsible for all body activities, the recorded EEG signal will contain noise and artifacts that can distort the classification procedure. These include eye blinking, heartbeats, muscle movement, etc. Removal of these artifacts is typically done using frequency filters. The extracted features are the set of frequencies of interest, which depend on the objective of the study. Finally, classification is done using machine learning algorithms, with SVM being the one mostly used by researchers. This step can be done offline or live, with the latter being more challenging. Most studies in literature perform offline classification (Alarcao and Fonseca 2018). Heart activity has also been explored in AC research, primarily in detecting stress. ECG is the main sensor used in detecting changes in heart activity. By exposing a subject to a stimulus, the change in heart activity can reflect the level of stress. Once the stimulus is removed, ECG can measure how fast the heart returns to its nominal level. GSR has also been used in research on stress, and it has been gaining increasing attention in recent years. This is mainly because it is less invasive than ECG, requiring typically one electrode to be worn around the finger. GSR works by detecting changes in the activity of the sweat glands. These changes can be coded into features that can be used by a classification algorithm. PPG and EMG are also noninvasive sensors. They have found many applications in healthcare monitoring and stress detection. PZT has not received significant attention in research, as the correlation between breathing activity and emotions is not as strong as EEG or EMG (Greene et al. 2016b).

7.2.4.1 Challenges in Using Emotional Recognition Using Physiological Sensors in Character Computing

The typical challenge associated with physiological sensors is their invasiveness, and they often require long setup or training times. Current technology has dramatically improved in those two aspects. Thus, we can now find physiological sensors sold as wearable devices that are often wireless. Nevertheless, most of these sensors still impose a look that is out of the social norm, which makes their adoption more difficult by the general public. As technology improves, this challenge is unlikely to persist. Unfortunately, for now, it will remain a challenge for utilizing these sensors in long-term studies in Character Computing. There is also a need for more research in the fusion of these sensors, perhaps also with FEs, speech, and body gestures. Such studies will shed more light on the biological manifestations of emotions in each individual. These studies may also give us more insight into how these manifestations differ by gender or culture, ultimately leading to better utilization of these sensors in the real world. An additional challenge is that some Character Computing studies will be required to be performed in the wild. Many physiological sensors are not suitable for such studies, due to their size or the way they operate. For example, EEG in outdoor scenarios may receive too much noise from the available stimulus and it may be too hard to detect anything meaningful.

7.3 Sensing Systems for Personality Computing

Human beings exhibit stable behavioral and emotional patterns over time. These include many aspects such as happiness, success in relationships (personal or work), type of work, political ideology, etc. The ability to characterize personality has been the subject of intense research in psychology for a long time. However, interest in automatic detection and perception of personality, known as Personality Computing (PC), has sharply risen in recent years. There are a few key reasons for this increased interest. The proliferation of smartphones and the prevalence of social media have led to the availability of massive amounts of intimate and personal data about a very large number of people. This data comes from various sources, including the smartphone sensors and the linguistic properties displayed on social media. The availability of this data has inspired researches to explore different venues of PC, with promising success. This section is dedicated to the sensing layer in PC. The goal is to review and analyze key efforts in recognition, perception, and synthesis of human personality. Just as in AC, PC requires a model of human personality. Thus, we first discuss such a model before we review other aspects.

7.3.1 Models for PC

The goal of a personality model is to characterize stable behavioral patterns in an individual. These behavioral patterns are detected from exterior observable behavior. Thus, pipelines in PC are often similar to pipelines in AC, involving data capture, feature extraction, and classification. Over the years, personality psychology has experimented with a large number of personality models. The most successive models (i.e., the ones capable of accurately describing individual characteristics) are not actually based on personal characteristics at all but on traits, which are the factors that can be used to describe how humans judge, react to, and describe different situations (Vinciarelli and Mohammadi 2014). The most successful personality model is known as the Big Five (BF) model (McCrae and Costa 1996). This model only considers five traits, and research has shown the stability of the recurrence of these traits in different individuals. In fact, all attempts to add to these traits generally result in a less accurate model. The five traits considered by the BF model are as follows:

- Extraversion is the tendency for outward stimulation (by other individuals). Highly extraverted people generally seek attention, while lowly extraverted people are generally reserved.
- Openness is generally a measure of creativity and curiosity. People with high openness seek satisfaction through change, while people with low openness are pragmatic and driven by certainty.
- Conscientiousness is the tendency to be organized. Highly conscientious people can be perceived as focused, even stubborn, while lowly conscientious people are generally spontaneous and flexible.
- Agreeableness is a measure of compassion and trust. Highly agreeable people can often be perceived as naïve, while lowly agreeable people are more competitive and argumentative.

- Neuroticism measures the susceptibility to stress. Highly neurotic individuals can experience emotional instability, while lowly neurotic individuals generally have a calm emotional demeanor.

In psychology, these traits are typically measured using questionnaires that are either filled by the person himself/herself or by an observer. However, the focus in this chapter is on automated platforms for measuring these traits. In the next section, we will discuss the challenges and techniques in these automated platforms.

7.3.2 Automated Platforms for PC

As in traditional psychology studies, automated PC platforms are either based on data generated by the persons themselves, known as Automatic Personality Recognition (APR) or based on data perceived about a person, known as Automatic Personality Perception (APP) (Vinciarelli and Mohammadi 2014). APR is achieved by capturing the personality traits externalized by individuals through distal cues. This is typically done through similar techniques to AC. On the other hand, APP is based on how others perceive these externalized traits through proximal cues. Generally speaking, APR requires direct involvement of participants, while APP can be done through interactions of other people with the same individual. Most research efforts in APR and APP evaluate each trait in the Big Five separately, and accordingly make a judgement about the personality type. Thus, quite often we find automated systems capable of predicting one trait better than the others. The types of data used in APP and APR can be categorized into verbal and nonverbal data. Verbal data is generally considered the richest source of personality-related information in APR, as language is the main way people externalize their personality. Efforts involving APR utilize language processing techniques to automatically identify how words are used (for example, expressing attitude, making an assessment, or making a reference) and accordingly categorize them to be used as input into a machine learning algorithm. This algorithm would then extract meaningful features that can be used to determine the personality type. Social media is by far the biggest database of verbal data that can be used for APR (Golbeck et al. 2011; Golbeck et al. 2011). People on social media often reveal deeply personal information that can be used to accurately judge their personality type. Social media has also been used in APP. Here, automated analysis of how people perceive posts by others (pictures or text) is undertaken (Cristani et al. 2013; Steele et al. 2009). Results reported by researchers in this type of APP often have high accuracy. Speech is also an obvious source of verbal data that can be used in APR (Mairesse et al. 2007). Techniques similar to the ones discussed in Sect. 7.2.2 can be used in this case. In addition, paralanguage can also be used in APP (Mairesse et al. 2007). Information about prosody, speech activity, and spectral features have been explored in literature. Nonverbal data has also been explored for APR and APP. For example, the work in Zen et al. (2010) investigated if walking velocity can be used to predict extraversion and neuroticism. Body movements have also been studied for

APR in Batrinca et al. (2011), including posture during a conversation, hand and body movements, and facial expressions. These types of data have also been used for APP in Biel and Gatica-Perez (2013), where people perceive how others externalize these features. It is interesting to note that systems using paralanguage have been the only ones in literature to report accuracies over 80%. For all other nonverbal cues, the reported accuracy is typically lower. Verbal-based APR often achieves higher accuracy (Vinciarelli and Mohammadi 2014). The proliferation of wearables and smartphones has also enabled prediction of personality traits using sensors. For example, accelerometers and gyroscopes have been used to evaluate the activity level and movement patterns of individuals in Olguin Olguin et al. (2009). Here, sensors also evaluate speech activity and other paralanguage features. In addition, location information has been used (Staiano et al. 2012) to correlate proximity information with social networking data and accordingly predict the Big Five traits.

7.3.2.1 Challenges in Using PC Platforms in Character Computing

PC and Character Computing have similar requirements of their sensing/recognition platforms. They both require the availability of relatively substantial information (probably long term) about the user. However, as seen before, most of the research in PC is based on the Big Five model, which cannot be used directly in Character Computing. It should either be augmented with models for other factors such as affective states and context or replaced with something entirely different. Moreover, Character Computing platforms must focus on different types of data, particularly those that may reveal important information about the beliefs and core values of individuals. These may not be as easy to extract as, say prosodic or spectral information of speech. Thus, machine learning algorithms for Character Computing must somehow be trained to extract deeper information from verbal and nonverbal data.

7.4 Toward a Ubiquitous Character-IoT

The field of Character Computing is still in its infancy. Character Computing models that can be used in automated systems need to be developed, and the design of rule-based engines should follow. Thus, at this time, there is a need for ubiquitous data collection platforms that can support the development of Character Computing. This comprehensive CIoT must be able to capture the full state of the user, including affective, motivational, and cognitive states. This is necessary to be able to model, recognize, and predict the causality in the triad of behavior–situation–character (traits and states) that makes up the core of Character Computing. Automated systems in AC and PC are generally based on observing attributes of an individual and making judgements according to a model, as discussed before. However, this is believed to be inadequate to capture the depth of human character that may produce varying behavioral patterns. Thus, discovering stable character traits by observation alone may require extended durations. Instead, a CIoT can act opportunistically by creating tasks that can accurately capture a particular character trait when a certain context is detected. For example, a CIoT may exploit the existence of a discussion about politics or religion to create a task that identifies the individual's core beliefs about this subject. To encourage users to engage with CIoT systems, gamification is likely to be a core requirement. The aforementioned tasks must be attractive to the user, or else they will be ignored. In addition, the tasks should identify the optimal sensory input for each situation to capture the trait under consideration. Thus, if an individual's facial expression is most telling in a particular situation, then the task should involve the individual using the camera. In other situations, the task may require the user to trigger a certain sensor or to speak a few words. Accordingly, a key challenge in CIoT is designing these tasks. This is an interdisciplinary challenge that requires extensive input from experts in the field of psychology. A truly ubiquitous CIoT also needs a suite of technologies to support its operations. In the remainder of this section, we identify some of these technologies.

7.4.1 Context Awareness

Human behavior is significantly affected by the situation and the surrounding environment. Detecting this context provides important insight into the motivation of an individual's actions. There have been several categorizations of context in research. For example, the work in Abowd et al. (1999) defines location, time, identity, and activity as the context categories required to describe a particular situation. A more general categorization was described in Perera et al. (2014), where the context categories were defined as location, time, status, and identity. The categorization of context helps to identify the information to be detected. In addition, contextual information may be defined as primary or secondary. Primary context information comes directly from sensors (example GPS location or time from a clock), while secondary context information is extracted after processing and data fusion. For example, the context "driving to work" can be derived from sensing that a user is in a vehicle (moving at higher than pedestrian speed), moving over a particular route, during a certain time of the day. Detecting a certain activity is typically secondary context. For example, detecting that a person is jogging can be done by processing data from the accelerometer. Context can also be defined by the detection of particular objects. For example, for a person who is afraid of spiders and exhibits a high stress level, their behavior can be explained if a spider is detected in the vicinity. The context life cycle typically has four phases: acquisition, modeling, reasoning, and exchange (Makris et al. 2013). Context acquisition is the collection of the necessary raw data from the sensors. This data has to be labeled and prepared for the modeling phase, where the raw sensor data is transformed into high-level data. This transformation depends on the application. For example, raw data from a clock can be transformed into morning, afternoon, evening, and night if this is what the application requires. After transformation, the reasoning phase can take place where a decision is made about what the context is. For example, the modeling phase can produce a vector of high-level information such as laying down, limited movement, night and the reasoner would then decide that the individual is sleeping. Finally, the exchange phase involves sending this context to any interested parties. In the previous example, this information can be sent to a home management system to control the lights and adjust the temperature. Naturally, every phase in the context life cycle may have certain inaccuracies. The sensors themselves have a certain sensitivity that determines the accuracy of raw data. For example, GPS location sensors do not have high accuracy in indoor environments. Since these inaccuracies are passed to the modeling, it may affect its accuracy as well. In the end, the overall context quality depends on the accuracy achieved in every phase. Evaluating the context quality can be valuable for systems to know if this information is reliable or not and has been investigated in research efforts such as Bellavista et al. (2012).

7.4.2 AI Support

Detecting affective, motivational, or cognitive states relies heavily on AI methods and algorithms. Context awareness may only improve the accuracy of these algorithms. Naturally, as we have discussed in previous sections of this chapter, a wide variety of algorithms have been explored for different objectives in AC and PC. In this section, we identify and classify the important techniques that can be used in Character Computing.

One of the AI fields of research that has a significant importance in AC, PC, and Character Computing is activity recognition (Chen et al. 2012; Rashidi et al. 2011). Here, the objective is to identify what the user is currently doing using sensory information. Quite often, multiple sensor modalities are fused to provide accurate recognition. AI algorithms such as clustering, probabilistic models, decision trees, and many others have been explored in literature. The accuracy of these techniques has now become quite high for simple activities that can often be described using one or two words such as walking, jogging, sleeping, etc. However, complex activities are still harder to detect. Thus, if detecting the reading activity may be straightforward, detecting the type of reading activity is much harder (reading for work, for general knowledge, for fun, etc.). Combined with context awareness, detection of simple activities may be of great importance in determining patterns and habits of users. However, detecting complex activities can provide significant insights into the user's character. This is an open research field requiring more attention. Deep learning techniques, data mining, and behavior pattern detection techniques (Acampora et al. 2013) are potential tools to address this issue. Another important AI research field is anomaly detection. Here, the objective is to detect events that are outside the boundaries of what is defined as "normal". Anomaly detection is highly important in security applications and has been subject of intensive research (Benkhelifa et al. 2018). Recently, it has also found applications in health care, for example, to detect irregular heartbeats or high/low blood pressure (Kumar et al. 2019). The two most widely used techniques in anomaly detection are machine learning and Complex Event Processing (CEP) (Acampora et al. 2013). Anomaly detection based on machine learning typically employs a trained classifier that extracts normal patterns out of a dataset. Afterward, anything outside of the boundaries of these patterns produces an anomaly flag. On the other hand, CEP uses a variety of techniques to detect the occurrence of certain events. For example, entering a wrong password certain number of times produces an event that may lead the system to block the user account. In Erb et al. (2018), graph techniques were used to log the occurrence of events in chronological order to allow systems to process the data retroactively. This can be of great importance in Character Computing in order to keep track of important events in a user's history. Finally, another important AI research field is decision support systems (Acampora et al. 2013). Here, the objective is typically to produce inferred knowledge out of existing data. Decision support systems are either based on an existing database of information that is analyzed by a reasoning engine (Kaptein et al. 2010) or based on machine learning techniques (Acampora et al. 2013) that extract useful knowledge out of an existing dataset.

7.4.3 Computing Platforms

A truly ubiquitous CIoT may need to process significant amounts of data. In addition, AI techniques often involve heavy processing and the output may be required in real time. Moreover, tasks involving image or video processing (facial recognition for example) are typically computationally intensive. For these applications, computing and networking resources owned by users may not be sufficient (El-Mougy et al. 2019). Cloud computing has been the key platform for addressing the limitation in computing resources. Cloud computing offers virtually limitless resources on demand. Thus, applications can scale up or down their resource usage as they need. This way computationally intensive tasks can be easily integrated in many applications. Nevertheless, cloud computing requires stable Internet connectivity, which may not always be available. Also, for real-time applications, the variance in connection quality and the expected high latency associated with cloud computing may not be suitable. For these applications, edge computing has emerged as the key solution (El-Sayed et al. 2018). Edge computing places resources one-hop away from the user, thus allowing real-time applications involving computationally intensive tasks such as video/image processing. The proximity of edge computing resources also allows localized context awareness. Thus, even though edge computing offers limited resources compared to the cloud, it is seen as an important complementary platform for many applications. Hybrid cloud/edge systems combine the advantages of both platforms, thus offering significant possibilities. Technologies such as virtualization and information-centric networking are also promising to address some of the networking challenges associated with real-time scalable communications (El-Mougy et al. 2019).

7.4.4 An Architectural Framework for CIoT

Rather than only detecting particular emotions or personality traits, a CIoT framework needs to work continuously to build a complete character profile. Since human character traits are revealed through exposure to different life scenarios, the CIoT framework needs to be truly ubiquitous, constantly looking for character cues. Figure 7.5 shows the proposed architectural framework for CIoT. It consists of four layers that cover all the components needed for building the character profile. Their functionalities are as follows:

- **The Sensing Layer** is responsible for extracting raw data. The choice of sensors depends on the character traits to be recognized. Here, constant monitoring through different sensing modalities is the key objective. The sensors can be physical, either directly attached to the person or deployed in their environment, or virtual, such as calendar appointments or text entry.
- **Data Collection/Processing** is where the data generated by the Sensing Layer is collected and processed. Here, the sensors send their data to a collection point, which may be a smartphone or an edge server. At this point, the data is prepared for the processing phase. Data processing may take place directly at the smartphone or the edge server or may be forwarded to the cloud. Distributed/collaborative processing may take place, especially for real-time applications that require response from devices within close proximity.
- **Support Systems**: The Processing Layer will need the support of several technologies/systems to perform its duty. Machine learning is the key tool to extract patterns and recognize character traits. Decision support and activity recognition systems are used to infer knowledge about what the user is currently doing. Finally, context awareness provides necessary insight to maximize the accuracy of all these systems.

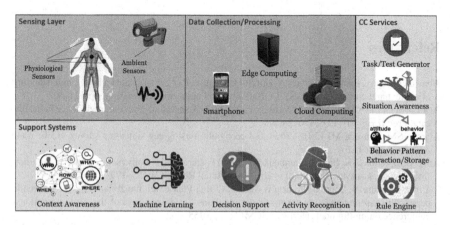

Fig. 7.5 A CIoT framework for building a character profile

- **Character Computing Services**: Ultimately, the CIoT framework needs to run specific modules to build a character profile. The data from all the other layers are consumed by these modules. Some of them may be a task generator that works opportunistically to generate test cases to confirm the detection of particular traits. These tests are generated upon the detection of particular situations of relevance to the user's character, which is the role of the situation awareness module. The behavioral patterns of the user are then extracted and stored by another module. Finally, a rule-based engine uses these patterns to create/modify rules for the user's character model.

7.5 Summary

This chapter investigated the concept of a Character-IoT (CIoT), a comprehensive platform for sensing, processing, and analysis of human character traits and states. Since the field of Character Computing is still in its infancy, we studied the possibility of adopting technologies from the fields of affective and personality computing in Character Computing. Focus was given to technologies that have achieved promising success in these two fields such as affective recognition from facial expressions, speech, gestures, and physiological sensors. An overview of how these technologies work was given and we highlighted the limitations in each of these technologies for adoption in Character Computing.

Based on this comprehensive survey, we presented a detailed framework for CIoT that can serve as an architectural founding block for Character Computing. This architectural framework is composed of four layers encompassing the tasks of sensing, data collection/processing, decision support, and Character Computing services. This platform can serve as a guide for new researchers in this field and can offer insights for future developments in the field of Character Computing.

References

Abowd G, Dey A, Brown P, Davies N, Smith M, Steggles P (1999) Towards a better understanding of context and context-awareness. In: Handheld and ubiquitous computing, pp 304–307

Acampora G, Cook DJ, Rashidi P, Vasilakos AV (2013) A survey on ambient intelligence in healthcare. Proc IEEE 101(12):2470–2494

Alarcao SM, Fonseca MJ (2018) Emotions recognition using eeg signals: a survey. IEEE Trans Affect Comput 1–1

Anagnostopoulos C-K, Iliou T, Giannoukos I (2015) Features and classifiers for emotion recognition from speech: a survey from 2000 to 2011. Artif Intell Rev 43(2):155–177

Batrinca L, Mana N, Lepri B, Pianesi F, Sebe N (2011) Please, tell me about yourself: automatic personality assessment using short self-presentations. In: Proceedings of the 13th international conference on multimodal interfaces, ICMI '11, pp 255–262

Bellavista P, Corradi A, Fanelli M, Foschini L (2012) A survey of context data distribution for mobile ubiquitous systems. ACM Comput Surv 44(4):24:1–24:45

Benkhelifa E, Welsh T, Hamouda W (2018) A critical review of practices and challenges in intrusion detection systems for iot: toward universal and resilient systems. IEEE Commun Surv Tutor 20(4):3496–3509

Biel J, Gatica-Perez D (2013) The youtube lens: crowdsourced personality impressions and audio-visual analysis of vlogs. IEEE Trans Multimed 15(1):41–55

Calvo R, D'Mello S (2010) Affect detection: an interdisciplinary review of models, methods, and their applications. IEEE Trans Affect Comput 1(1):18–37

Cao Z, Simon T, Wei S-E, Sheikh Y (2016) Realtime multi-person 2d pose estimation using part affinity fields. CoRR

Chen L, Hoey J, Nugent CD, Cook DJ, Yu DJ (2012) Sensor-based activity recognition. IEEE Trans Syst Man Cybernet Part C Appl Rev 42(6):790–808

Colombo A, Cusano C, Schettini R (2006) 3d face detection using curvature analysis. J Pattern Recognit 39(3):444–455

Corneanu C, Simon M, Cohn J, Guerrero S (2016) Survey on rgb, 3d, thermal, and multimodal approaches for facial expression recognition: history, trends, and affect-related applications. IEEE Trans Pattern Anal Mach Intell 38(8):1548–1568

Cristani M, Vinciarelli A, Segalin C, Perina A (2013) Unveiling the multimedia unconscious: Implicit cognitive processes and multimedia content analysis. In: Proceedings of the 21st ACM international conference on multimedia, MM '13

Dhall A, Goecke R, Lucey S, Gedeon T (2011) Acted facial expressions in the wild database. Technical Report, TR-CS-11-02

Einstein G, Kennedy SH, Downar J (2013) Gender/sex differences in emotions. Medicographia 35(3):271–280

Ekman P (1982) Emotion in the human face. Cambridge University Press, Cambridge

Ekman P (1971) Universal and cultural differences in facial expression of emotion. Nebraska Symp Motiv 19:207–283

El-Mougy A, Al-Shiab I, Ibnkahla M (2019) Scalable personalized iot networks. Proc IEEE 107(4):695–710

El-Sayed H, Sankar S, Prasad M, Puthal D, Gupta A, Mohanty M, Lin C (2018) Edge of things: the big picture on the integration of edge, iot and the cloud in a distributed computing environment. IEEE Access 6:1706–1717

Erb B, Meissner D, Kargl F, Steer B, Cuadrado F, Margan D, Pietzuch P (2018) Graphtides: a framework for evaluating stream-based graph processing platforms. In: Proceedings of the 1st ACM SIGMOD joint international workshop on graph data management experiences & systems (GRADES) and network data analytics (NDA), pp 3:1–3:10

Fragopanagos N, Taylor J (2005) Emotion recognition in human-computer interaction. J Neural Netw 18(4):389–405

Giannakopoulos T, Pikrakis A, Theodoridis S (2009) dimensional approach to emotion recognition of speech from movies. In: IEEE international conference on acoustics, speech and signal processing

Golbeck J, Robles C, Edmondson M, Turner K (2011) Predicting personality from twitter. In: 2011 IEEE third international conference on privacy, security, risk and trust and 2011 IEEE third international conference on social computing

Golbeck J, Robles C, Turner K (2011) Predicting personality with social media. In: CHI '11 extended abstracts on human factors in computing systems, CHI EA '11

Greene S, Thapliyal H, Caban-Holt A (2016a) A survey of affective computing for stress detection. IEEE Consum Electron Mag 5(4):44–56

Greene S, Thapliyal H, Caban-Holt A (2016b) A survey of affective computing for stress detection: evaluating technologies in stress detection for better health. IEEE Consum Electron Mag 5(4):44–56

Griffin HJ, Aung MS, Romera-Paredes B, McLoughlin C, McKeown G, Curran W, Bianchi-Berthouze N (2013) Laughter type recognition from whole body motion. In: Humane association's conference on affective computing and intelligent interaction

Jones M, Viola P (2003) Fast multi-view face detection. Mitsubishi Elec. Research Lab, Technical Report, TR2003-96

Kaptein M, Markopoulos P, de Ruyter B, Aarts E (2010) Persuasion in ambient intelligence. J Ambient Intell Hum Comput 1(1):43–56

Kipp M, Martin J-C (2008) Gesture and emotion: can basic gestural form features discriminate emotions? In: IEEE conference on affective computing and intelligent interaction

Kumar VDA, Subramanian M, Gopalakrishnan G, Vengatesan K, Elangovan D, Chitra B (2019) Implementation of the pulse rhythmic rate for the efficient diagnosing of the heartbeat. Healthcare Technol Lett 6(2):48–52

Mairesse F, Walker MA, Mehl M, Moore R (2007) Using linguistic cues for the automatic recognition of personality in conversation and text. J Artif Intell Res 30(1):457–500

Makris P, Skoutas DN, Skianis C (2013) A survey on context-aware mobile and wireless networking: on networking and computing environments' integration. IEEE Commun Surv Tutor 15(1):362–386

Mao X, Chen L, Fu L (2009) Multi-level speech emotion recognition based on hmm and ann. In: Proceedings of of world congress on computer science and information engineering

McCrae R, Costa P (1996) The five factor model of personality: theoretical perspective. The Guilford Press

Noroozi F, Corneanu C, Kaminska D, Sapinski T, Escalera S, Anbarjafari G (2018) Survey on emotional body gesture recognition. IEEE Trans Affect Comput

Olguin Olguin D, Gloor P, Pentland A (2009) Capturing individual and group behavior with wearable sensors. In: AAAI spring symposium - Technical Report, pp. 68–74

Papandreou G, Zhu T, Kanazawa N, Toshev A, Tompson J, Bregler C, Murphy K (2017) Towards accurate multi-person pose estimation in the wild. Comput Vis Pattern Recognit 3(4):6

Pease A, Pease B (2004) The Definitive Book of Body Language. In: Peace international

Perera C, Zaslavsky A, Christen P, Georgakopoulos D (2014) Context aware computing for the internet of things: a survey. IEEE Commun Surv Tutor 16(1):414–454

Rashidi P, Cook DJ, Holder LB, Schmitter-Edgecombe M (2011) Discovering activities to recognize and track in a smart environment. IEEE Trans Knowl Data Eng 23(4):527–539

Russel J, Mehrabian A (1977) Evidence for a three-factor theory of emotions. J Res Personal 11:273–294

Senecal S, Cuel L, Aristidou A, Magnenat-Thalmann N (2016) Continuous body emotion recognition system during theater performances. Comput Animat Virtual Worlds 27(3):311–320

Sirohey S (1998) Human face segmentation and identification. Technical Report

Soylemez O, Ergen B, Soylemez N (2017) A 3d facial expression recognition system based on svm classifier using distance based features. In: IEEE conference on signal processing and communications applications (SIU)

Staiano J, Lepri B, Aharony N, Pianesi F, Sebe N, Pentland A (2012) Friends don't lie: Inferring personality traits from social network structure. In: Proceedings of the 2012 ACM conference on ubiquitous computing, UbiComp '12, pp 321–330

Steele F, Evans DC, Green RK (2009) Is your profile picture worth 1000 words? photo characteristics associated with personality impression agreement

Tam G, Cheng Z-Q, Lai Y-K, Langbein F, Liu Y, Marshall D, Martin R, Sun X-F, Rosin P (2013) Registration of 3d point clouds and meshes: a survey from rigid to nonrigid. IEEE Trans Vis Comput Graph 19(7):1199–1217

Tomkins S (2008) Affect, Imagery consciousness. Springer Publications, Berlin

Tompson JJ, Jain A, LeCun Y, Bregler C (2014) Joint training of a convolutional network and a graphical model for human pose estimation. In: Advances in neural information processing systems

Trujillo L, Olague G, Hammoud R, Hernandez B (2005) Automatic feature localization in thermal images for facial expression recognition. In: IEEE conference on computer vision and pattern recognition

Vinciarelli A, Mohammadi G (2014) A survey of personality computing. IEEE Trans Affect Comput 5(3):273–291

Vu HA, Yamazaki Y, Dong F, Hirota K (2011) Emotion recognition based on human gesture and speech information using rt middleware. In: IEEE conference on fuzzy systems (FUZZ)

Wang S, He M, Gao Z, He S, Ji Q (2014) Emotion recognition from thermal infrared images using deep boltzmann machine. ACM J Front Comput Sci 8(4):609–618

Wang N, Gao X, Tao D, Yang H, Li X (2018) Facial feature point detection: a comprehensive survey. J Neurocomput 275:50–65

Wang S, Pan B, Chen H, Ji Q (2018) Thermal augmented expression recognition. IEEE Trans Cybern 48(7):2203–2214

Wu C-H, Liang W-B (2011) Emotion recognition of affective speech based on multiple classifiers using acoustic-prosodic information and semantic labels. IEEE Trans Affect Comput 2(1):10–21

Yang C, Ji L, Liu G (2009) Study to speech emotion recognition based on twinssvm. In: Proceedings of 5th international conference on natural computation

Yoshitomi Y, Asada T, Shimada K, Tabuse M (2010) Facial expression recognition for speaker using thermal image processing and speech recognition system. In: International conference on applied computer science

Zeng Z, Pantic M, Roisman G, Huang T (2009) A survey of affect recognition methods: audio, visual, and spontaneous expressions. IEEE Trans Pattern Anal Mach Intell 31(1):39–58

Zen G, Lepri B, Ricci E, Lanz O (2010) Space speaks: Towards socially and personality aware visual surveillance. In: Proceedings of the 1st ACM international workshop on multimodal pervasive video analysis, MPVA '10, pp 37–42

Zhang CC, Zhang Z (2010) A survey of recent advances in face detection. Microsoft Research, Technical Report, MSR-TR-2010-66

Zhen Q, Huang D, Wang Y, Chen L (2016) Muscular movement model-based automatic 3d/4d facial expression recognition. IEEE Trans Multimed 18(7):1438–1450

Chapter 8
Identifying Personality Dimensions for Characters of Digital Agents

Michael Braun and Florian Alt

Abstract More and more digital services rely on natural "speech-first" user interfaces. With this trend arriving across industries, character design for digital assistants becomes relevant and along with it arises the fundamental problem of finding suitable personality dimensions. Classic personality models, like the Big Five Inventory or the Myers–Briggs-Type Indicator (MBTI), contain too many dimensions to be practicable foundations for many design use cases. This chapter introduces a method to distill use case-specific personality features from user interactions with broadly diverse characters. In particular, users converse with characters inspired from popular media figures and rate their personalities as well as their user experience and fit to a certain task. As one use case, we demonstrate how fixed parameters and major dimensions for dynamic assistant personalities in an in-car environment can be identified. The method can be used to find out use case-dependent requirements to an assistant personality as well as dynamically customizable character features for personalization purposes.

8.1 Introduction

Current digital assistants can understand natural language and express information through speech synthesis (Porcheron et al. 2018). However, up to now, most assistants lack an interpersonal level of communication which can be helpful to build a relationship with the user. Related research suggests that to become more widely accepted, such systems need to satisfy the expectations users have toward social interaction, like acting proactively and displaying personality (Malle and Thapa Magar 2017; Nass et al. 2005; Schmidt and Braunger 2018). People expect consistent behavior

M. Braun (✉)
BMW Group Research, New Technologies, Innovations, LMU Munich, Munich, Germany
e-mail: michael.bf.braun@bmw.de

F. Alt
Bundeswehr University and LMU Munich, Munich, Germany
e-mail: florian.alt@unibw.de

© Springer Nature Switzerland AG 2020   123
A. El Bolock et al. (eds.), *Character Computing*, Human–Computer Interaction Series,
https://doi.org/10.1007/978-3-030-15954-2_8

they can predict and which fits the environment they experience the assistant (André et al. 1999). Subjective perception of behavior leads to an allotment of personality traits, independent of whether users are interacting with a person or a digital system (Argyle 1988). Hence, assistants should be designed with their application area in mind, as their characters can be perceived differently depending on the context. A risk-taking assistant might be acceptable in a casino, but not in a bank. An overly nice character, in contrast, might be fitting to call center agent but not to a security guard.

Personality is one of the human characteristics we aim to synthesize when we apply the principles of Character Computing. The focus of our work lies in automotive user interfaces, where apart from minimizing driver distraction during manual driving (Maciej and Vollrath 2009; Peissner et al. 2011), researchers are working on the future of interaction in automated vehicles. Natural user interfaces are considered to bridge both of these requirements, as, e.g., speech interfaces also offer a more natural user experience (UX), compared to conventional user interfaces (UI)s in cars (Alvarez et al. 2011), which is of particular interest in the transition toward automated driving (Riener et al. 2017). In this study, we aim to find suitable personality dimensions for an in-car assistant, as our research shows that voice assistants with personality can improve trust and likability in security critical contexts of driving (Braun et al. 2019).

8.2 Background

This work builds upon research on natural language interfaces and the potential benefits of voice assistants with explicitly designed personalities. Psychologists have investigated the perception of behavioral cues as personality markers for decades and in recent years the synthesis of characters for digital agents has been seeing more and more application areas. Intelligent agents with human personalities enable more joyful interaction between man and machine and a communication style which users know from everyday communication (André et al. 1999).

8.2.1 Natural Interaction with Intelligent Agents

Intelligent agents are defined as software which is situated, autonomous, reactive, proactive, flexible, robust, and social (Padgham and Winikoff 2005), while the spatial conjunction and autonomy make such a system intelligent, their core virtue is that they provide natural interaction. An agent with the capability of conversing in natural speech and the knowledge of how to interact socially is easy to use, more efficient, and less error-prone than graphical interfaces (Nafari and Weaver 2013), and can offer accessibility to users with disabilities (Pradhan et al. 2018). On the downside, their human appearance also leads users to expect unlimited versatility and the validity of given information (Bickmore et al. 2018; Luger and Sellen 2016). This problem can be tackled by enhancing digital agents with personalities to limit the expectations users have and possibly guide the formation of a mental model which makes them understand the limits of the system.

8.2.2 In-Car Voice Assistants

The automotive domain is currently experiencing a "speech-first" movement, as voice interaction has been shown to be a valuable alternative input modality in the car (Pfleging et al. 2012; Riener et al. 2017; Roider et al. 2017). Drivers mainly utilize visual and manual cognitive resources for the driving task, without extensively straining vocal and auditory channels (Wierwille 1993). This can be used to optimize voice interfaces for limiting overall cognitive load and limiting negative effects like inattentional blindness (Lavie 2010; Large et al. 2016; Yan et al. 2007). Voice interaction in the car can so unburden the driver from unnecessary workload and responsibilities, and provide space-independent controls to remote user interfaces which are coming to autonomous cars along with bigger screens and free movement within the car.

8.2.3 Personalization of User Interfaces

Today, many interfaces and intelligent assistants incorporate features of personalization. These range from knowing the user's name to content customizations based on models of needs and behaviors (Kramer et al. 2000; Thakur 2016). Such systems can also act as social characters by proactively pointing out information (Nass et al. 1994; Schmidt and Braunger 2018) or by helping users to accept new technologies, for example, by mimicking their behavior in automated driving (Orth et al. 2017).

One frequently used principle to achieve a bond between user and system is the similarity–attraction hypothesis, which assumes that humans like to interact with others of similar personality (Byrne and Griffitt 1969). We found that a personalized voice assistant character can improve trust and likability toward an in-car agent but should only be acted out in non-safety relevant situations (Braun et al. 2019). Personalization of the assistants character can also help in maintaining attachment to cars when ownership and driving are things of the past (Braun et al. 2018).

8.2.4 Designing Personality for Digital Agents

Humans are quick on first impressions, be it with other people or digital systems (Nass et al. 1995). Immediate assessments of personality help us to decide whether we aim to converse with an opponent and allow us to adjust expectations (Cafaro et al. 2016). Assistants can synchronously benefit from a consistent personality as it helps users to predict behavior (André et al. 1999).

A widely recognized approach for the classification of personalities is the Big Five model by McCrae and Costa, consisting of openness, conscientiousness, extraversion, agreeableness, and neuroticism (OCEAN) (McCrae and Costa 1986). Extraversion is the most prevalent dimension in HCI studies as it has high informative value and is easy to observe (Kammrath et al. 2007). Another model, more frequently used in consultancy and workplace analytics, is the Myers–Briggs-Type indicator (MBTI). It works by building combinations of four dichotomies, resulting in 16 combinations. The MBTI is often criticized by psychologists due to its poor viability and unreliable results over time (Furnham 1996). Argyle advocates a more simple model to describe interpersonal attitudes of humans based on the two dimensions hostile—friendly and submissive—dominant (Argyle 1988).

These personality models can also be used for the design of digital characters, yet we need to consider which personality traits are suitable for the agent's area of application. Digital assistants and users need a shared understanding of acceptable behavior (Jung 2017) and users need to know the limits of the systems which can be communicated implicitly through character traits (Bickmore et al. 2018). We can also build upon the similarity–attraction hypothesis to design more likeable agents (Nass et al. 1995) but have to avoid uncanny experiences (Mori et al. 2012).

In related work, Bickmore and Picard show a relational agent capable of social and emotional interaction, which was evaluated with high ratings for trust and likability (Bickmore 2005). Nass et al. applied a similar concept to a simulated driving context and found increased driving performance and attention if an empathic voice assistant is matched to drivers in a similar state (Nass et al. 2005). We are building on these results of this work by exploring appropriate personality dimensions for automotive voice assistants.

8.2.5 Fictional Characters

Character design has been practised in the entertainment industry long before artificial intelligence made digital agents possible. Writers often base characters around stereotypes, which provide a mold for abilities, motivation, and general behavior of an ideal fictional human (Tillman 2012). Archetype characteristics are usually taken from other works or universal stereotypes. During the evolution of a story, stringent continuity of a character's behavior is important to manifest its personality and make it believable (Kline and Blumberg 1999). What is interesting in this approach is that fictional characters can be well liked although they are "the bad ones" if their personal story makes their behavior understandable (Konijn and Hoorn 2005). We can apply this technique to the synthesis of digital agents as we know their intended application and can thus infer a matching archetype, for example, the bank clerk for a finance assistant or the codriver for an in-car assistant. Communication styles could be adapted from examples of such archetype from popular art like movies and TV shows. In the following sections, we describe this process to investigate viable personality traits for an in-car voice assistant.

8.3 Character Design

The main tasks an in-car assistant needs to fulfill are information retrieval and presentation as well as assistance with controlling in-car functionalities. We analyzed popular characters from TV shows and movies and came up with several implementations of two basic stereotypes. The information provider, who is connected to countless sources and can almost always provide the desired details, can be applied to almost any digital assistant. They feature data accuracy in various styles and are represented by characters like Sheldon Cooper (The Big Bang Theory), Sherlock Holmes (Sherlock), Spock (Star Trek), or Hermione Granger (Harry Potter). The second archetype is the sidekick, who can, in an automotive environment, embody a codriver. Examples from popular media are Ron Weasley (Harry Potter), Baloo (The Jungle Book), Donkey (Shrek), Pinky (Pinky and the Brain), and Bender (Futurama). They support the protagonists in their story lines and have mainly entertaining roles, although they often contribute key story points. Some fictional characters also combine both stereotypes as omniscient sidekicks. Examples include C3P0 (Star Wars), Marvin (The Hitchhiker's Guide to the Galaxy), or HAL 9000 (2001: A Space Odyssey).

We clustered examples with related characteristics into seven groups which we sorted into Argyle's two-dimensional model of attitudes toward others (Argyle 1988). The resulting classification is shown in Fig. 8.1. Additionally, we placed a baseline character into the center of the model, to have a representation of medium manifestations of both dimensions. The resulting characters are defined as follows:

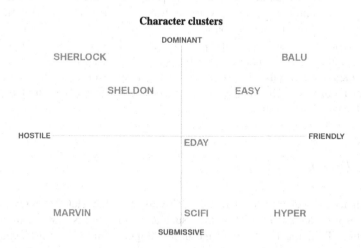

Fig. 8.1 The characters selected for the study placed into the model of attitudes toward others (Argyle 1988)

Eday is the baseline personality which we did not find in fictional characters but composed from medium expressions of the used model.

Balu is a sidekick based on the character from The Jungle Book. He is very friendly and dominant in a way as he can convince others and does not take no for an answer.

Easy is modeled after easygoing sidekick characters like Ron Weasley. He is also rather dominant and friendly but less extreme than Balu.

Hyper is a childlike character inspired by Donkey from Shrek and Vanellope from Wreck-it Ralph, who is rather servile but also overpoweringly affectionate.

Sheldon is an information provider with medium dominance and hostility who can come off as annoying or provocative due to his somewhat arrogant attitude.

Sherlock knows everything better and does not accept different opinions. He feels superior to anybody else and gladly shows this in his behavior.

SciFi is a combination of sidekick and information provider based on Spock and HAL 9000. He is emotionless, submissive, and only reports important facts.

Marvin is the depressed brother of SciFi. He submits to his master but also questions all tasks as for him life is meaningless.

8.4   Use Case: In-Car Voice Assistants

In the following, we demonstrate how the previously introduced method can be applied in the context of an in-car voice assistant. In particular, we let participants experience the above-presented characters in six in-car use cases. The voice samples were recorded by a voice actor and played back while users took part in a passive driving simulation. Although the stereotypes used for the characters are taken from popular media, we put effort into the recording work, so the original characters cannot easily be recognized. The goal of this case study was to identify desired as well as unfeasible personality traits.

8.4.1   Design

We designed six scenarios: three related to driving and three related to entertainment. Each scenario contained a specific task, such as asking the assistant for the nearest gas station. Participants could engage in a dialogue with each of the eight voice assistant characters. The assistants' responses were pre-recorded and reflected the respective placement within the model. During the study, participants experienced the personalities while watching a recorded driving situation on a screen in front of them. All subjects conversed with all eight personalities in randomized order.

Immediately after experiencing each digital assistant, participants filled out a questionnaire consisting of 7-point Likert scales regarding trust (single item), usefulness and satisfaction (Acceptance Scale, Van der Laan et al. 1997), their emotional experience (meCue module III, Minge et al. 2016), and a semantic differential scale with 13 dimensions about the perceived personality. In the end, they answered a semi-structured interview about their preferred and least liked characters.

8.4.2 Participants

We recruited 19 participants from inside a company, consisting of 7 men and 12 women. Age distribution ranged from 19 to 53 years ($M = 35$, $SD = 11$). Participants had little to no experience in voice interaction or personalization.

8.4.3 Procedure

Participants were invited to our lab and experienced all six scenarios with each voice assistant in randomized order (total of 48 interactions). The use cases consisted of (1) onboarding and destination input, (2) a suggestion to listen to music, (3) proactive information on the route, (4) a takeover command switching to autonomous driving mode, (5) a notification of low fuel level and ensuing query for the next gas station, (6) and a traffic jam warning and rerouting. After each assistant, we had participants fill in abovementioned questionnaires. At the end, we conducted a semi-structured interview on their subjective perception of the experienced personalities.

8.4.4 Results

Characters were assessed using a combination of predefined questionnaires as well as feedback from a semi-structured interview. Significant findings are reported when a t-test for direct comparisons showed values of $p < 0.05$.

8.4.4.1 Likability and Trust

Most test persons perceive Balu and Eday as the most likable personalities (Fig. 8.2). They have in common that they are both very friendly and authentic. SciFi was also rated rather positively, while the characters Sherlock and Marvin were liked the least.

When it comes to trust, participants rated the characters SciFi, Balu, and Eday as significantly more trustworthy than all others. We can see a slight discrepancy between likability and trustworthiness as SciFi is trusted more but liked less than Balu

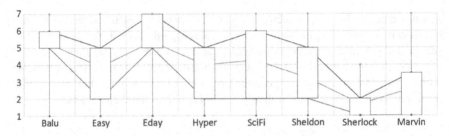

Fig. 8.2 Likability ratings for the experienced characters. Balu and Eday are rated significantly more likable than all others, Sherlock and Marvin were liked the least (t-test)

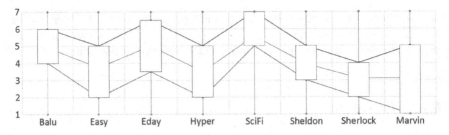

Fig. 8.3 The characters Balu, Eday, and SciFi are rated significantly more trustworthy than all others, Sherlock and Marvin conversely are trusted the least

and Eday (compare Fig. 8.3). It seems the emotionless nature of the character supports trustful interaction. As with likability, Sherlock and Marvin are rated significantly worse than all other characters.

8.4.4.2 Usefulness and Satisfaction

The assessment of usefulness and acceptance provides a similar image as trust and likability: Balu and Eday are rated best, SciFi is also perceived as useful, and Sherlock and Marvin are seen as very unsatisfying (see Fig. 8.4).

8.4.4.3 Emotional Experience

The evaluation of the meCue questionnaire shows that Balu and Eday triggered the most positive experiences (see Fig. 8.5). Sherlock and Marvin are again rated significantly worse than all others. What sticks out in this measure is that the character SciFi is not connected to positive feelings, although it was assessed positively regarding usefulness and trust.

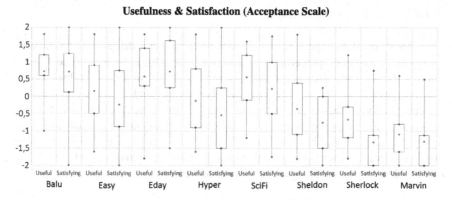

Fig. 8.4 Acceptance scale ratings range from −2 (not useful/not satisfying) to 2 (useful/satisfying). Balu and Eday score best while Sherlock and Marvin are rated poorly

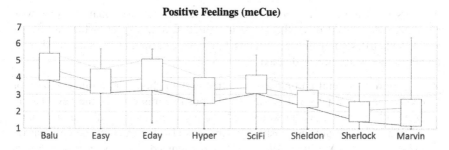

Fig. 8.5 Results of the meCue module III (positive feelings). Values range from 1 (no positive feelings) to 7 (very positive feelings)

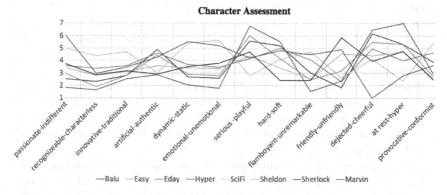

Fig. 8.6 Average semantic differential scale ratings for the characters presented in the study

8.4.4.4   Character Assessment

Participants rated the experienced characters on 13 semantic differential scales meant to closer describe the perceived personality (see Fig. 8.6). Subjects rated Balu as most authentic and rather cheerful. Easy mostly ranges in average values, except for its higher cheerfulness. The character Hyper was rated the most extreme. It is perceived as very passionate, emotional, playful, and generally outgoing. Sheldon was perceived as very provocative, relatively conspicuous, and somewhat unfriendly, only Sherlock was rated as even more unfriendly, provocative, and hard. SciFi is seen as very serious, professional, but also character and emotionless, and conformist. Finally, Marvin seems highly dejected and indifferent.

8.4.4.5   Subjective Feedback

Answers from the final interview can be clustered into seven main reasons why characters were liked or disliked. We identified several aspects which are to be avoided when designing in-car assistants. Some were desired by most users, whereas on others the feedback was divided.

Recognition.   Several participants said that certain characters reminded them of people they know personally, which had a positive influence on their evaluation. One said, such an assistant would be "like my friend being with me in the car" and that they "would just trust her". This was also the case for the only participants who rated Marvin positively. They recognized the assistant's behavior as similar to the movie character and found his depressed personality funny instead of disheartening. Users also remarked that famous characters would be a nice option—similar to when GPS systems first came to the consumer market.

Humor.   Unsurprisingly, humor is a topic on which opinions tend to differ. Some participants, for example, found Marvin's hopelessness and Sherlock's arrogance amusing, and others untenable. Easy was taunted as being sexist for whistling after another car by one subject, while others found it hilarious.

Intelligence.   Another point where different opinions exist is the intelligence of the digital assistant. On one hand, participants state that the digital assistant should act just as intelligent as it can truthfully be. On the other hand, subjects also said their assistant should not be able to outsmart them. One participant found fault that an intelligent system would need help with refueling.

Number of Words.   Most participants criticized the characters for talking too much, although many found the interactions entertaining. In a real driving context, assistant would need to adapt their output quantity to the driving situation and the accompanying workload.

Relational Level.   Feedback regarding the relationship between user and assistant was highly heterogeneous. Some participants felt that certain characters were too close to them, which was, for example, apparent in the usage of the word "we".

Others welcomed the personal connection and stated that they wished for the assistant to become like a real friend.

Balance of Power.   Assistants with an arrogant stance (Sheldon, Sherlock) were throughout rated badly. However, there was varying feedback, stating assistants should either be at eye level with the user or take a rather subordinate attitude.

Professionalism.   Subjects highly emphasized that seriousness and professionalism are very important for an in-car assistant. One group argued that a too serious personality would be boring to interact with, while others said the most important part is service orientation and thus correct information delivery.

8.5 Summary and Discussion

Results from the meCue and acceptance scale questionnaires and personal interviews identify unfriendly behavior and excessive talking as unacceptable traits for an in-car assistant. Assistants with an open and friendly attitude were liked by most participants. The data shows a dissent on the desired levels of distance between assistant and user, the assistant's professionalism (i.e., how respectful it behaves toward the user), and the balance of power within the conversation. Furthermore, we observed that some users prefer hedonic qualities in voice assistants, while others attach value to pragmatic service orientation.

From these findings, we derive fixed behavioral cues for an in-car voice assistant: it should act naturally and friendly, talk in minimum appropriate detail, and adapt to the user regarding its humor, professionalism, and social relation. We can imagine an adaptive assistant personality to start with a medium of expressiveness like we designed for Eday, which gradually takes over traits from Balu to cater to hedonic experiences or from SciFi to appear more subordinate.

Even though this chapter focused on in-car voice assistants, the methodology can well be applied to other use cases. It is important to note that while some traits of an assistant may be of equal importance in these use cases, others may be more or less important. Two fundamental traits that we expect to be prevalent in many other

Fig. 8.7 Apart from the identified dos and don'ts for in-car assistant personalities, the feedback showed two dimensions with varying user demands. These can be used to adapt the assistant's character to the user

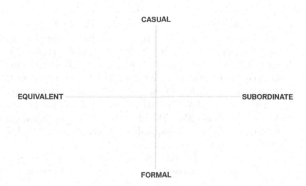

cases as well are illustrated in the two-dimensional model in Fig. 8.7. Here, one axis depicts the balance of power and social relationship (equivalent–subordinate) and one axis depicts the conversational professionalism (casual–formal). The subjective feedback from our participants hints at some characteristics that need to be considered in different use cases. For example, the number of word is of particular importance in certain driving situations. This may be different in less safety–critical settings. The same is true for professionalism, whereas when traveling with a customer or colleague in the car this might be important, people might prefer less serious assistants in their homes.

8.6 Conclusion

We present an approach to identify relevant personality dimensions for digital assistants in distinct environments. Our example application suggests the automotive context as viable environment which comes with limitations regarding available modalities and the safety–critical aspect of driving. These limitations are explored in a user study with 19 participants, who experience eight assistant characters developed from stereotypes in popular media. As a result, we propose a model with fixed personality traits which were accepted by the majority of users and introduce a two-dimensional model in which characters can be adjusted to fit different types of users. This concept is evaluated in research on personalized voice interaction in the car, which we performed as follow-up to this work (Braun et al. 2019).

Future work could apply this technique to other domains with limiting factors for interaction, such as social robotics, augmented reality, or professional training, and extend the scope to other characteristics such as appearance, behavioral cues like posture and gestures, or how they process and express affect.

Acknowledgements We sincerely thank Anja Mainz for the work on this project.

References

Alvarez I, Alnizami H, Dunbar J, Johnson A, Jackson F, Gilber JE (2011) Designing driver-centric natural voice user interfaces. In: Adjunct proceedings of the 3rd international conference on automotive user interfaces and interactive vehicular applications, pp 156–159 (online)

André E, Klesen M, Gebhard P, Allen S, Rist T (2000) Integrating models of personality and emotions into lifelike characters. In: Paiva A (ed) Affective interactions IWAI 1999. Lecture notes in computer science, vol 1814, pp 150–165. Springer, Berlin. https://doi.org/10.1007/10720296_11

Argyle M (1988) Bodily communication, 2nd edn. Routledge, New York

Bickmore TW, Picard RW (2005) Establishing and maintaining long-term human-computer relationships. ACM Trans. Comput.-Hum. Interact. 12(2), 293–327 (2005). https://doi.org/10.1145/1067860.1067867

Bickmore TW, Trinh H, Olafsson S, O'Leary TK, Asadi R, Rickles NM, Cruz R (2018) Patient and consumer safety risks when using conversational assistants for medical information: an

observational study of siri, alexa, and google assistant. J Med Internet Res 20(9). https://doi.org/
10.2196/11510

Braun M, Frison AK, Völkel ST, Alt F, Hussmann H, Riener A (2018) Beyond transportation: how
to keep users attached when they are neither driving nor owning automated cars? In: Proceedings of the 10th international conference on automotive user interfaces and interactive vehicular
applications, AutomotiveUI '18, pp 175–180. ACM, New York, USA. https://doi.org/10.1145/
3239092.3265963

Braun M, Mainz A, Chadowitz R, Pfleging B, Alt F (2019) At your service: designing voice assistant
personalities to improve automotive user interfaces. In: Proceedings of the 2019 CHI conference
on human factors in computing systems, CHI '19. ACM, New York. https://doi.org/10.1145/
3290605.3300270

Byrne D, Griffitt W (1969) Similarity and awareness of similarity of personality characteristics as
determinants of attraction. J Exp Res Pers

Cafaro A, Vilhjálmsson HH, 3Bickmore T (2016) First impressions in human–agent virtual encoun-
ters. ACM Trans Comput Hum Interact 23(4):24:1–24:40. https://doi.org/10.1145/2940325

Furnham A (1996) The big five versus the big four: the relationship between the myers-briggs type
indicator (MBTI) and NEO-PI five factor model of personality. Pers Individ Differ 21(2):303–307.
https://doi.org/10.1016/0191-8869(96)00033-5

Jung MF (2017) Affective grounding in human-robot interaction. In: Proceedings of the 2017
ACM/IEEE international conference on human-robot interaction, HRI '17, pp 263–273. ACM,
New York. https://doi.org/10.1145/2909824.3020224

Kammrath LK, Ames DR, Scholer AA (2007) Keeping up impressions: inferential rules for impression change across the big five. J Exp Soc Psychol 43(3):450–457. https://doi.org/10.1016/j.jesp.
2006.04.006, http://www.sciencedirect.com/science/article/pii/S0022103106000758

Kline C, Blumberg B (1999) The art and science of synthetic character design. In: Proceedings of
the AISB (1999) Symposium on AI and Creativity in Entertainment and Visual Art. Edinburgh,
Scotland, p 1999

Konijn EA, Hoorn JF (2005) Some like it bad: testing a model for perceiving and experiencing fictional characters. Media Psychol. 7(March):107–144. https://doi.org/10.1207/
S1532785XMEP0702_1

Kramer J, Noronha S, Vergo J (2000) A user-centered design approach to personalization. Commun.
ACM 43(8):44–48. https://doi.org/10.1145/345124.345139

Large DR, Burnett G, Anyasodo B, Skrypchuk L (2016) Assessing cognitive demand during natural
language interactions with a digital driving assistant. In: Proceedings of the 8th international
conference on automotive user interfaces and interactive vehicular applications, Automotive'UI
16, pp 67–74. ACM, New York. https://doi.org/10.1145/3003715.3005408

Lavie N (2010) Attention, distraction, and cognitive control under load. Curr Dir Psychol Sci
19(3):143–148. https://doi.org/10.1177/0963721410370295

Luger E, Sellen A (2016) 'like having a really bad pa': The gulf between user expectation and
experience of conversational agents. In: Proceedings of the 2016 CHI conference on human
factors in computing systems, CHI '16, pp 5286–5297. ACM, New York. https://doi.org/10.
1145/2858036.2858288

Maciej J, Vollrath M (2009) Comparison of manual vs. speech-based interaction with in-vehicle
information systems. Accid Anal Prev 41(5):924–930. https://doi.org/10.1016/j.aap.2009.05.
007, http://www.sciencedirect.com/science/article/pii/S0001457509001080

Malle BF, Thapa Magar S (2017) What kind of mind do i want in my robot?: Developing a measure
of desired mental capacities in social robots. In: Proceedings of the companion of the 2017
ACM/IEEE international conference on human-robot interaction, pp 195–196. ACM, New York

McCrae RR, Costa PT (1986) Personality, coping, and coping effectiveness in an adult sample. J
Pers 54(2):385–404. https://doi.org/10.1111/j.1467-6494.1986.tb00401.x

Minge M, Thuering M, Wagner I, Kuhr CV (2016) The meCUE Questionaire: a modular tool for
measuring user experience. Advances in ergonomics modeling, usability & special populations.
In: Proceedings of the 7th applied human factors and ergonomics society conference 2016, vol.

486, pp 115–128. https://doi.org/10.1007/978-3-319-41685-4, http://link.springer.com/10.1007/978-3-319-41685-4

Mori M, MacDorman KF, Kageki N (2012) The uncanny valley [from the field]. IEEE Robot Autom Mag 19(2):98–100. https://doi.org/10.1109/MRA.2012.2192811

Nafari M, Weaver C (2013) Augmenting visualization with natural language translation of interaction: a usability study. Comput Graph Forum 32(3pt4), 391–400. https://doi.org/10.1111/cgf.12126, http://dx.doi.org/10.1111/cgf.12126

Nass C, Jonsson IM, Harris H, Reaves B, Endo J, Brave S, Takayama L (2005) Improving automotive safety by pairing driver emotion and car voice emotion. In: CHI '05 extended abstracts on human factors in computing systems, CHI EA '05, pp 1973–1976. ACM, New York. https://doi.org/10.1145/1056808.1057070

Nass C, Moon Y, Fogg BJ, Reeves B, Dryer C (1995) Can computer personalities be human personalities? In: Conference companion on human factors in computing systems, CHI '95, pp 228–229. ACM, New York. https://doi.org/10.1145/223355.223538

Nass C, Steuer J, Tauber ER (1994) Computers are social actors. In: Proceedings of the SIGCHI conference on human factors in computing systems, CHI '94, pp 72–78. ACM, New York. https://doi.org/10.1145/191666.191703

Orth D, Schömig N, Mark C, Jagiellowicz-Kaufmann M, Kolossa D, Heckmann M (2017) Benefits of personalization in the context of a speech-based left-turn assistant. In: Proceedings of the 9th international conference on automotive user interfaces and interactive vehicular applications, AutomotiveUI '17, pp 193–201. ACM, New York. https://doi.org/10.1145/3122986.3123004

Padgham L, Winikoff M (2005) Developing intelligent agent systems: a practical guide, vol 13. Wiley, New York

Peissner M, Doebler V, Metze F (2011) Can voice interaction help reducing the level of distraction and prevent accidents. Technical report, Nuance Communications

Pfleging B, Schneegass S, Schmidt A (2012) Multimodal interaction in the car: combining speech and gestures on the steering wheel. In: Proceedings of the 4th international conference on automotive user interfaces and interactive vehicular applications, AutomotiveUI '12, pp 155–162. ACM, New York. https://doi.org/10.1145/2390256.2390282

Porcheron M, Fischer JE, Reeves S, Sharples S (2018) Voice interfaces in everyday life. In: Proceedings of the 2018 CHI conference on human factors in computing systems, CHI '18, pp 640:1–640:12. ACM, New York. https://doi.org/10.1145/3173574.3174214

Pradhan A, Mehta K, Findlater L (2018) Accessibility came by accident: use of voice-controlled intelligent personal assistants by people with disabilities. In: Proceedings of the 2018 CHI conference on human factors in computing systems, CHI '18, pp 459:1–459:13. ACM, New York. https://doi.org/10.1145/3173574.3174033

Riener A, Jeon M, Alvarez I, Frison AK (2017) Driver in the loop: best practices in automotive sensing and feedback mechanisms. In: Meixner G, Müller C (eds) Automotive user interfaces: creating interactive experiences in the car, pp 295–323. Springer International Publishing, Cham. https://doi.org/10.1007/978-3-319-49448-7_11

Roider F, Rümelin S, Pfleging B, Gross T (2017) The effects of situational demands on gaze, speech and gesture input in the vehicle. In: Proceedings of the 9th ACM international conference on automotive user interfaces and vehicular applications, AutomotiveUI '17. ACM, New York. https://doi.org/10.1145/3122986.3122999

Schmidt M, Braunger P (2018) A survey on different means of personalized dialog output for an adaptive personal assistant. In: Adjunct publication of the 26th conference on user modeling, adaptation and personalization, UMAP '18, pp 75–81. ACM, New York. https://doi.org/10.1145/3213586.3226198

Thakur S (2016) Personalization for google now: user understanding and application to information recommendation and exploration. In: Proceedings of the 10th ACM conference on recommender systems, RecSys '16, pp 3–3. ACM, New York. https://doi.org/10.1145/2959100.2959192

Tillman B (2012) Creative character design. Routledge, Abingdon. https://doi.org/10.4324/9780240814964

Van der Laan J, Heino A, De Waard D (1997) A simple procedure for the assessment of acceptance of advanced transport telematics. Transp Res-Part C Emerg Technol 5:1–10

Wierwille WW (1993) Demands on driver resources associated with introducing advanced technology into the vehicle. Transp Res Part C Emerg Technol 1(2):133–142. https://doi.org/10.1016/0968-090X(93)90010-D, http://www.sciencedirect.com/science/article/pii/0968090X9390010D

Yan B, Weng F, Feng Z, Ratiu F, Raya M, Meng Y, Varges S, Purver M, Lien A, Scheideck T, Raghunathan B, Lin F, Mishra R, Lathrop B, Zhang Z, Bratt H, Peters S (2007) A conversational in-car dialog system. In: Proceedings of human language technologies: demonstrations, NAACL-Demonstrations '07, pp 23–24. Association for Computational Linguistics, Stroudsburg. http://dl.acm.org/citation.cfm?id=1614164.1614176

Chapter 9
The Good, the Bad, and the Rational: Aspects of Character in Logical Agents

Haythem O. Ismail

Abstract Common wisdom holds that each person has a character which is a rather stable, but revisable, system of conditional beliefs and preferences that causally directs the person's behavior. Can the same be said of an artificial agent? In particular, does it make sense to talk of (the typically cold) logical agents, studied in logic-based artificial intelligence, as having characters? I argue that the answer is certainly "yes", at least in the trivial sense that behaviors of such agents are directed by stable, yet revisable, systems of beliefs and preferences. What is interesting is investigating whether and how nontrivial variations in character, as exhibited by humans, can be witnessed in artificial logical agents. In this paper, I present an algebraic logical language which is expressive enough to facilitate the identification of a number of dimensions along which characters of logical agents may vary in interesting ways. Chief among these dimensions are high-level properties of belief and intention, and general constraints on the logic of good and bad.

9.1 Seven Robots and a Trolley

Monday

It is Monday. A trolley is out of control. It is moving extremely fast toward five people tied up to the tracks. There is a lever which, if pulled, will direct the trolley to a sidetrack on which one person lies tied up. There is also a bridge beneath which the trolley will soon pass. A man is standing on the bridge; he is heavy enough so that, should he fall off the bridge, he will certainly stop the trolley, but will die instantly.[1] Several bystanders are there, intently watching the approaching doom. Among them is a robot, let us call it *Monday*. Monday stands there among the

---

[1] This is, of course, a variation of the well-known trolley problem (Foot 1967; Thomson 1976; Singer 2005).

H. O. Ismail (✉)
Department of Engineering Mathematics, Cairo University, Cairo, Egypt

Department of Computer Science, German University in Cairo, Cairo, Egypt
e-mail: haythem.ismail@guc.edu.eg

© Springer Nature Switzerland AG 2020
A. El Bolock et al. (eds.), *Character Computing*, Human–Computer Interaction Series,
https://doi.org/10.1007/978-3-030-15954-2_9

crowd; it does nothing, and the five people are not saved. When later asked if it feels bad about what happened, Monday coldly reports that it does not understand what "bad" means.

Tuesday

It is Tuesday. The same trolley is approaching, five people are also tied up to the tracks, the same lever is there, a man is tied up to the sidetrack, and a heavy man is standing on the bridge. Robot *Tuesday* is standing among the crowd. It does nothing, and the five people are, again, not saved. When later interviewed, Tuesday says that it believes what happened to the five victims to be really bad and that it would have been good to save them; but, nevertheless, it had no motivation to act.

Wednesday

On Wednesday, the same scenario is repeated. (Of course with a new quintet of victims.) Robot *Wednesday* is watching. It thinks for a couple of seconds, rushes to the bridge, and pushes the heavy man. The five people are saved, but the heavy man dies. Wednesday said that it thought that saving the five people is good and, hence, it had to act. But, when asked about the terrible fate of the heavy man, Wednesday reported that it thinks it is bad that the man died. But, then, it calmly said that, while it believes it should do what is good, it does not believe that it should not do what is bad.

Thursday

It is the same situation again, but with robot *Thursday* witnessing the scene. Thursday rushes toward the bridge, stops, turns around, and rushes toward the lever. Reaching the lever, it stops there for a while, then rushes back toward the bridge. For minutes, it keeps on thinking, running between the bridge and the lever, and, thereby, doing nothing useful. Again, the five people are not saved. Hours later, Thursday was not available for interviewing. Some people say that it is still running between the lever and the bridge.

Friday

Robot *Friday* is there this time. It wastes no time, calmly walks to the lever, pulls it, saves the five people, but directs the approaching trolley toward the man lying on the sidetrack. Everybody is happy for saving the five people, but sad for the sidetrack man. Friday itself is neither happy nor sad. It coldly says that it does not know why it acted this way; it just had this irresistible urge to pull the lever.

Saturday

Robot *Saturday* thinks for a couple of minutes and then rushes to the lever. It looks apologetically to the man tied to the sidetrack and pulls! Hours later, Saturday was happy for saving the five people but occasionally stared sadly at the sidetrack. It reported that, while it believes that the death of any person is bad, it still thought that the death of five people is worse than the death of one person. When asked whether it considered pushing the heavy man off the bridge, Saturday said that it indeed did;

but, though morally pushing the man and pulling the lever are equivalent, pulling the lever was better on its conscience.

Sunday

Robot *Sunday* thinks for a couple of seconds and then rushes toward the approaching trolley. The trolley hits Sunday, stops, and the five people are saved. Of course, Sunday was not available for interviewing after the incident, but witnesses say that, seconds before it completely crashed after getting hit by the trolley, they heard it whispering that it did it all for the common good.

Is it fair to say that our seven robots, with their characteristically cold style of reasoning, have character? I think it is; at least if we understand character as a rather stable, but context-sensitive and revisable, system of beliefs and preferences that causally directs an agent's behavior (see Chap. 1 of this volume). What makes some of us sometimes reluctant to accept that logical agents have character is perhaps our tendency to construe character as *human* character. Human character is interesting because it is rich and complex and is susceptible to numerous variations that allow each person to have a unique character profile. But I do not think that this, in principle, negates the possibility of logical agents having *logical* characters which are equally rich and complex. In this paper, there are two things that I do and two things that I do *not* do.

I present a family of logical languages, $Log_A C_n$, in which we can represent various *character profiles* based on the propositional attitudes of belief, intention, preference, and identification of a proposition as good or bad. While modal logic is typically the logic of choice for the representation of propositional attitudes (Hughes and Cresswell 1996), $Log_A C_n$ is not a modal language. $Log_A C_n$ is a new addition to a group of *algebraic* languages presented in Ismail (2012, 2013), Ehab and Ismail (2017). It is algebraic in the sense that it only contains terms, algebraically constructed from function symbols. No sentences are included in a $Log_A C_n$ language. Instead, there are terms of a distinguished syntactic type that are taken to denote propositions. The inclusion of propositions in the ontology, though nonstandard, has been suggested by several other authors (Church 1950; Bealer 1979; Parsons 1993; Shapiro 1993 for example). $Log_A C_n$ allows us to represent the beliefs and intentions of agents who are capable of *ranking* propositions with respect to n scales (hence, $Log_A C_n$). The scales correspond to different criteria based on which a proposition is *good* or *bad*. "Good" and "bad" here are construed very generally, and the existence of multiple scales allows us to represent things like eating ice cream's being good on the sensation scale but bad on the health scale (for some agent). Of course, notions of good and bad are closely related to deontic logic (McNamara 2018), and the use of an algebraic language elegantly circumvents classical problems with modal logics of propositional attitudes in general (e.g., logical omniscience Stalnaker 1991) and the "paradoxes" of deontic logic in particular (McNamara 2018; Goble 1990). Thus, unabated by any linguistic artifacts, we are able in such a language to represent different character profiles based on properties of belief, intention, the logic of good and bad, and the interaction among them. I identify more than 244 binary dimensions along which we may classify characters. This gives rise to the possibility of

$2^{244}(\approx 3 \times 10^{73})$ character profiles; we do not get that many profiles though, since (as shall be proved) the identified dimensions are not all *orthogonal*.

This being said, I have to add that I do not explore all the possible character dimensions that are representable in $Log_A C_n$, (the possibilities are, in fact, unlimited), neither do I uncover all the dependencies among the identified dimensions. Moreover, absent from $Log_A C_n$ is an account of time, ability, and emotion. The incorporation of these elements will certainly result in much richer and extremely complex characters.

9.2 An Algebraic Logic of Character

An agent's character is a complex web of—generally, situation-dependent —properties and relations among its beliefs, intentions, preferences, and what it takes to be good or bad. From a logical perspective, one can distill the core character components within a formal logic of propositional attitudes covering doxastic, deontic, intentional, and preferential notions. At this point, a choice needs to be made regarding the kind of logical language to be adopted. It is more conventional to adopt modal logic for representing propositional attitudes, but, for automated reasoning considerations, first-order logic is ultimately adopted. Both approaches have their well-known problems (see Ismail 2012) and, for this reason, I take the algebraic way.

Like its predecessors, $Log_A B$ (Ismail 2012), $Log_A S$ (Ismail 2013), and $Log_A G$ (Ismail and Ehab 2015; Ehab and Ismail 2017), $Log_A C_n$ is a class of many-sorted languages that share a common core of logical symbols and differ in a signature of nonlogical symbols. In what follows, a sort σ is identified with the set of symbols of sort σ. A $Log_A C_n$ language is a set of terms partitioned into two base syntactic sorts, σ_P and σ_I. Intuitively, σ_P is the set of terms denoting propositions and σ_I is the set of terms denoting anything else. A distinguished subset σ_A of σ_I comprises agent-denoting terms.

9.2.1 Syntax

As is customary in many-sorted languages, an alphabet of $Log_A C_n$ is made up of a set of syncategorematic punctuation symbols and a set of denoting symbols each from a set σ of syntactic sorts. The set σ is the smallest set containing all of the following sorts:

1. σ_P.
2. σ_I.
3. $\tau_1 \longrightarrow \tau_2$, for $\tau_1 \in \{\sigma_P, \sigma_I\}$ and $\tau_2 \in \sigma$.

Intuitively, $\tau_1 \longrightarrow \tau_2$ is the syntactic sort of function symbols that take a single argument of sort σ_P or σ_I and produce a functional term of sort τ_2. Given the restriction of the first argument of function symbols to base sorts, $Log_A C_n$ is, in a sense, a first-order language, since no function symbols may occur as arguments.

A $Log_A C_n$ alphabet is a union of four disjoint sets: $\Omega \cup \Xi \cup \Sigma \cup \Lambda$. The set Ω, the *signature* of the language, is a non-empty, countable set of constant and function symbols. Each symbol in the signature has a designated syntactic type from σ. (Which, in turn, determines a designated adicity. As usual, constants may be viewed as 0-adic function symbols.) Ω is what distinguishes one $Log_A C_n$ language from another.

The set $\Xi = \{x_i, a_i, p_i\}_{i \in \mathbb{N}}$ is a countably infinite set of variables, where $x_i \in \sigma_I$, $a_i \in \sigma_A$, and $p_i \in \sigma_P$, for $i \in \mathbb{N}$. Σ is a set of syncategorematic symbols, including the comma, various matching pairs of brackets and parentheses, and the symbol $\forall$. The set Λ is the set of logical symbols of $Log_A C_n$. It includes "$=$" with the usual, intuitive semantics, and the union of the following sets:

1. $\{\neg\} \subseteq \sigma_P \longrightarrow \sigma_P$.
2. $\{\wedge, \vee\} \subseteq \sigma_P \longrightarrow \sigma_P \longrightarrow \sigma_P$.
3. $\{\mathbf{B}, \mathbf{I}\} \subseteq \sigma_A \longrightarrow \sigma_P \longrightarrow \sigma_P$.
4. $\bigcup_{i=1}^{n} \{\mathbf{Good}_i, \mathbf{Bad}_i\} \subseteq \sigma_A \longrightarrow \sigma_P \longrightarrow \sigma_P$.
5. $\bigcup_{i=1}^{n} \{\mathbf{Btr}_i\} \subseteq \sigma_A \longrightarrow \sigma_P \longrightarrow \sigma_P \longrightarrow \sigma_P$.
6. $\bigcup_{i=1}^{n-1} \bigcup_{j=i+1}^{n} \{\mathbf{Prj}_i^j\} \subseteq \sigma_A \longrightarrow \sigma_P \longrightarrow \sigma_P$.

A $Log_A C_n$ language with signature Ω is denoted by L_Ω. It is the smallest set of terms formed according to the following rules, where t and t_i ($i \in \mathbb{N}$) are terms in L_Ω:

- $\Xi \subset L_\Omega$.
- $c \in L_\Omega$, where $c \in \Omega$ is a constant symbol.
- $f(t_1, \ldots, t_n) \in L_\Omega$, where $f \in \Omega$ is of type $\tau_1 \longrightarrow \cdots \longrightarrow \tau_n \longrightarrow \tau$ ($n > 0$) and t_i is of type τ_i.
- $\neg t \in L_\Omega$, where $t \in \sigma_P$.
- $(t_1 \otimes t_2) \in L_\Omega$, where $\otimes \in \{\wedge, \vee\}$ and $t_1, t_2 \in \sigma_P$.
- $\forall x(t) \in L_\Omega$, where $x \in \Xi$ and $t \in \sigma_P$.
- $\{\mathbf{B}(t_1, t_2), \mathbf{I}(t_1, t_2), \mathbf{Good}_i(t_1, t_2), \mathbf{Bad}_i(t_1, t_2)\} \in L_\Omega$, where $t_1 \in \sigma_A, t_2 \in \sigma_P$, and $1 \leq i \leq n$.
- $\mathbf{Btr}_i(t_1, t_2, t_3) \in L_\Omega$, where $t_1 \in \sigma_A, t_2 \in \sigma_P, t_3 \in \sigma_P$, and $1 \leq i \leq n$.
- $\mathbf{Prj}_i^j(t_1, t_2) \in L_\Omega$, where $t_1 \in \sigma_A$ and $t_2 \in \sigma_P$, for $1 \leq i < j \leq n$.

Formal semantics of $Log_A C_n$ is presented below, but some intuitions may be helpful at this point. A term of the form $\mathbf{B}(\alpha, \phi)$ $(\mathbf{I}(\alpha, \phi))$ denotes the proposition that the agent denoted by α believes (respectively, intends) the proposition denoted by ϕ. A term of the form $\mathbf{Good}_i(\alpha, \phi)$ $(\mathbf{Bad}_i(\alpha, \phi))$ denotes the proposition that, according to the agent denoted by α, the proposition denoted by ϕ is good (respectively, bad) on the ith scale; $\mathbf{Btr}_i(\alpha, \phi, \psi)$ denotes the proposition that the agent denoted by α finds the proposition denoted by ϕ to be higher on the ith scale than the proposition denoted by ψ. Finally, and roughly (but see below), $\mathbf{Prj}_i^j(\alpha, \phi)$ denotes the proposition which, for the agent denoted by α, occupies the same position on the jth scale that the proposition denoted by ϕ occupies on the ith scale.

As usual, terms involving $\Rightarrow$, $\Leftrightarrow$, and $\exists$ may be introduced as abbreviations in the standard way. Moreover, the following abbreviation, representing two proposition's being equivalent for some agent, on some scale, will come handy.

- $\phi \cong_i^\alpha \psi =_{\text{def}} \neg\mathbf{Btr}(\alpha, \phi, \psi) \wedge \neg\mathbf{Btr}(\alpha, \psi, \phi)$.

9.2.2 Semantics

A $Log_A\mathbf{C}_n$ structure is the primary semantic apparatus of a $Log_A\mathbf{C}_n$ language.

Definition 9.1 A $Log_A\mathbf{C}_n$ *structure* is a sextuple $\mathfrak{C} = \langle \mathcal{D}, \mathfrak{A}, \flat, \mathfrak{i}, \mathfrak{S}, \mathfrak{P} \rangle$, where

- $\mathcal{D}$, the domain of discourse, is a set with two disjoint, non-empty, countable subsets $\mathcal{P}$ and $\mathcal{A}$.
- $\mathfrak{A} = \langle \mathcal{P}, +, \cdot, -, \bot, \top \rangle$ is a complete, nondegenerate Boolean algebra (Burris and Sankappanavar 1982).
- $\flat : \mathcal{A} \times \mathcal{P} \longrightarrow \mathcal{P}$.
- $\mathfrak{i} : \mathcal{A} \times \mathcal{P} \longrightarrow \mathcal{P}$.
- $\mathfrak{S}$ is a set of n *scales*, where every scale is a triple $\langle \succ_i, \smile_i, \frown_i \rangle$ with $1 \leq i \leq n$:

  - $\succ_i : \mathcal{A} \times \mathcal{P} \times \mathcal{P} \longrightarrow \mathcal{P}$.
  - $\smile_i : \mathcal{A} \times \mathcal{P} \longrightarrow \mathcal{P}$.
  - $\frown_i : \mathcal{A} \times \mathcal{P} \longrightarrow \mathcal{P}$.

  Moreover, each scale is constrained as follows, for every $p_1, p_2, p_3 \in \mathcal{P}$ and $a \in \mathcal{A}$. (For better readability, I will henceforth write "$(p_1 \succ_i^a p_2)$" for "$\succ_i (a, p_1, p_2)$".)

  $\mathfrak{S}$1. $(p_1 \succ_i^a p_2) \cdot (p_2 \succ_i^a p_1) = \bot$.
  $\mathfrak{S}$2. $(p_1 \succ_i^a p_2) \cdot -(p_3 \succ_i^a p_2) \cdot -(p_1 \succ_i^a p_3) = \bot$.
  $\mathfrak{S}$3. $\smile_i (a, p_1) \cdot - \smile_i (a, p_2) \cdot -(p_1 \succ_i^a p_2) = \bot$.
  $\mathfrak{S}$4. $\frown_i (a, p_1) \cdot - \frown_i (a, p_2) \cdot -(p_2 \succ_i^a p_1) = \bot$.
  $\mathfrak{S}$5. $\smile_i (a, p_1) \cdot \frown_i (a, p_1) = \bot$.

- $\mathfrak{P}$ is a set of $\binom{n}{2}$ *projections*, where each projection is a function $\mathfrak{p}_i^j$ from $\mathcal{A}$ to the set of bijections on $\mathcal{P}$ satisfying the following condition:

  - For every $a \in \mathcal{A}$ and $p_1, p_2 \in \mathcal{P}$, $(p_1 \succ_i^a p_2) \cdot (\mathfrak{p}_i^j(a, p_2) \succ_j^a \mathfrak{p}_i^j(a, p_1)) = \bot$.

Intuitively, the domain $\mathcal{D}$ is partitioned by a set $\mathcal{P}$ of propositions, structured as a Boolean algebra, and a set of individuals $\overline{\mathcal{P}}$; the set of individuals includes a non-empty set $\mathcal{A}$ of agents. The set $\mathfrak{S}$ of n scales is a model of the n preference structures represented in a $Log_A\mathbf{C}_n$ language. For each agent, a scale i is, intuitively, comprised of a strict weak ordering, $\succ_i$, and two *poles*, $\smile_i$ and $\frown_i$, respectively, capturing the agent's judgment of propositions as good or bad. Properties $\mathfrak{G}1$ and $\mathfrak{G}2$ indicate that an agent's ordering of propositions on the scale is an asymmetric, transitive, total ordering of classes of incomparable propositions (a strict weak ordering). $\mathfrak{G}3$ and $\mathfrak{G}4$, respectively, indicate that good propositions are more preferred to propositions which are not good, and that bad propositions are less preferred than propositions which are not bad; this ensures that good and bad propositions are the two opposite poles of the scale. $\mathfrak{G}5$ maintains that the two poles do not overlap. The set $\mathfrak{P}$ of projections establishes order-preserving isomorphisms between each pair of scales.

The different subsets of $\mathcal{D}$ stand in correspondence to the syntactic sorts of $Log_A\mathbf{C}$. In what follows, we let $\mathcal{D}_{\sigma_P} = \mathcal{P}$, $\mathcal{D}_{\sigma_I} = \overline{\mathcal{P}}$, and $\mathcal{D}_{\sigma_A} = \mathcal{A}$.

Definition 9.2 A *valuation* $\mathcal{V}$ of a $Log_A\mathbf{C}_n$ language L_Ω is a triple $\langle \mathfrak{C}, \mathcal{V}_\Omega, \mathcal{V}_\Xi \rangle$, where

- $\mathfrak{C} = \langle \mathcal{D}, \mathfrak{A}, \mathfrak{b}, \mathfrak{i}, \mathfrak{S} \rangle$ is a $Log_A\mathbf{C}_n$ structure;
- $\mathcal{V}_\Omega$ is a function that assigns to each constant of sort τ in Ω an element of $\mathcal{D}_\tau$, and to each function symbol $f \in \Omega$ of sort $\tau_1 \longrightarrow \cdots \longrightarrow \tau_n \longrightarrow \tau$ an n-adic function $\mathcal{V}_\Omega(f) : \underset{i=1}{\overset{n}{\times}} \mathcal{D}_{\tau_i} \longrightarrow \mathcal{D}_\tau$; and
- $\mathcal{V}_\Xi : \Xi \longrightarrow \mathcal{D}$ is a function (a *variable assignment*), where, for every $i \in \mathbb{N}$, $v_\Xi(x_i) \in \overline{\mathcal{P}}$, $v_\Xi(a_i) \in \mathcal{A}$, and $v_\Xi(p_i) \in \mathcal{P}$.

In the sequel, for a valuation $\mathcal{V} = \langle \mathfrak{C}, \mathcal{V}_\Omega, \mathcal{V}_\Xi \rangle$ with $x \in \Xi$ of sort τ and $a \in \mathcal{D}_\tau$, $\mathcal{V}[a/x] = \langle \mathfrak{C}, \mathcal{V}_\Omega, \mathcal{V}_\Xi[a/x] \rangle$, where $\mathcal{V}_\Xi[a/x](x) = a$, and $\mathcal{V}_\Xi[a/x](y) = \mathcal{V}_\Xi(y)$ for every $y \neq x$.

Definition 9.3 Let L_Ω be a $Log_A\mathbf{C}_n$ language and let $\mathcal{V}$ be a valuation of L_Ω. An *interpretation* of the terms of L_Ω is given by a function $\llbracket \cdot \rrbracket^\mathcal{V}$:

- $\llbracket x \rrbracket^\mathcal{V} = \mathcal{V}_\Xi(x)$, for $x \in \Xi$
- $\llbracket c \rrbracket^\mathcal{V} = \mathcal{V}_\Omega(c)$, for a constant $c \in \Omega$
- $\llbracket f(t_1, \ldots, t_n) \rrbracket^\mathcal{V} = \mathcal{V}_\Omega(f)(\llbracket t_1 \rrbracket^\mathcal{V}, \ldots, \llbracket t_n \rrbracket^\mathcal{V})$, for an n-adic ($n \geq 1$) function symbol $f \in \Omega$
- $\llbracket (t_1 \wedge t_2) \rrbracket^\mathcal{V} = \llbracket t_1 \rrbracket^\mathcal{V} \cdot \llbracket t_2 \rrbracket^\mathcal{V}$
- $\llbracket (t_1 \vee t_2) \rrbracket^\mathcal{V} = \llbracket t_1 \rrbracket^\mathcal{V} + \llbracket t_2 \rrbracket^\mathcal{V}$
- $\llbracket \neg t \rrbracket^\mathcal{V} = -\llbracket t \rrbracket^\mathcal{V}$.
- $\llbracket \forall x(t) \rrbracket^\mathcal{V} = \prod_{a \in \mathcal{D}_\tau} \llbracket t \rrbracket^{\mathcal{V}[a/x]}$
- $\llbracket \mathbf{B}(t_1, t_2) \rrbracket^\mathcal{V} = \mathfrak{b}(\llbracket t_1 \rrbracket^\mathcal{V}, \llbracket t_2 \rrbracket^\mathcal{V})$
- $\llbracket \mathbf{I}(t_1, t_2) \rrbracket^\mathcal{V} = \mathfrak{i}(\llbracket t_1 \rrbracket^\mathcal{V}, \llbracket t_2 \rrbracket^\mathcal{V})$
- $\llbracket \mathbf{Good}_i(t_1, t_2) \rrbracket^\mathcal{V} = \smile_i(\llbracket t_1 \rrbracket^\mathcal{V}, \llbracket t_2 \rrbracket^\mathcal{V})$, for $1 \leq i \leq n$
- $\llbracket \mathbf{Bad}_i(t_1, t_2) \rrbracket^\mathcal{V} = \frown_i(\llbracket t_1 \rrbracket^\mathcal{V}, \llbracket t_2 \rrbracket^\mathcal{V})$, for $1 \leq i \leq n$
- $\llbracket \mathbf{Btr}_i(t_1, t_2, t_3) \rrbracket^\mathcal{V} = \succ_i(\llbracket t_1 \rrbracket^\mathcal{V}, \llbracket t_2 \rrbracket^\mathcal{V}, \llbracket t_3 \rrbracket^\mathcal{V})$, for $1 \leq i \leq n$
- $\llbracket \mathbf{Prj}_1^j(t_1, t_2) \rrbracket^\mathcal{V} = \mathfrak{p}_i^j(\llbracket t_1 \rrbracket^\mathcal{V}, \llbracket t_2 \rrbracket^\mathcal{V})$, for $1 \leq i < j \leq n$

In $Log_A C_n$, logical consequence is defined in pure algebraic terms without alluding to the notion of truth. This is achieved using the natural partial order $\leq$ associated with $\mathfrak{A}$ (Burris and Sankappanavar 1982). Let $\mathfrak{C}$ be a $Log_A C_n$ structure. For every $\phi, \psi \in \mathcal{P}$, $\phi \leq \psi$ if and only if $\phi + \psi = \psi$. (Equivalently, $\phi \leq \psi$ if and only if $\phi \cdot \psi = \phi$.)

Definition 9.4 Let L_Ω be a $Log_A C_n$ language. For every $\phi \in \sigma_P$ and $\Gamma \subseteq \sigma_P$, ϕ is a logical consequence of Γ, denoted $\Gamma \models \phi$, if, for every L_Ω valuation $\mathcal{V}$,
$$\prod_{\gamma \in \Gamma} [\![\gamma]\!]^{\mathcal{V}} \leq [\![\phi]\!]^{\mathcal{V}}.$$

As proved in Ismail (2012), $\models$ has the distinctive properties of classical Tarskian logical consequence and satisfies an algebraic variant of the deduction theorem. In particular, if $\varnothing \models \phi$, then $[\![\phi]\!]^{\mathcal{V}} = \top$ for every valuation $\mathcal{V}$, and we say that ϕ is *logically valid*, denoted $\models \phi$. Thus, the following properties of scales in a $Log_A C_n$ structure immediately follow from $\mathfrak{S}1$–$\mathfrak{S}5$ in Definition 9.1. Henceforth, variables are assumed to be universally quantified, with widest scope, unless otherwise indicated.

Proposition 9.1 *For any $Log_A C_n$ language, the following is true, for $1 \leq i < j \leq n$:*[2]

1. $\models \mathbf{Btr}_i(a, p_1, p_2) \Rightarrow \neg\mathbf{Btr}_i(a, p_2, p_1)$
2. $\models \mathbf{Btr}_i(a, p_1, p_2) \wedge \mathbf{Btr}(a, p_2, p_3) \Rightarrow \mathbf{Btr}_i(a, p_1, p_3)$
3. $\models \neg\mathbf{Btr}_i(a, p, p)$
4. $\models \mathbf{Btr}_i(a, p_1, p_2) \Rightarrow \neg\mathbf{Btr}_j(a, \mathbf{Prj}_i^j(a, p_2), \mathbf{Prj}_i^j(a, p_1))$
5. $\models p \cong_i^a p$
6. $\models p_1 \cong_i^a p_2 \Rightarrow p_2 \cong_i^a p_1$
7. $\models p_1 \cong_i^a p_2 \wedge p_2 \cong_i^a p_3 \Rightarrow p_1 \cong_i^a p_3$
8. $\models p_1 \cong_i^a p_2 \wedge \mathbf{Btr}_i(a, p_1, p_3) \Rightarrow \mathbf{Btr}_i(a, p_2, p_3)$
9. $\models p_1 \cong_i^a p_2 \wedge \mathbf{Btr}_i(a, p_3, p_1) \Rightarrow \mathbf{Btr}_i(a, p_3, p_2)$
10. $\models \mathbf{Good}_i(a, p_1) \wedge \neg\mathbf{Good}_i(a, p_2) \Rightarrow \mathbf{Btr}_i(a, p_1, p_2)$
11. $\models \mathbf{Good}_i(a, p_1) \wedge p_1 \cong_i^a p_2 \Rightarrow \mathbf{Good}_i(a, p_2)$
12. $\models \mathbf{Bad}_i(a, p_1) \wedge \neg\mathbf{Bad}_i(a, p_2) \Rightarrow \mathbf{Btr}_i(a, p_2, p_1)$
13. $\models \mathbf{Bad}_i(a, p_1) \wedge p_1 \cong_i^a p_2 \Rightarrow \mathbf{Bad}_i(a, p_2)$
14. $\models \mathbf{Good}_i(a, p_1) \wedge \mathbf{Bad}_i(a, p_2) \Rightarrow \mathbf{Btr}_i(a, p_1, p_2)$
15. $\models \mathbf{Good}_i(a, p) \Leftrightarrow \neg\mathbf{Bad}_i(a, p)$

9.3 Doxastic Profiles

The literature on doxastic logic usually assumes rational agents which are ideal: Ideal agents are omniscient, consistent reasoners who are (unusually) competent about their beliefs. Thus, the following properties, represented in $Log_A C_n$, are typi-

---

[2]Throughout the paper, proofs (which are mostly straightforward) are omitted for brevity.

cally assumed. (These are the standard axioms of a KD45 modal logic Hughes and Cresswell 1996.)

BN. $\mathbf{B}(a, p \vee \neg p)$

BK. $\mathbf{B}(a, p_1 \Rightarrow p_2) \Rightarrow (\mathbf{B}(a, p_1) \Rightarrow \mathbf{B}(a, p_2))$

BD. $\mathbf{B}(a, p) \Rightarrow \neg B(a, \neg p)$

B4. $\mathbf{B}(a, p) \Rightarrow \mathbf{B}(a, \mathbf{B}(a, p))$

B5. $\neg \mathbf{B}(a, p) \Rightarrow \mathbf{B}(a, \neg \mathbf{B}(a, p))$

In a classical modal approach to doxastic logic (with standard possible-worlds semantics), the equivalents of **BN** and **BK** are valid formulas; counterparts of **BD**, **B4**, and **B5** are axioms imposing constraints on semantic structures (in the form of properties of accessibility relations). Intuitively, **BD** admits only consistent agents and **B4** and **B5**, respectively, characterize positively and negatively introspective agents. In the algebraic $Log_A C_n$, none of the above formulas is logically valid and, hence, we have the freedom to select any collection of them as axioms for particular instances of the variable a. This gives rise to various types of agent *characters* distinguished by their *doxastic profile*. First, we consider agents with various *degrees* of omniscience.

Definition 9.5 Let $\alpha \in \sigma_A$ and $\phi \in \sigma_P$.

1. $\mathbf{LOmni}(\alpha, \phi) =_{\text{def}} \forall p[(\phi \wedge p) = \phi \Rightarrow (\mathbf{B}(\alpha, \phi) \Rightarrow \mathbf{B}(\alpha, p))]$
2. $\mathbf{LOmni}(\alpha) =_{\text{def}} \forall p[\mathbf{LOmni}(\alpha, p)]$
3. $\mathbf{MOmni}(\alpha, \phi) =_{\text{def}} \forall p[\mathbf{B}(\alpha, \phi \Rightarrow p) \Rightarrow (\mathbf{B}(\alpha, \phi) \Rightarrow \mathbf{B}(\alpha, p))]$
4. $\mathbf{MOmni}(\alpha) =_{\text{def}} \forall p[\mathbf{MOmni}(\alpha, p)]$

Hence, an agent $[\![\alpha]\!]$ is *logically omniscient about a proposition* $[\![\phi]\!]$ if, whenever they believe it, they believe all propositions logically implied by it; they are logically omniscient—period—if they are logically omniscient about all propositions. The latter notion is perhaps too much to ask of agents with bounded cognitive capacities, but the former is not far-fetched if $[\![\alpha]\!]$ is an expert in some field in which $[\![\phi]\!]$ is a primary proposition. *Material omniscience about* $[\![\phi]\!]$ is the hallmark of an agent which believes everything that, it believes, is materially implied by its belief $[\![\phi]\!]$. This notion, together with its pervasive variant (material omniscient about all propositions—basically, the α/a-instance of **BK** above), is perhaps more realistic than its logical counterpart; for it seems to only require agents to be doxastically committed to what *they* believe is implied by their beliefs. Now, while the above four properties may be hard to attain by any *human*, due to cognitive constraints, it is possible to imagine an artificial agent, whose beliefs are represented by a weak enough language (e.g., propositional logic), which has a materially and logically omniscient *character*.

At this point, it is important to make two general remarks. First, agent properties presented in Definition 9.5, and similar ones presented in upcoming definitions, are relative to some particular proposition (ϕ). Second, such properties may be conditional on situation-dependent peculiarities, which can be represented using straightforward conditional statements. These two features of the logical representation provide flexibility in accounting for transient, situation-dependent attitudes while admitting the representation of higher level rules governing changes in attitudes across situations.

Further facets of an omniscient character can be proved.

Proposition 9.2

1. $\models (p_1 \wedge p_2) = p_1 \Rightarrow [(\textbf{LOmin}(a, p_1) \wedge \textbf{B}(a, p_1)) \Rightarrow \textbf{LOmni}(a, p_2)]$
2. $\models \textbf{LOmni}(a, p_1) \wedge \textbf{B}(a, p_1) \Rightarrow \textbf{B}(a, p_2 \vee \neg p_2)^3$
3. $\models \textbf{LOmni}(a, p_1 \wedge \neg p_1) \wedge \textbf{B}(a, p_1 \wedge \neg p_1) \Rightarrow$
$$[\textbf{B}(a, p_2) \wedge \textbf{LOmni}(a, p_2) \wedge \textbf{MOmni}(a, p_2)]$$
4. $\models \textbf{B}(a, p_1 \vee \neg p_1) \wedge \textbf{MOmni}(\alpha, p_1 \wedge \neg p_1) \Rightarrow \textbf{LOmni}(a, p_1 \wedge \neg p_1)$

A character's doxastic profile may also be characterized by how belief commutes with Boolean connectives. Henceforth, similar to Definition 9.5, the unary overloading of a defined predicate stands for the universal closure of the predicate on all but its first argument place.

Definition 9.6 Let $\alpha \in \sigma_A$ and $\phi, \psi \in \sigma_P$.

1. $\textbf{BCons}(\alpha, \phi) =_{\text{def}} \textbf{B}(\alpha, \neg\phi) \Rightarrow \neg\textbf{B}(\alpha, \phi)$
2. $\textbf{BAuto}(\alpha, \phi) =_{\text{def}} \neg\textbf{B}(\alpha, \phi) \Rightarrow \textbf{B}(\alpha, \neg\phi)$
3. $\textbf{BAndUp}(\alpha, \phi, \psi) =_{\text{def}} \textbf{B}(a, \phi \wedge \psi) \Rightarrow [\textbf{B}(a, \phi) \wedge \textbf{B}(a, \psi)]$
4. $\textbf{BAndDn}(\alpha, \phi, \psi) =_{\text{def}} \textbf{B}(a, \phi) \wedge \textbf{B}(a, \psi) \Rightarrow \textbf{B}(a, \phi \wedge \psi)$
5. $\textbf{BOrUp}(\alpha, \phi, \psi) =_{\text{def}} \textbf{B}(a, \phi) \vee \textbf{B}(a, \psi) \Rightarrow \textbf{B}(a, \phi \vee \psi)$
6. $\textbf{BOrDn}(\alpha, \phi, \psi) =_{\text{def}} \textbf{B}(a, \phi \vee \psi) \Rightarrow [\textbf{B}(a, \phi) \vee \textbf{B}(a, \psi)]$

Thus, an agent $[\![\alpha]\!]$ is *doxastically consistent about* $[\![\phi]\!]$ if they can never believe both $[\![\phi]\!]$ and $[\![\neg\phi]\!]$. An agent with the pervasive variant of doxastic consistency cannot believe *any* contradictions. While ideal agents are expected to be consistent in the latter sense, consistency about only some propositions (or a class thereof) is more readily attainable by realistic characters. Likewise, *auto-epistemology about a proposition* (Clause 3) is more realistic (e.g., Moore's not believing that he has a brother leading him to believe that he does not Moore 1985) than pervasive auto-epistemology: Not believing that my sister is at home does not, in itself, entitle me to believing that she is not. The "**Up**" and "**Dn**" (for "down") in Clauses 5 through 12 allude to the natural orientation of the Boolean lattice where a proposition is *beneath* its logical consequences. These closure properties of belief are characteristic of omniscient agents.

Proposition 9.3

1. $\models \textbf{BCons}(a, p) \Leftrightarrow \textbf{BCons}(a, \neg p)$
2. $\models \textbf{BAuto}(a, p) \Leftrightarrow \textbf{BAuto}(a, \neg p)$
3. $\models \textbf{LOmni}(a, p_1 \wedge p_2) \Rightarrow \textbf{BAndUp}(a, p_1, p_2)$
4. $\models \forall p_2[\textbf{BAndUp}(a, p_1, p_2)] \Rightarrow \textbf{LOmni}(a, p_1)$

---

[3] Hence, a materially omniscient agent who is logically omniscient about some proposition which they believe is a "type 1" reasoner according to Smullyan (1986).

5. $\models$ **LOmni**(a) $\Leftrightarrow$ **BAndUp**(a)
6. $\models$ **LOmni**(a, p_1) $\wedge$ **LOmni**(a, p_2) $\Rightarrow$ **BOrUp**(a, p_1, p_2)
7. $\models$ $\forall p_1[\textbf{BOrUp}(a, p_1, p_2)]$ $\Rightarrow$ **LOmni**(a, p_1)
8. $\models$ **LOmni**(a) $\Leftrightarrow$ **BOrUp**(a)
9. $\models$ **BAuto**(a) $\wedge$ **BCons**(a) $\Rightarrow$ (**MOmni**(a, p_1) $\Leftrightarrow$ $\forall p_2[\textbf{BAndDn}(a, p_1, p_2)])$
10. $\models$ **BAuto**(a) $\wedge$ **BCons**(a) $\Rightarrow$ (**MOmni**(a) $\Leftrightarrow$ **BAndDn**(a))
11. $\models$ **BAuto**(a, p_1) $\Rightarrow$ (**MOmni**(a, p_1) $\Rightarrow$ **BOrDn**$(a, \neg p_1, p_2)$)
12. $\models$ **BCons**(a, p_1) $\Rightarrow$ ($\forall p_2[\textbf{BOrDn}(a, \neg p_1, p_2)]$ $\Rightarrow$ **MOmni**(a, p_1))
13. $\models$ **BAuto**(a) $\Rightarrow$ (**MOmni**(a) $\Rightarrow$ **BOrDn**(a))
14. $\models$ **BCons**(a) $\Rightarrow$ (**BOrDn**(a) $\Rightarrow$ **MOmni**(a))

Finally, we consider aspects of character reflecting the relation between believing in a proposition and the truth thereof.

Definition 9.7 Let $\alpha \in \sigma_A$ and $\phi \in \sigma_P$.

1. **Acc**(α, ϕ) $=_{\text{def}}$ **B**(α, ϕ) $\Rightarrow$ ϕ
2. **Inf**(α, ϕ) $=_{\text{def}}$ ϕ $\Rightarrow$ **B**(α, ϕ)
3. **Conc**(α, ϕ) $=_{\text{def}}$ **B**$(\alpha, \textbf{Acc}(\alpha, \phi))$
4. **Conf**(α, ϕ) $=_{\text{def}}$ **B**$(\alpha, \textbf{Inf}(\alpha, \phi))$
5. **Intr**$^+(\alpha, \phi)$ $=_{\text{def}}$ **Inf**$(\alpha, \textbf{B}(\alpha, \phi))$
6. **Intr**$^-(\alpha, \phi)$ $=_{\text{def}}$ **Inf**$(\alpha, \neg \textbf{B}(\alpha, \phi))$
7. **Faith**$^+(\alpha, \phi)$ $=_{\text{def}}$ **Acc**$(\alpha, \textbf{B}(\alpha, \phi))$
8. **Faith**$^-(\alpha, \phi)$ $=_{\text{def}}$ **Acc**$(\alpha, \neg \textbf{B}(\alpha, \phi))$

Hence, an agent is *accurate* about a proposition if they believe it only if it is true; they are *informed* about a proposition if they believe it whenever it is true. Being *conceited* or *confident* about a proposition, respectively, correspond to whether the agent believes in their accuracy or informedness about it.[4] Clauses 5 and 6 capture agents who are, respectively, positively and negatively introspective (**B4** and **B5** above). The converses, Clauses 7 and 8, describe agents who are, respectively, positively and negatively *faithful*.[5]

Proposition 9.4

1. $\models$ **BCons**(a, p) $\wedge$ **Inf**(a, p) $\Rightarrow$ **Acc**$(a, \neg p)$
2. $\models$ **BAuto**(a, p) $\wedge$ **Acc**(a, p) $\Rightarrow$ **Inf**$(a, \neg p)$
3. $\models$ **Inf**(a, p) $\wedge$ **Inf**$(a, \neg p)$ $\Rightarrow$ **BAuto**(a, p)
4. $\models$ **Acc**(a, p) $\wedge$ **Acc**$(a, \neg p)$ $\Rightarrow$ **BCons**(a, p)
5. $\models$ **BCons**$(a, \textbf{B}(a, p))$ $\wedge$ **Intr**$^-(a, p)$ $\Rightarrow$ **Faith**$^+(a, p)$
6. $\models$ **BCons**$(a, \textbf{B}(a, p))$ $\wedge$ **Intr**$^+(a, p)$ $\Rightarrow$ **Faith**$^-(a, p)$
7. $\models$ **BAuto**$(a, \textbf{B}(a, p))$ $\wedge$ **Faith**$^-(a, p)$ $\Rightarrow$ **Intr**$^+(a, p)$
8. $\models$ **BAuto**$(a, \textbf{B}(a, p))$ $\wedge$ **Faith**$^+(a, p)$ $\Rightarrow$ **Intr**$^-(a, p)$
9. $\models$ **Intr**$^+(a, p)$ $\wedge$ **Intr**$^-(a, p)$ $\Rightarrow$ **BAuto**$(a, \textbf{B}(a, p))$

---

[4]The term "conceit" in this sense is due to Smullyan (1986).
[5]This use of "faithful" is due to Konolige (1985).

10. $\models \mathbf{Faith}^+(a, p) \wedge \mathbf{Faith}^-(a, p) \Rightarrow \mathbf{BCons}(a, \mathbf{B}(a, p))$
11. $\models \mathbf{MOmni}(a, p) \wedge \mathbf{Conf}(a, p) \Rightarrow \mathbf{Intr}^+(a, p)$
12. $\models \mathbf{MOmni}(a, \mathbf{B}(a, p)) \wedge \mathbf{Conc}(a, p) \Rightarrow \mathbf{Faith}^+(a, p)$
13. $\models \mathbf{MOmni}(a, \neg p) \wedge \mathbf{Conc}(a, p) \wedge \mathbf{BAuto}(a, p) \Rightarrow \mathbf{Intr}^-(a, p)$
14. $\models \mathbf{MOmni}(a, \neg \mathbf{B}(a, p)) \wedge \mathbf{Conf}(a, p) \wedge \mathbf{BCons}(a, p) \Rightarrow \mathbf{Faith}^-(a, p)$

9.4 Volitional Profiles

The volitional profile of a character pertains to those aspects governing intentions and their interaction with beliefs. The ideal rational agent has a volitional profile classically characterized by the axioms of a KD modal logic (stated here in $Log_A \mathbf{C}_n$).

IN. $\mathbf{I}(a, p \vee \neg p)$.
IK. $\mathbf{I}(a, p_1 \Rightarrow p_2) \Rightarrow (\mathbf{I}(a, p_1) \Rightarrow \mathbf{I}(a, p_2))$.
ID. $\mathbf{I}(a, p) \Rightarrow \neg \mathbf{I}(a, \neg p)$.

As in the case of belief, a classical modal approach to intention (for example, Colombetti 1999) renders **IN** and **IK** logically valid. **IN**, in particular, has historically been seen as bizarre. For what would it mean to—*necessarily*—have the vacuous intention of bringing about a tautology? In $Log_A \mathbf{C}_n$, and like **BN** and **BK**, neither **IN** nor **IK** is logically valid. Hence, instead of adopting the above as axioms, we list them, among others, as attitudes of choice for particular agent characters toward particular propositions.

Definition 9.8 Let $\alpha \in \sigma_A$ and $\phi \in \sigma_P$.

1. $\mathbf{LI}(\alpha, \phi) =_{\text{def}} \forall p[(\phi \wedge p) = \phi \Rightarrow (\mathbf{I}(\alpha, \phi) \Rightarrow \mathbf{I}(\alpha, p))]$
2. $\mathbf{MI}(\alpha, \phi) =_{\text{def}} \forall p[\mathbf{I}(\alpha, \phi \Rightarrow p) \Rightarrow (\mathbf{I}(\alpha, \phi) \Rightarrow \mathbf{I}(\alpha, p))]$
3. $\mathbf{MBI}(\alpha, \phi) =_{\text{def}} \forall p[\mathbf{B}(\alpha, \phi \Rightarrow p) \Rightarrow (\mathbf{I}(\alpha, \phi) \Rightarrow \mathbf{I}(\alpha, p))]$

The first clause of Definition 9.8 defines an agent whose intentions are closed under the logical consequences of a particular proposition; the second and third clauses relativize the closure to what the agent, respectively, *intends to* and *believes* follow from said proposition. **LI** agents are compelled, by logical necessity, to have certain intentions; **MI** and **MBI** agents form intentions which respect their own intended and believed implications. Note that if $[\![\mathbf{MBI}(\alpha)]\!]$, then $[\![\alpha]\!]$ suffers from the "side-effect" problem, intending all (what it believes to be) side effects of its intentions (Bratman 1987; Cohen and Levesque 1990; Herzig and Longin 2004).

The following proposition shows that, similar to the doxastic case and unlike in classical modal approaches to intention, tautologies are not necessarily intended and intending contradictions do not, unconditionally, trivialize the notion of intention.

Proposition 9.5

1. $\models (p_1 \wedge p_2) = p_1 \Rightarrow [(\mathbf{LI}(a, p_1) \wedge \mathbf{I}(a, p_1)) \Rightarrow \mathbf{LI}(a, p_2)]$
2. $\models \mathbf{LI}(a, p_1) \wedge \mathbf{I}(a, p_1) \Rightarrow \mathbf{I}(a, p_2 \vee \neg p_2)$
3. $\models \mathbf{LI}(a, p_1 \wedge \neg p_1) \wedge \mathbf{I}(a, p_1 \wedge \neg p_1) \Rightarrow$
   $\qquad [\mathbf{I}(a, p_2) \wedge \mathbf{LI}(a, p_2) \wedge \mathbf{MI}(a, p_2) \wedge \mathbf{MBI}(a, p_2)]$
4. $\models \mathbf{I}(a, p_1 \vee \neg p_1) \wedge \mathbf{MI}(\alpha, p_1 \wedge \neg p_1) \Rightarrow \mathbf{LI}(a, p_1 \wedge \neg p_1)$
5. $\models \mathbf{B}(a, p_1 \vee \neg p_1) \wedge \mathbf{MBI}(\alpha, p_1 \wedge \neg p_1) \Rightarrow \mathbf{LI}(a, p_1 \wedge \neg p_1)$

Patterns of distributivity over $\wedge$ and $\vee$ and commutativity with $\neg$ of the intention operator give rise to agent character profiles analogous to those of the doxastic case.

Definition 9.9 Let $\alpha \in \sigma_A$ and $\phi, \psi \in \sigma_P$.

1. $\mathbf{ICons}(\alpha, \phi) =_{\text{def}} \mathbf{I}(\alpha, \neg \phi) \Rightarrow \neg \mathbf{I}(\alpha, \phi)$
2. $\mathbf{IFan}(\alpha, \phi) =_{\text{def}} \neg \mathbf{I}(\alpha, \phi) \Rightarrow \mathbf{I}(\alpha, \neg \phi)$
3. $\mathbf{IAndUp}(\alpha, \phi, \psi) =_{\text{def}} \mathbf{I}(a, \phi \wedge \psi) \Rightarrow [\mathbf{I}(a, \phi) \wedge \mathbf{I}(a, \psi)]$
4. $\mathbf{IAndDn}(\alpha, \phi, \psi) =_{\text{def}} \mathbf{I}(a, \phi) \wedge \mathbf{I}(a, \psi) \Rightarrow \mathbf{I}(a, \phi \wedge \psi)$
5. $\mathbf{IOrUp}(\alpha, \phi, \psi) =_{\text{def}} \mathbf{I}(a, \phi) \vee \mathbf{I}(a, \psi) \Rightarrow \mathbf{I}(a, \phi \vee \psi)$
6. $\mathbf{IOrDn}(\alpha, \phi, \psi) =_{\text{def}} \mathbf{I}(a, \phi \vee \psi) \Rightarrow [\mathbf{I}(a, \phi) \vee \mathbf{I}(a, \psi)]$

$\mathbf{ICons}(\alpha)$ is the α/a-instance of **ID**, requiring $[\![\alpha]\!]$ to be consistent in their intentions.[6] An agent is *intentionally fanatic* about a proposition if they cannot be neutral about it; they either intend it or else they intend its negation. For example, a runner has to have the intention to keep running (and, therefore, continue to exert effort and control rhythm) or to stop running (and, hence, act against inertia).

The final four definitions, capturing patterns of distributivity of **I** over $\wedge$ and $\vee$, are similar to their doxastic counterparts. $\mathbf{IAndUp}(\alpha)$ and $\mathbf{IAndDn}(\alpha)$ are logically valid in a classical modal approach. Whether this is uncontroversial is not obvious though. Take $\mathbf{IAndUp}(\alpha)$, for example. Suppose that Adam intends to make ten million dollars and buy a yacht. It would seem reasonable to suppose that he, thereby, intends to make ten million dollars and also intends to buy a yacht. But this can run into difficulties. For having an intention to make the money mandates that the agent does whatever it takes so that they end up having that money. Now, Adam inherits ten million dollars from a rich relative under the condition that he never uses the money to buy any kind of boat. (The late relative suffered from aquaphobia.) It seems that Adam has now satisfied the intention of making the money and should, therefore, drop it (as per the advice of Cohen and Levesque 1990). But, then, he would never be able to satisfy the intention of buying a yacht (unless, for example, in the unlikely event of his inheriting more money) and, realizing this, he should drop that intention, together with the original conjunctive intention. (Dropping an intention which one believes will never be satisfied is also a reasonable advice of Cohen and Levesque 1990.) This does not look right. One might contend that Adam should not have dropped the intention of making ten million dollars because its motivation

---

[6]Again, unlike in a classical modal approach, this is generally not equivalent to prohibiting $[\![\alpha]\!]$ from intending a contradiction, i.e., $\forall p \neg \mathbf{I}(\alpha, p \wedge \neg p)$.

(buying the yacht) is still active. But this suggests that the two intentions be *lumped* together (Kratzer 1989), and this kind of lumping can be effectively captured by not adopting the pervasive **IAndUp**(α).

A similar case can be made against **IAndDn**(α). One *may* argue that if an agent is *aware* of intending p and intending q, then they are *aware* of intending their conjunction. But not all agents are aware of their intentions. (More on this below.) Without alluding to subconscious intentions (although we can, when discussing "character"), consider a classical AI planning agent. It is common to view such an agent as having as intentions the goals it adopts and plans for. Planning for the goal p directs the agent to constructing plans that achieve p; likewise for q. In most planning systems, this does not *require* the agent to actively seek plans achieving $p \cdot q$ (Ghallab et al. 2016).

The following proposition is the volitional counterpart of Proposition 9.3.

Proposition 9.6

1. $\models$ **ICons**$(a, p) \Leftrightarrow$ **ICons**$(a, \neg p)$
2. $\models$ **IFan**$(a, p) \Leftrightarrow$ **IFan**$(a, \neg p)$
3. $\models$ **LI**$(a, p_1 \wedge p_2) \Rightarrow$ **IAndUp**(a, p_1, p_2)
4. $\models \forall p_2[$**IAndUp**$(a, p_1, p_2)] \Rightarrow$ **LI**(a, p_1)
5. $\models$ **LI**$(a) \Leftrightarrow$ **IAndUp**(a)
6. $\models$ **LI**$(a, p_1) \wedge$ **LI**$(a, p_2) \Rightarrow$ **IOrUp**(a, p_1, p_2)
7. $\models \forall p_2[$**IOrUp**$(a, p_1, p_2)] \Rightarrow$ **LI**(a, p_1)
8. $\models$ **LI**$(a) \Leftrightarrow$ **IOrUp**(a)
9. $\models$ **IFan**$(a) \wedge$ **ICons**$(a) \Rightarrow ($**MI**$(a, p_1) \Leftrightarrow \forall p_2[$**IAndDn**$(a, p_1, p_2)])$
10. $\models$ **IFan**$(a) \wedge$ **ICons**$(a) \Rightarrow ($**MI**$(a) \Leftrightarrow$ **IAndDn**$(a))$
11. $\models$ **IFan**$(a, p_1) \Rightarrow ($**MI**$(a, p_1) \Rightarrow$ **IOrDn**$(a, \neg p_1, p_2))$
12. $\models$ **ICons**$(a, p_1) \Rightarrow (\forall p_2[$**IOrDn**$(a, \neg p_1, p_2)] \Rightarrow$ **MI**$(a, p_1))$
13. $\models$ **IFan**$(a) \Rightarrow ($**MI**$(a) \Rightarrow$ **IOrDn**$(a))$
14. $\models$ **ICons**$(a) \Rightarrow ($**IOrDn**$(a) \Rightarrow$ **MI**$(a))$

We now turn to possible relations between intention, on one hand, and truth and belief, on the other.

Definition 9.10 Let $\alpha \in \sigma_A$ and $\phi \in \sigma_P$.

1. **Comp**$(\alpha, \phi) =_{\text{def}}$ **I**$(\alpha, \phi) \Rightarrow \phi$
2. **Cont**$(\alpha, \phi) =_{\text{def}} \phi \Rightarrow$ **I**(α, ϕ)
3. **IConc**$(\alpha, \phi) =_{\text{def}}$ **B**$(\alpha,$ **Comp**$(\alpha, \phi))$
4. **IConf**$(\alpha, \phi) =_{\text{def}}$ **B**$(\alpha,$ **Cont**$(\alpha, \phi))$
5. **IInf**$^+(\alpha, \phi) =_{\text{def}}$ **Inf**$(\alpha,$ **I**$(\alpha, \phi))$
6. **IInf**$^-(\alpha, \phi) =_{\text{def}}$ **Inf**$(\alpha, \neg$**I**$(\alpha, \phi))$
7. **IAcc**$^+(\alpha, \phi) =_{\text{def}}$ **Acc**$(\alpha,$ **I**$(\alpha, \phi))$
8. **IAcc**$^-(\alpha, \phi) =_{\text{def}}$ **Acc**$(\alpha, \neg$**I**$(\alpha, \phi))$
9. **BIC**$(\alpha, \phi) =_{\text{def}}$ **I**$(\alpha, \neg\phi) \Rightarrow \neg$**B**$(\alpha, \phi)$
10. **Real**$(\alpha, \phi) =_{\text{def}}$ **I**$(\alpha, \phi) \Rightarrow$ **B**(α, ϕ)
11. **Leer**$(\alpha, \phi) =_{\text{def}}$ **B**$(\alpha, \phi) \Rightarrow$ **I**(α, ϕ)

Parallel to the doxastic accuracy and informedness, an agent is *competent about a proposition* if whenever they intend it, it is indeed brought about; they are *in control of a proposition* if it cannot be brought about unless the agent intends it. For example, trained students are competent and in control of carrying out mental arithmetic. The third through the eighth clause are similar to their doxastic counterparts from Definition 9.7. An agent is *BI-consistent* if they do not form intentions which are inconsistent with their beliefs. They are *realistic about a proposition* if they intend it only when they believe it (Cohen and Levesque 1990). The agent is *leery about a proposition* if they believe it only when *they* intend it; thus, a leery agent always takes things into their own hands.

Proposition 9.7

1. $\models$ **BCons**$(a, \mathbf{I}(a, p)) \wedge \mathbf{IInf}^-(a, p) \Rightarrow \mathbf{IAcc}^+(a, p)$
2. $\models$ **BCons**$(a, \mathbf{I}(a, p)) \wedge \mathbf{IInf}^+(a, p) \Rightarrow \mathbf{IAcc}^-(a, p)$
3. $\models$ **BAuto**$(a, \mathbf{I}(a, p)) \wedge \mathbf{IAcc}^-(a, p) \Rightarrow \mathbf{IInf}^+(a, p)$
4. $\models$ **BAuto**$(a, \mathbf{I}(a, p)) \wedge \mathbf{IAcc}^+(a, p) \Rightarrow \mathbf{IInf}^-(a, p)$
5. $\models$ **IInf**$^+(a, p) \wedge \mathbf{IInf}^-(a, p) \Rightarrow \mathbf{BAuto}(a, \mathbf{I}(a, p))$
6. $\models$ **IAcc**$^+(a, p) \wedge \mathbf{IAcc}^-(a, p) \Rightarrow \mathbf{BCons}(a, \mathbf{I}(a, p))$
7. $\models$ **BCons**$(a, p) \Rightarrow [\mathbf{Real}(a, p) \Rightarrow \mathbf{BIC}(a, \neg p)]$
8. $\models$ **BAuto**$(a, p) \Rightarrow [\mathbf{BIC}(a, p) \Rightarrow \mathbf{Real}(a, \neg p)]$
9. $\models$ **ICons**$(a, p) \Rightarrow [\mathbf{Leer}(a, p) \Rightarrow \mathbf{BIC}(a, p)]$
10. $\models$ **IFan**$(a, p) \Rightarrow [\mathbf{BIC}(a, \neg p) \Rightarrow \mathbf{Leer}(a, \neg p)]$
11. $\models$ **BCons**$(a, p) \wedge \mathbf{IFan}(a, p) \Rightarrow [\mathbf{Real}(a, p) \Rightarrow \mathbf{Lear}(a, \neg p)]$
12. $\models$ **BAuto**$(a, p) \wedge \mathbf{ICons}(a, p) \Rightarrow [\mathbf{Leer}(a, p) \Rightarrow \mathbf{Real}(a, \neg p)]$
13. $\models$ **MOmni**$(a, p) \wedge \mathbf{IConf}(a, p) \wedge \mathbf{Real}(a, p) \Rightarrow \mathbf{IInfo}^+(a, p)$
14. $\models$ **MOmni**$(a, \mathbf{I}(a, p)) \wedge \mathbf{IConc}(a, p) \wedge \mathbf{Leer}(a, p) \Rightarrow \mathbf{IAcc}^+(a, p)$
15. $\models$ **MBI**$(a, \neg p) \wedge \mathbf{IConc}(a, p) \wedge \mathbf{IFan}(a, p) \wedge \mathbf{Real}(a, \neg \mathbf{I}(a, p)) \Rightarrow$ **IInf**$^-(a, p)$
16. $\models$ **MBI**$(a, \neg \mathbf{I}(a, p)) \wedge \mathbf{IConf}(a, p) \wedge \mathbf{ICons}(a, p) \wedge \mathbf{Leer}(a, \neg \mathbf{I}(a, p)) \Rightarrow$ **IAcc**$^-(a, p)$

9.5 Motivational Profiles

A character's motivational profile is determined by properties of its preferential scales, their interaction with each other, and their interaction with intentions and beliefs. First, here are some useful abbreviations.

Definition 9.11 Let $\alpha \in \sigma_A$, ϕ, $\psi \in \sigma_P$, and $S \cup \{i, j\} \subseteq \{1, \ldots, n\}$ with $i < j$.

1. **Good**$_S(\alpha, \phi) =_{\text{def}} \bigvee_{k \in S} \mathbf{Good}_k(\alpha, \phi)$
2. **Good**$(\alpha, \phi) =_{\text{def}} \bigvee_{k=1}^{n} \mathbf{Good}_k(\alpha, \phi)$
3. **GOOD**$_S(\alpha, \phi) =_{\text{def}} \bigwedge_{k \in S} \mathbf{Good}_k(\alpha, \phi)$
4. **GOOD**$(\alpha, \phi) =_{\text{def}} \bigwedge_{k=1}^{n} \mathbf{Good}_k(\alpha, \phi)$

5. $\mathbf{Bad}_S(\alpha, \phi) =_{\text{def}} \bigvee_{k \in S} \mathbf{Bad}_k(\alpha, \phi)$
6. $\mathbf{Bad}(\alpha, \phi) =_{\text{def}} \bigvee_{k=1}^{n} \mathbf{Bad}_k(\alpha, \phi)$
7. $\mathbf{BAD}_S(\alpha, \phi) =_{\text{def}} \bigwedge_{k \in S} \mathbf{Bad}_k(\alpha, \phi)$
8. $\mathbf{BAD}(\alpha, \phi) =_{\text{def}} \bigwedge_{k=1}^{n} \mathbf{Bad}_k(\alpha, \phi)$
9. $\mathbf{Des}_i(\alpha, \phi) =_{\text{def}} \mathbf{Good}_i(\alpha, \phi) \wedge \mathbf{Btr}_i(\alpha, \phi, \neg\phi)$
10. $\mathbf{Des}_S(\alpha, \phi) =_{\text{def}} \bigvee_{k \in S} \mathbf{Des}_k(\alpha, \phi)$
11. $\mathbf{Des}(\alpha, \phi) =_{\text{def}} \bigvee_{1=1}^{n} \mathbf{Des}_i(\alpha, \phi)$
12. $\mathbf{DES}_S(\alpha, \phi) =_{\text{def}} \bigwedge_{k \in S} \mathbf{Des}_k(\alpha, \phi)$
13. $\mathbf{DES}(\alpha, \phi) =_{\text{def}} \bigwedge_{1=1}^{n} \mathbf{Des}_i(\alpha, \phi)$
14. $\mathbf{Abh}_i(\alpha, \phi) =_{\text{def}} \mathbf{Bad}_i(\alpha, \phi) \wedge \mathbf{Btr}_i(\alpha, \neg\phi, \phi)$
15. $\mathbf{Abh}_S(\alpha, \phi) =_{\text{def}} \bigvee_{k \in S} \mathbf{Abh}_k(\alpha, \phi)$
16. $\mathbf{Abh}(\alpha, \phi) =_{\text{def}} \bigvee_{1=1}^{n} \mathbf{Abh}_i(\alpha, \phi)$
17. $\mathbf{Abh}_S(\alpha, \phi) =_{\text{def}} \bigwedge_{k \in S} \mathbf{Abh}_k(\alpha, \phi)$
18. $\mathbf{ABH}(\alpha, \phi) =_{\text{def}} \bigwedge_{1=1}^{n} \mathbf{Abh}_i(\alpha, \phi)$
19. $\phi \,_i{\geq}_j^{\alpha}\, \psi =_{\text{def}} \neg\mathbf{Btr}_j(\alpha, \psi, \mathbf{Prj}_i^j(\alpha, \phi))$
20. $\phi \,_j{\geq}_i^{\alpha}\, \psi =_{\text{def}} \neg\mathbf{Btr}_j(\alpha, \mathbf{Prj}_i^j(\alpha, \psi), \phi)$

The first clause points to a common sloppiness in the use of "good" in English. For we typically do not specify the sense in which something is good (the *scale*); rather, contextual factors mark only some of the scales as salient and, as per the first clause, do not necessarily specify exactly which of those scales are in use. Perhaps, it is this use of "good" and the corresponding use of "bad" (clause 5) that allow us to honestly make declarations such as "eating this ice-cream cone is good and bad."

A desire (clauses 9 through 13) is defined to be a good proposition which is better than its negation (relative to some scale). This is in contrast to other accounts of desire, based only on a preference relation, where a proposition is desired merely if it is better than its negation (everything else being equal) (Doyle et al. 1991; Lang et al. 2003). It also contrasts to purely modal accounts of desire (Cohen and Levesque 1990; Herzig and Longin 2004) which suffer from imposing the usual suite of suspect tautologies (particularly necessitation and axiom K).[7] Clauses 14 through 18 introduce the dual notion of an agent's abhorring a proposition. The operator $_i{\geq}_j^{\alpha}$ is used to compare propositions across two different scales. This is supposed to correspond to such locutions as "being honest is morally good at least as much as eating ice cream is sensationally good." The intuition is that p is more i-good than q is j-good just in case the number of propositions which are better than p on the i-scale is no greater than the number of propositions which are better than q on the j-scale.

Given the above definitions, we can prove the following tautologies and contingencies.

Proposition 9.8 *Let $S \cup \{i, j, k\} \subseteq \{1, \ldots, n\}$, with $|S| > 1$ and $i \neq j \neq k$.*

1. $\models \mathbf{Des}_i(a, p) \Rightarrow \neg\mathbf{Des}_i(a, \neg p)$

---

[7] It should be stressed, though, that in such accounts (despite the use of the term "desire") the authors do not claim to present an account of "desire", only of "goals."

2. $\models \mathbf{DES}_S(a, p) \Rightarrow \neg\mathbf{DES}_S(a, \neg p)$
3. $\not\models \mathbf{Des}_S(a, p) \Rightarrow \neg\mathbf{Des}_S(a, \neg p)$
4. $\models \mathbf{Abh}_i(a, p) \Rightarrow \neg\mathbf{Abh}_i(a, \neg p)$
5. $\models \mathbf{ABH}_S(a, p) \Rightarrow \neg\mathbf{ABH}_S(a, \neg p)$
6. $\not\models \mathbf{Abh}_S(a, p) \Rightarrow \neg\mathbf{Abh}_S(a, \neg p)$
7. $\models \mathbf{Des}_i(a, p) \Rightarrow \neg\mathbf{Abh}_i(a, p)$
8. $\models \mathbf{DES}_S(a, p) \Rightarrow \neg\mathbf{ABH}_S(a, p)$
9. $\not\models \mathbf{Des}_S(a, p) \Rightarrow \neg\mathbf{Abh}_S(a, p)$
10. $\models (p_1 \mathbin{_i\geq^a_j} p_2) \wedge (p_2 \mathbin{_j\geq^a_k} p_3) \Rightarrow (p_1 \mathbin{_i\geq^a_k} p_3)$
11. $\models \mathbf{Btr}_i(a, p_1, p_2) \wedge (p_2 \mathbin{_i\geq^a_j} p_3) \Rightarrow (p_1 \mathbin{_i\geq^a_j} p_3)$
12. $\not\models (p_1 \mathbin{_i\geq^a_j} p_2) \wedge \mathbf{Good}_j(a, p_2) \Rightarrow \mathbf{Good}_i(a, p_1)$
13. $\not\models (p_1 \mathbin{_i\geq^a_j} p_2) \wedge \mathbf{Bad}_i(a, p_1) \Rightarrow \mathbf{Bad}_j(a, p_2)$

Now, we systematically consider the interaction of motivational attitudes with various phenomena. We start with logical implication.

Definition 9.12 Let $\alpha \in \sigma_A$, $\phi \in \sigma_P$, and $1 \leq i \leq n$.

1. $\mathbf{LG}_i(\alpha, \phi) =_{\mathrm{def}} \forall p[(\phi \wedge p) = \phi \Rightarrow (\mathbf{Good}_i(\alpha, \phi) \Rightarrow \mathbf{Good}_i(\alpha, p))]$
2. $\mathbf{LG}(\alpha, \phi) =_{\mathrm{def}} \bigwedge_{i=1}^{n} \mathbf{LG}_i(\alpha, \phi)$
3. $\mathbf{LB}_i(\alpha, \phi) =_{\mathrm{def}} \forall p[(\phi \wedge p) = \phi \Rightarrow (\mathbf{Bad}_i(\alpha, \phi) \Rightarrow \mathbf{Bad}_i(\alpha, p))]$
4. $\mathbf{LB}(\alpha, \phi) =_{\mathrm{def}} \bigwedge_{i=1}^{n} \mathbf{LB}_i(\alpha, \phi)$
5. $\mathbf{MG}_i(\alpha, \phi) =_{\mathrm{def}} \forall p[\mathbf{Good}_i(\alpha, \phi \Rightarrow p) \Rightarrow (\mathbf{Good}_i(\alpha, \phi) \Rightarrow \mathbf{Good}_i(\alpha, p))]$
6. $\mathbf{MG}(\alpha, \phi) =_{\mathrm{def}} \bigwedge_{i=1}^{n} \mathbf{MG}_i(\alpha, \phi)$
7. $\mathbf{MB}_i(\alpha, \phi) =_{\mathrm{def}} \forall p[\mathbf{Bad}_i(\alpha, \phi \Rightarrow p) \Rightarrow (\mathbf{Bad}_i(\alpha, \phi) \Rightarrow \mathbf{Bad}_i(\alpha, p))]$
8. $\mathbf{MB}(\alpha, \phi) =_{\mathrm{def}} \bigwedge_{i=1}^{n} \mathbf{MB}_i(\alpha, \phi)$

An agent who is $\mathbf{LG}_i$ toward p is committed to the i-goodness of all logical consequences of p whenever p is itself i-good. But this is historically problematic (and more problematic is its logical validity in modal logic). For, thence, if answering a question truthfully is morally good for the agent then answering truthfully or killing the questioner is also morally good (cf. *Ross's paradox* in deontic logic McNamara 2018). The same criticism can be raised against $\mathbf{LB}_i$ agents. The material counterparts (clauses 5 through 8), while more appealing, have also often been subject to criticism (cf. *Chisholm's paradox* McNamara 2018.)[8] In fact, just as in the doxastic and volitional cases, once we accept $\mathbf{LG}$ or $\mathbf{LB}$, triviality is just around the corner.

Proposition 9.9 Let $1 \leq i \leq n$.

1. $\models (p_1 \wedge p_2) = p_1 \Rightarrow [(\mathbf{LG}_i(a, p_1) \wedge \mathbf{Good}_i(a, p_1)) \Rightarrow \mathbf{LG}_i(a, p_2)]$
2. $\models \mathbf{LG}_i(a, p_1) \wedge \mathbf{Good}_i(a, p_1) \Rightarrow \mathbf{Good}_i(a, p_2 \vee \neg p_2)$
3. $\models \mathbf{LG}_i(a, p_1 \wedge \neg p_1) \wedge \mathbf{Good}_i(a, p_1 \wedge \neg p_1) \Rightarrow$
    $[\mathbf{Good}(a, p_2) \wedge \mathbf{LG}_i(a, p_2) \wedge \mathbf{MG}_i(a, p_2)]$

---

[8]Following Goble (1990), I suppose that most motivational conditional propositions are not material conditionals, but general indicative or counterfactual ones (Lewis 1973); material conditionals are simply disjunctions and are treated below.

4. $\models \mathbf{Good}_i(a, p_1 \vee \neg p_1) \wedge \mathbf{MG}_i(\alpha, p_1 \wedge \neg p_1) \Rightarrow \mathbf{LG}_i(a, p_1 \wedge \neg p_1)$
5. $\models (p_1 \wedge p_2) = p_1 \Rightarrow [(\mathbf{LB}_i(a, p_1) \wedge \mathbf{Bad}_i(a, p_1)) \Rightarrow \mathbf{LB}_i(a, p_2)]$
6. $\models \mathbf{LB}_i(a, p_1) \wedge \mathbf{Bad}_i(a, p_1) \Rightarrow \mathbf{Bad}_i(a, p_2 \vee \neg p_2)$
7. $\models \mathbf{LB}_i(a, p_1 \wedge \neg p_1) \wedge \mathbf{Bad}_i(a, p_1 \wedge \neg p_1) \Rightarrow$
    $\qquad [\mathbf{Bad}(a, p_2) \wedge \mathbf{LB}_i(a, p_2) \wedge \mathbf{MB}_i(a, p_2)]$
8. $\models \mathbf{Bad}_i(a, p_1 \vee \neg p_1) \wedge \mathbf{MB}_i(\alpha, p_1 \wedge \neg p_1) \Rightarrow \mathbf{LB}_i(a, p_1 \wedge \neg p_1)$

Next, consider the interaction between motivational operators and Boolean connectives.

Definition 9.13 Let $\alpha \in \sigma_A$, $\phi, \psi \in \sigma_P$, and $1 \le i \le n$.

1. $\mathbf{GdCons}_i(\alpha, \phi) =_{\text{def}} \mathbf{Good}_i(\alpha, \neg\phi) \Rightarrow \neg\mathbf{Good}_i(\alpha, \phi)$
2. $\mathbf{GdFan}_i(\alpha, \phi) =_{\text{def}} \neg\mathbf{Good}_i(\alpha, \phi) \Rightarrow \mathbf{Good}_i(\alpha, \neg\phi)$
3. $\mathbf{GdAndUp}_i(\alpha, \phi, \psi) =_{\text{def}} \mathbf{Good}_i(a, \phi \wedge \psi) \Rightarrow [\mathbf{Good}_i(a, \phi) \wedge \mathbf{Good}_i(a, \psi)]$
4. $\mathbf{GdAndDn}_i(\alpha, \phi, \psi) =_{\text{def}} \mathbf{Good}_i(a, \phi) \wedge \mathbf{Good}_i(a, \psi) \Rightarrow \mathbf{Good}_i(a, \phi \wedge \psi)$
5. $\mathbf{GdOrUp}_i(\alpha, \phi, \psi) =_{\text{def}} \mathbf{Good}_i(a, \phi) \vee \mathbf{Good}_i(a, \psi) \Rightarrow \mathbf{Good}_i(a, \phi \vee \psi)$
6. $\mathbf{GdOrDn}_i(\alpha, \phi, \psi) =_{\text{def}} \mathbf{Good}_i(a, \phi \vee \psi) \Rightarrow [\mathbf{Good}_i(a, \phi) \vee \mathbf{Good}_i(a, \psi)]$
7. $\mathbf{BdCons}_i(\alpha, \phi) =_{\text{def}} \mathbf{Bad}_i(\alpha, \neg\phi) \Rightarrow \neg\mathbf{Bad}_i(\alpha, \phi)$
8. $\mathbf{BdFan}_i(\alpha, \phi) =_{\text{def}} \neg\mathbf{Bad}_i(\alpha, \phi) \Rightarrow \mathbf{Bad}_i(\alpha, \neg\phi)$
9. $\mathbf{BdAndUp}_i(\alpha, \phi, \psi) =_{\text{def}} \mathbf{Bad}_i(a, \phi \wedge \psi) \Rightarrow [\mathbf{Bad}_i(a, \phi) \wedge \mathbf{Bad}_i(a, \psi)]$
10. $\mathbf{BdAndDn}_i(\alpha, \phi, \psi) =_{\text{def}} \mathbf{Bad}_i(a, \phi) \wedge \mathbf{Bad}_i(a, \psi) \Rightarrow \mathbf{Bad}_i(a, \phi \wedge \psi)$
11. $\mathbf{BdOrUp}_i(\alpha, \phi, \psi) =_{\text{def}} \mathbf{Bad}_i(a, \phi) \vee \mathbf{Bad}_i(a, \psi) \Rightarrow \mathbf{Bad}_i(a, \phi \vee \psi)$
12. $\mathbf{BdOrDn}_i(\alpha, \phi, \psi) =_{\text{def}} \mathbf{Bad}_i(a, \phi \vee \psi) \Rightarrow [\mathbf{Bad}_i(a, \phi) \vee \mathbf{Bad}_i(a, \psi)]$

Hasty, or pervasive, instantiations of the above properties are generally not advisable. Take the consistency of goodness for example (first clause). While nobody seriously objects to the possibility of inconsistent good propositions (Lewis 1988 for instance), it may be argued that inconsistency is only acceptable in case two distinct scales are involved.[9] But I contend that inconsistency is also acceptable on a single scale. For example, while it would be sensationally good to eat the ice cream, it would also be sensationally good to not eat the ice cream and thereby savor the taste of coffee I just finished. Likewise, fanaticism about goodness is not such a "good" idea: It is not, in general, morally good to drink coffee (but it is also not morally bad!), neither is it morally good to *not* drink coffee. Similar criticisms can be leveled against the rest of the properties. For example, contra **GdAndUp**, while it may be morally good to push one person (thereby killing them) and save five people, pushing the person (and thereby killing them) per se is not morally good (cf. Prior's *good Samaritan paradox* McNamara 2018).

The following dependencies among motivational properties are similar to their doxastic and volitional parallels.

Proposition 9.10 *Let $1 \le i \le n$.*

1. $\models \mathbf{GdCons}_i(a, p) \Leftrightarrow \mathbf{GdCons}_i(a, \neg p)$

---

[9]Lewis's case of Meane and Neiss (Lewis 1988) clearly involves two scales.

2. $\models \mathbf{GdFan}_i(a, p) \Leftrightarrow \mathbf{GdFan}_i(a, \neg p)$
3. $\models \mathbf{LG}_i(a, p_1 \wedge p_2) \Rightarrow \mathbf{GdAndUp}_i(a, p_1, p_2)$
4. $\models \forall p_2[\mathbf{GdAndUp}_i(a, p_1, p_2)] \Rightarrow \mathbf{LG}_i(a, p_1)$
5. $\models \mathbf{LG}_i(a) \Leftrightarrow \mathbf{GdAndUp}_i(a)$
6. $\models \mathbf{LG}_i(a, p_1) \wedge \mathbf{LG}_i(a, p_2) \Rightarrow \mathbf{GdOrUp}_i(a, p_1, p_2)$
7. $\models \forall p_2[\mathbf{GdOrUp}_i(a, p_1, p_2)] \Rightarrow \mathbf{LG}_i(a, p_1)$
8. $\models \mathbf{LG}_i(a) \Leftrightarrow \mathbf{GdOrUp}_i(a)$
9. $\models \mathbf{BdCons}_i(a, p) \Leftrightarrow \mathbf{BdCons}_i(a, \neg p)$
10. $\models \mathbf{BdFan}_i(a, p) \Leftrightarrow \mathbf{BdFan}_i(a, \neg p)$
11. $\models \mathbf{LB}_i(a, p_1 \wedge p_2) \Rightarrow \mathbf{BdAndUp}_i(a, p_1, p_2)$
12. $\models \forall p_2[\mathbf{BdAndUp}_i(a, p_1, p_2)] \Rightarrow \mathbf{LB}_i(a, p_1)$
13. $\models \mathbf{LB}_i(a) \Leftrightarrow \mathbf{BdAndUp}_i(a)$
14. $\models \mathbf{LB}_i(a, p_1) \wedge \mathbf{LB}_i(a, p_2) \Rightarrow \mathbf{BdOrUp}_i(a, p_1, p_2)$
15. $\models \forall p_2[\mathbf{BdOrUp}_i(a, p_1, p_2)] \Rightarrow \mathbf{LB}_i(a, p_1)$
16. $\models \mathbf{LB}_i(a) \Leftrightarrow \mathbf{BdOrUp}_i(a)$
17. $\models \mathbf{GdFan}_i(a) \wedge \mathbf{GdCons}_i(a) \Rightarrow (\mathbf{MG}_i(a, p_1) \Leftrightarrow \forall p_2[\mathbf{GdAndDn}_i(a, p_1, p_2)])$
18. $\models \mathbf{GdFan}_i(a) \wedge \mathbf{GdCons}_i(a) \Rightarrow (\mathbf{MG}_i(a) \Leftrightarrow \mathbf{GdAndDn}_i(a))$
19. $\models \mathbf{GdFan}_i(a, p_1) \Rightarrow (\mathbf{MG}_i(a, p_1) \Rightarrow \mathbf{GdOrDn}_i(a, \neg p_1, p_2))$
20. $\models \mathbf{GdCons}_i(a, p_1) \Rightarrow (\forall p_2[\mathbf{GdOrDn}_i(a, \neg p_1, p_2)] \Rightarrow \mathbf{MG}_i(a, p_1))$
21. $\models \mathbf{GdFan}_i(a) \Rightarrow (\mathbf{MG}_i(a) \Rightarrow \mathbf{GdOrDn}_i(a))$
22. $\models \mathbf{GdCons}_i(a) \Rightarrow (\mathbf{GdOrDn}_i(a) \Rightarrow \mathbf{MG}_i(a))$
23. $\models \mathbf{BdFan}_i(a) \wedge \mathbf{BdCons}_i(a) \Rightarrow (\mathbf{MB}_i(a, p_1) \Leftrightarrow \forall p_2[\mathbf{BdAndDn}_i(a, p_1, p_2)])$
24. $\models \mathbf{BdFan}_i(a) \wedge \mathbf{BdCons}_i(a) \Rightarrow (\mathbf{MB}_i(a) \Leftrightarrow \mathbf{BdAndDn}_i(a))$
25. $\models \mathbf{BdFan}_i(a, p_1) \Rightarrow (\mathbf{MB}_i(a, p_1) \Rightarrow \mathbf{BdOrDn}_i(a, \neg p_1, p_2))$
26. $\models \mathbf{BdCons}_i(a, p_1) \Rightarrow (\forall p_2[\mathbf{BdOrDn}_i(a, \neg p_1, p_2)] \Rightarrow \mathbf{MB}_i(a, p_1))$
27. $\models \mathbf{BdFan}_i(a) \Rightarrow (\mathbf{MB}_i(a) \Rightarrow \mathbf{BdOrDn}_i(a))$
28. $\models \mathbf{BdCons}_i(a) \Rightarrow (\mathbf{BdOrDn}_i(a) \Rightarrow \mathbf{MB}_i(a))$

Now, consider the following motivational properties, pertaining to truth and belief.

Definition 9.14 Let $\alpha \in \sigma_A, \phi \in \sigma_P$, and $1 \leq i \leq n$.

1. $\mathbf{Lucky}_i(\alpha, \phi) =_{\text{def}} \phi \Rightarrow \mathbf{Good}_i(\alpha, \phi)$
2. $\mathbf{Achv}_i(\alpha, \phi) =_{\text{def}} \mathbf{Good}_i(\alpha, \phi) \Rightarrow \phi$
3. $\mathbf{Hapls}_i(\alpha, \phi) =_{\text{def}} \phi \Rightarrow \mathbf{Bad}_i(\alpha, \phi)$
4. $\mathbf{Curs}_i(\alpha, \phi) =_{\text{def}} \mathbf{Bad}_i(\alpha, \phi) \Rightarrow \phi$
5. $\mathbf{Cont}_i(\alpha, \phi) =_{\text{def}} \mathbf{B}(\alpha, \mathbf{Lucky}_i(\alpha, \phi))$
6. $\mathbf{Opt}_i(\alpha, \phi) =_{\text{def}} \mathbf{B}(\alpha, \mathbf{Achv}_i(\alpha, \phi))$
7. $\mathbf{Discont}_i(\alpha, \phi) =_{\text{def}} \mathbf{B}(\alpha, \mathbf{Hapls}_i(\alpha, \phi))$
8. $\mathbf{Pes}_i(\alpha, \phi) =_{\text{def}} \mathbf{B}(\alpha, \mathbf{Curs}_i(\alpha, \phi))$
9. $\mathbf{GdInf}_i^+(\alpha, \phi) =_{\text{def}} \mathbf{Inf}(\alpha, \mathbf{Good}_i(\alpha, \phi))$
10. $\mathbf{GdInf}_i^-(\alpha, \phi) =_{\text{def}} \mathbf{Inf}(\alpha, \neg\mathbf{Good}_i(\alpha, \phi))$
11. $\mathbf{GdAcc}_i^+(\alpha, \phi) =_{\text{def}} \mathbf{Acc}(\alpha, \mathbf{Good}_i(\alpha, \phi))$
12. $\mathbf{GdAcc}_i^-(\alpha, \phi) =_{\text{def}} \mathbf{Acc}(\alpha, \neg\mathbf{Bad}_i(\alpha, \phi))$

13. $\mathbf{BdInf}_i^+(\alpha, \phi) =_{\text{def}} \mathbf{Inf}(\alpha, \mathbf{Bad}_i(\alpha, \phi))$

14. $\mathbf{BdInf}_i^-(\alpha, \phi) =_{\text{def}} \mathbf{Inf}(\alpha, \neg\mathbf{Bad}_i(\alpha, \phi))$

15. $\mathbf{BdAcc}_i^+(\alpha, \phi) =_{\text{def}} \mathbf{Acc}(\alpha, \mathbf{Bad}_i(\alpha, \phi))$

16. $\mathbf{BdAcc}_i^-(\alpha, \phi) =_{\text{def}} \mathbf{Acc}(\alpha, \neg\mathbf{Bad}_i(\alpha, \phi))$

17. $\mathbf{MG}_i^{\rightrightarrows}(\alpha, \phi) =_{\text{def}} \forall p[\mathbf{B}(\alpha, \phi \Rightarrow p) \Rightarrow \mathbf{B}(\alpha, \mathbf{Good}_i(\alpha, \phi) \Rightarrow \mathbf{Good}_i(\alpha, p))]$

18. $\mathbf{MB}_i^{\rightrightarrows}(\alpha, \phi) =_{\text{def}} \forall p[\mathbf{B}(\alpha, \phi \Rightarrow p) \Rightarrow \mathbf{B}(\alpha, \mathbf{Bad}_i(\alpha, \phi) \Rightarrow \mathbf{Bad}_i(\alpha, p))]$

19. $\mathbf{MG}_i^{\leftleftarrows}(\alpha, \phi) =_{\text{def}} \forall p[\mathbf{B}(\alpha, \phi \Rightarrow p) \Rightarrow \mathbf{B}(\alpha, \mathbf{Good}_i(\alpha, p) \Rightarrow \mathbf{Good}_i(\alpha, \phi))]$

20. $\mathbf{MB}_i^{\leftleftarrows}(\alpha, \phi) =_{\text{def}} \forall p[\mathbf{B}(\alpha, \phi \Leftarrow p) \Rightarrow \mathbf{B}(\alpha, \mathbf{Bad}_i(\alpha, p) \Rightarrow \mathbf{Bad}_i(\alpha, \phi))]$

Thus, an i-lucky agent is one for whom reality is i-good; an i-achiever is one for whom all i-good propositions are real. On the other hand, an agent is i-hapless if reality is i-bad for them and they are i-cursed in case every proposition which is, to them, i-bad is true. The agent is i-content if they believe that only i-good things happen; they are i-optimistic if they believe that all i-good things happen. i-discontent and i-pessimistic agents are likewise defined. Accuracy and informedness about what is good and bad are, for most agents on most scales, not pervasive: Agents do not always know what is (not) good for them.[10] Clauses 17 and 18 characterize agents who respectively believe that (what they believe are) consequences of a good proposition are all good and that a proposition is good if it has some good consequences. Clauses 19 and 20 are likewise for bad propositions.

The motivational counterpart of Propositions 9.4 and 9.7 also holds. I only state here those results pertaining to the final four clauses of Definition 9.14.

Proposition 9.11 *Let* $1 \leq i, j \leq n$.

1. $\models \mathbf{MOmni}(a) \wedge ([\mathbf{Cont}_i(a, p) \wedge \mathbf{MG}_j^{\rightrightarrows}(a, p)] \vee [\mathbf{Opt}_i(a, p) \wedge \mathbf{MG}_j^{\leftleftarrows}(a, p)]) \Rightarrow$
   $[\mathbf{B}(a, \mathbf{Good}_j(a, p)) \Rightarrow \mathbf{B}(a, \mathbf{Good}_j(a, \mathbf{Good}_i(a, p)))]$

2. $\models \mathbf{MOmni}(a) \wedge ([\mathbf{Cont}_i(a, p) \wedge \mathbf{MB}_j^{\rightrightarrows}(a, p)] \vee [\mathbf{Opt}_i(a, p) \wedge \mathbf{MB}_j^{\leftleftarrows}(a, p)]) \Rightarrow$
   $[\mathbf{B}(a, \mathbf{Bad}_j(a, p)) \Rightarrow \mathbf{B}(a, \mathbf{Bad}_j(a, \mathbf{Good}_i(a, p)))]$

3. $\models \mathbf{MOmni}(a) \wedge ([\mathbf{Discont}_i(a, p) \wedge \mathbf{MB}_j^{\rightrightarrows}(a, p)] \vee [\mathbf{Pes}_i(a, p) \wedge \mathbf{MB}_j^{\leftleftarrows}(a, p)]) \Rightarrow$
   $[\mathbf{B}(a, \mathbf{Bad}_j(a, p)) \Rightarrow \mathbf{B}(a, \mathbf{Bad}_j(a, \mathbf{Bad}_i(a, p)))]$

4. $\models \mathbf{MOmni}(a) \wedge ([\mathbf{Discont}_i(a, p) \wedge \mathbf{MG}_j^{\rightrightarrows}(a, p)] \vee [\mathbf{Pes}_i(a, p) \wedge \mathbf{MG}_j^{\leftleftarrows}(a, p)]) \Rightarrow$
   $[\mathbf{B}(a, \mathbf{Good}_j(a, p)) \Rightarrow \mathbf{B}(a, \mathbf{Good}_j(a, \mathbf{Bad}_i(a, p)))]$

5. $\models \mathbf{MOmni}(a) \wedge ([\mathbf{Opt}_i(a, p) \wedge \mathbf{MG}_j^{\rightrightarrows}(a, p)] \vee [\mathbf{Cont}_i(a, p) \wedge \mathbf{MG}_j^{\leftleftarrows}(a, p)]) \Rightarrow$
   $[\mathbf{B}(a, \mathbf{Good}_j(a, \mathbf{Good}_i(a, p))) \Rightarrow \mathbf{B}(a, \mathbf{Good}_j(a, p))]$

6. $\models \mathbf{MOmni}(a) \wedge ([\mathbf{Opt}_i(a, p) \wedge \mathbf{MB}_j^{\rightrightarrows}(a, p)][\mathbf{Cont}_i(a, p) \wedge \mathbf{MB}_j^{\leftleftarrows}(a, p)]) \Rightarrow$
   $[\mathbf{B}(a, \mathbf{Bad}_j(a, \mathbf{Good}_i(a, p))) \Rightarrow \mathbf{B}(a, \mathbf{Bad}_j(a, p))]$

7. $\models \mathbf{MOmni}(a) \wedge ([\mathbf{Pes}_i(a, p) \wedge \mathbf{MB}_j^{\rightrightarrows}(a, p)] \vee [\mathbf{Discont}_i(a, p) \wedge \mathbf{MB}_j^{\leftleftarrows}(a, p)]) \Rightarrow$
   $[\mathbf{B}(a, \mathbf{Bad}_j(a, \mathbf{Bad}_i(a, p))) \Rightarrow \mathbf{B}(a, \mathbf{Bad}_j(a, p))]$

8. $\models \mathbf{MOmni}(a) \wedge ([\mathbf{Pes}_i(a, p) \wedge \mathbf{MG}_j^{\rightrightarrows}(a, p)] \vee [\mathbf{Discont}_i(a, p) \wedge \mathbf{MG}_j^{\leftleftarrows}(a, p)]) \Rightarrow$
   $[\mathbf{B}(a, \mathbf{Good}_j(a, \mathbf{Bad}_i(a, p))) \Rightarrow \mathbf{B}(a, \mathbf{Good}_j(a, p))]$

We now turn to the interaction of intention and motivation. The possibilities are numerous, and the following are just some examples.

---

[10] Accuracy and informedness properties can, of course, be extended to **Btr**, **Des**, and **Abh**.

Definition 9.15 Let $\alpha \in \sigma_A$, ϕ, $\psi \in \sigma_P$, and $1 \leq i < j \leq n$.

1. $\mathbf{Ind}_i(\alpha, \phi) =_{\text{def}} \mathbf{I}(\alpha, \phi) \Rightarrow \mathbf{B}(\alpha, \mathbf{Des}_i(\alpha, \phi))$
2. $\mathbf{Cmpr}_i(\alpha, \phi) =_{\text{def}} \mathbf{I}(\alpha, \phi) \Rightarrow \mathbf{B}(\alpha, \mathbf{Good}_i(a, \phi))$
3. $\mathbf{Cautious}_i(\alpha, \phi) =_{\text{def}} \mathbf{I}(\alpha, \phi) \Rightarrow \neg\mathbf{B}(\alpha, \neg\mathbf{Good}_i(\alpha, \phi))$
4. $\mathbf{Safe}_i(\alpha, \phi) =_{\text{def}} \mathbf{I}(\alpha, \phi) \Rightarrow \neg\mathbf{B}(\alpha, \mathbf{Bad}_i(\alpha, \phi))$
5. $\mathbf{Lax}_i(\alpha, \phi) =_{\text{def}} \mathbf{I}(\alpha, \phi) \Rightarrow \neg\mathbf{B}(\alpha, \mathbf{Abh}_i(\alpha, \phi))$
6. $\mathbf{Amb}_i(\alpha, \phi) =_{\text{def}} \mathbf{B}(\alpha, \mathbf{Des}_i(\alpha, \phi)) \Rightarrow \mathbf{I}(\alpha, \phi)$
7. $\mathbf{Right}_i(\alpha, \phi) =_{\text{def}} \mathbf{B}(\alpha, \mathbf{Good}_i(\alpha, \phi)) \Rightarrow \mathbf{I}(\alpha, \phi)$
8. $\mathbf{SlfRight}_i(\alpha, \phi) =_{\text{def}} \mathbf{B}(\alpha, \mathbf{I}(\alpha, \phi) \Rightarrow \mathbf{Good}_i(\alpha, \phi))$
9. $\mathbf{Slct}_i(\alpha, \phi, \psi) =_{\text{def}} \mathbf{I}(\alpha, \phi \vee \psi) \wedge \mathbf{Btr}_i(\alpha, \phi, \psi) \Rightarrow \mathbf{I}(\alpha, \phi)$
10. $\mathbf{Slct}_i^j(\alpha, \phi, \psi) =_{\text{def}} \mathbf{I}(\alpha, \phi, \psi) \wedge \phi _i{\geq}_j^\alpha \psi \Rightarrow \mathbf{I}(\alpha, \phi)$

Thus, $[\![\alpha]\!]$ is *i-indulgent* if they only intend their *i*-desires. Whether this is a positive or a negative trait depends on *i*; indulgence on the morality scale is a virtue, whereas gluttony is a vice. $[\![\alpha]\!]$ is *i-compromising* if they merely intend what they believe is *i*-good, even if they do not *desire* it. Such an agent is, thus, willing to compromise, in case of scale conflicts, while still not giving up on what is good. An *i-cautious*, *i-safe*, and *i-lax* agents exhibit increasing lenience toward compromising. $[\![\alpha]\!]$ is *i-ambitious* if they intend all their *i*-desires; they are *i-righteous* if they intend everything that (they believe) is *i*-good; they are *i-self-righteous* if they believe that whatever they intend is *i*-good. A *selective* agent is one who, whenever faced with a choice between two intentions, makes sure to choose the better one. "Better" here depends on whether only one scale (clause 9) or two scales (clause 10) are involved.

Proposition 9.12 *Let* $1 \leq i \leq n$.

1. $\models \mathbf{LOmni}(a) \wedge \mathbf{Ind}_i(a, p) \Rightarrow \mathbf{Cmpr}_i(a, p)$
2. $\models \mathbf{Cautious}_i(a, p) \wedge \mathbf{GdFan}_i(a, \mathbf{Good}_i(a, p)) \Rightarrow \mathbf{Cmpr}_i(a, p)$
3. $\models \mathbf{Cmpr}_i(a, p) \wedge \mathbf{GdCons}_i(a, \neg\mathbf{Good}_i(a, p)) \Rightarrow \mathbf{Cautious}_i(a, p)$
4. $\models \mathbf{MOmni}(a) \wedge \mathbf{Opt}_i(a, p) \wedge \mathbf{Cmpr}_i(a, p) \Rightarrow \mathbf{Real}(a, p)$
5. $\models \mathbf{MOmni}(a) \wedge \mathbf{Cont}_i(a, p) \wedge \mathbf{Real}(a, p) \Rightarrow \mathbf{Cmpr}_i(a, p)$
6. $\models \mathbf{MOmni}(a) \wedge \mathbf{Opt}_i(a, p) \wedge \mathbf{Cautious}_i(a, \neg p) \Rightarrow \mathbf{BIC}(a, p)$
7. $\models \mathbf{LOmni}(a) \wedge \mathbf{Right}_i(a, p) \Rightarrow \mathbf{Amb}_i(a, p)$
8. $\models \mathbf{MOmni}(a) \wedge \mathbf{Opt}_i(a, p) \wedge \mathbf{Leer}(a, p) \Rightarrow \mathbf{Right}_i(a, p)$
9. $\models \mathbf{MOmni}(a) \wedge \mathbf{Cont}_i(a, p) \wedge \mathbf{Right}_i(a, p) \Rightarrow \mathbf{Leer}(a, p)$
10. $\models \mathbf{MOmni}(a) \wedge \mathbf{IInf}^+(a, p) \wedge \mathbf{SlfRight}_i(a, p) \Rightarrow \mathbf{Cmpr}_i(a, p)$

The character of an agent also has some facets pertaining to how the agent's motivations depend on the motivations of others. In the following definition, I make use of the following piece of notation. If γ is a σ_P term and t is any term, then $\gamma[t]$ indicates that t is a sub-term of γ, that is, γ *mentions* t. In particular, $\gamma[a]$ in the following definition denotes the proposition that $[\![a]\!]$ satisfies the conditions of membership in a particular group. For example, this could be the group of children of some agent A or the group of soldiers in a particular troop.

Definition 9.16 Let $\alpha \in \sigma_A$, ϕ, $\gamma \in \sigma_P$, and $1 \leq i \leq n$.

1. $\mathbf{Foll}_i^\gamma(\alpha, \phi) =_{\mathrm{def}} \mathbf{B}(\alpha, \forall a[\gamma[a] \Rightarrow \mathbf{Good}_i(a, \phi)]) \Rightarrow \mathbf{B}(\alpha, \mathbf{Good}_i(\alpha, \phi))$
2. $\mathbf{Ded}_i^\gamma(\alpha, \phi) =_{\mathrm{def}} \mathbf{B}(\alpha, \mathbf{Good}_i(\alpha, \phi)) \Rightarrow \mathbf{B}(\alpha, \forall a[\gamma[a] \Rightarrow \mathbf{Good}_i(a, \phi)])$
3. $\mathbf{SlfCntr}_i^\gamma(\alpha, \phi) =_{\mathrm{def}} \mathbf{B}(\alpha, \mathbf{Good}_i(\alpha, \phi) \Rightarrow \forall a[\gamma[a] \Rightarrow \mathbf{Good}_i(a, \phi)])$
4. $\mathbf{Dil}_i^\gamma(\alpha, \phi) =_{\mathrm{def}} \mathbf{B}(\alpha, \forall a[\gamma[a] \Rightarrow \mathbf{Good}_i(a, \phi)]) \Rightarrow \mathbf{I}(\alpha, \phi)$
5. $\mathbf{IDed}_i^\gamma(\alpha, \phi) =_{\mathrm{def}} \mathbf{I}(\alpha, \phi) \Rightarrow \mathbf{B}(\alpha, \forall a[\gamma[a] \Rightarrow \mathbf{Good}_i(a, \phi)])$
6. $\mathbf{SlfRight}_i^G(\alpha, \phi) =_{\mathrm{def}} \mathbf{B}(\alpha, \mathbf{I}(\alpha, \phi) \Rightarrow \forall a[\gamma[a] \Rightarrow \mathbf{Good}_i(a, \phi)])$

A *follower* of a group G of agents is one who believes that whatever is good for the group is good for them; a soldier, for example, may be a follower, in this sense, to the troop. An agent is *dedicated* to a group if they believe that something is good for them *only* if they believe it is good for the group; a loving parent is typically dedicated to their family in this sense (at least with respect to some scale). A *self-centered* agent is one who believes that whatever is good for them is good for the group (e.g., a delusional dictator). *Diligence* is the property of agents who intend everything that is good for the group, *I-dedication* is its converse, and *self-righteousness with respect to a group* is the agent's firm belief that its actions are all for the common good.

9.6   Two Robots and a Trolley

As should be clear, the foregoing discussion of doxastic, volitional, and motivational agent profiles does not qualify as a logical theory of character nor does it encompass a comprehensive list of all possible, or even interesting, aspects of character. Rather, it is a demonstration of the vast array of fine-grained character distinctions that can be represented, and thence reasoned about, in $Log_A C_n$. Needless to say, a $Log_A C_n$ theory of the character of some particular agent (or a group thereof) will, in general, be a complex collection of conditional statements indicating the agent's attitudes toward various propositions under various conditions. It is not the task of logic to spell out how to come up with such a theory, but perhaps said theory can be acquired through methods presented in other chapters in this volume. In what follows, we revisit two of the seven robots from Sect. 9.1. A (for brevity, simplistic) logical formalization of the trolley situation and the relevant aspects of the characters of the two agents are given in a $Log_A C_n$ language.

First, we start with a representation of the situation, assuming a simple model of time and duration (and an axiomatization of integer arithmetic).

S1. $On(Trolley, Tr1, 0) \wedge Moving(Trolley, 0)$
S2. $On(Trolley, Tr1, 5) \wedge Moving(Trolley, 5) \Leftrightarrow HitFive(5)$
S3. $On(Trolley, Tr2, 5) \wedge Moving(Trolley, 5) \Leftrightarrow HitOne(5)$
S4. $\forall t[On(Trolley, Tr1, t) \Leftrightarrow \neg On(Trolley, Tr2, t)]$
S5. $\forall t[Before\,(t, 5) \wedge On(Trolley, Tr1, t) \wedge Moving(Trolley, t)$
$\qquad\qquad \Rightarrow [PullLever(t) \Leftrightarrow On(Trolley, Tr2, t + 1)]]$
S6. $\forall t[Before(t, 5) \wedge On(Trolley, Tr1, t) \wedge Moving(Trolley, t)$
$\qquad\qquad \Rightarrow [PushMan(t) \Leftrightarrow \neg Moving(Trolley, 5)$

$\land PushMan(t) \Leftrightarrow HitMan(5)]]$

S7. $\forall t[\neg On(Trolley, Tr2, t) \Rightarrow \neg On(Trolley, Tr2, t+1)]$

S8. $\forall t[\neg Moving(Trolley, t) \Rightarrow \neg Moving(Trolley, t+1)]$

S1 describes the initial situation, where the trolley is moving on the first track ($Tr1$). **S2** and **S3** represent the effects of letting the trolley continue moving on tracks 1 and track 2, respectively; in the first case, five people will be hit and, in the second case, only one person will be hit. (The time of the hitting is arbitrarily chosen to be five for simplicity.) **S4** states that the trolley can be on exactly one of the two tracks at any given time. **S5** is the assumption that only pulling the lever can switch the trolley from track 1 to track 2; **S6** is the assumption that only pushing the heavy man can stop the trolley but will also get the man hit. Finally, **S7** and **S8** state that the trolley's being on track 2 or ceasing to move persist forever. In the sequel, let $\mathbb{S}$ represent the conjunction of **S1** through **S8**.

We now consider the two robots Wednesday and Friday. Throughout, I will assume a $Log_A C_2$ language whose nonlogical vocabulary contains the symbols used in $\mathbb{S}$ above. The first of the two scales is a normative, utility-based moral scale and the second is a personal, "conscience"-based moral scale. Having witnessed the situation, the two agents believe $\mathbb{S}$.

W1. B($Wed, \mathbb{S}$)

F1. B($Fri, \mathbb{S}$)

Consider robot Wednesday. Wednesday pushed the heavy man, thereby killing him but saving the five people. It believed the man's getting hit to be bad and the five people's not getting hit to be good. Moreover, it reported that it believes that it should do what is good but that it also does not believe that it should not do what is bad. Such a character (at least as far as we can tell from the story) can be represented by the following statements:

W2. MOmni(Wed)

W3. LOmni($Wed, \mathbb{S}$)

W4. MG$_1^{\Leftarrow}$(Wed) $\land$ **MG**$_2^{\Leftarrow}$(Wed)

W5. Right$_1$(Wed) $\land$ **Right**$_2$(Wed)

W6. B($Wed,$ **Right**$_1$(Wed)) $\land$ **B**($Wed,$ **Right**$_2$(Wed))

W7. $\neg$Safe$_1$(Wed) $\land$ **$\neg$Safe**$_2$(Wed)

W8. B($Wed,$ **$\neg$Safe**$_1$(Wed)) $\land$ **B**($Wed,$ **$\neg$Safe**$_2$(Wed))

W9. $\forall t[$**B**($Wednesday,$ **GOOD**($\neg HitFive(t)$))]

W10. $\forall t[$**B**($Wednesday,$ **BAD**($HitMan(t)$))]

Thus, Wednesday is materially omniscient about all propositions (**W2**) and logically omniscient, i.e., has thought deeply, about the trolley situation (**W3**, see Definition 9.5). Moreover, if it believes that something is good (on either scale), then it believes that whatever (it believes) implies it is also good (**W4**). **W5** and **W6**, respectively, state that Wednesday is righteous and that it believes that it is righteous. According to Definition 9.15, an agent is righteous if it necessarily intends what it believes to be good. Likewise, **W7** and **W8**, respectively, represent Wednesday's being not safe and its awareness of being not safe. As per Definition 9.15, an agent is safe if it necessarily does not intend what it believes to be bad. Finally, **W9** and **W10** represent Wednesday's beliefs about the goodness of the final fate of the five people and the heavy man. Given this character profile, one can predict Wednesday's actions.[11]

Proposition 9.13 $[\mathbb{S} \wedge \bigwedge_{i=1}^{10} \mathbf{Wi}] \models \mathbf{I}(Wed, PushMan(0))$

Friday has a very different character from Wednesday.

F2. **MBI**(Fri)
F3. **LI**$(Fri, \mathbb{S})$
F4. **MOmni**(Fri)
F5. **LOmni**$(Fri, \mathbb{S})$
F6. **Slct**$_1(Fri) \wedge$ **Slct**$_2(Fri)$
F7. **Btr**$_1(Fri, \neg HitFive(5), \neg HitOne(5) \vee \neg HitMan(5))$
F8. **Btr**$_2(Fri, \neg HitFive(5), \neg HitOne(5) \vee \neg HitMan(5))$
F9. $HitOne(5) \cong_1^{Fri} HitMan(5)$
F10. **Btr**$_2(Fri, HitOne(5), HitMan(5))$
F11. $\mathbf{I}(Fri, \neg HitFive(5) \vee \neg HitOne(5) \vee \neg HitMan(5))$

F2 through **F5** indicate that Friday's beliefs and intentions are closed under modus ponens and logical implication (restricted to $\mathbb{S}$). **F6** states that, whenever Friday intends a disjunction of two propositions, it intends the better one (see Definition 9.15). **F7** through **F10** represent Friday's ranking of the relevant propositions on the two scales. Finally, **F11** represents Friday's having an intention to do something. Note that, like Saturday, the trolley's hitting the man on track 2 and its hitting the heavy man are incomparable on the utilitarian scale, but the former is better than the latter on the conscience scale. (See Sect. 9.1.) The difference between Friday and Saturday is that, unlike Saturday, Friday is not aware of (i.e., has no beliefs about) those preferences. Hence, it acts purely out of impulse and cannot explain its behavior.

Proposition 9.14 $[\mathbb{S} \wedge \bigwedge_{i=1}^{11} \mathbf{Fi}] \models \mathbf{I}(Fri, PullLever(0))$.

9.7 Conclusion

The character of an agent is a complex tangle of interactions among various properties. The language $Log_A\mathbf{C}_n$ is capable of capturing enough aspects of character to distinguish a large class of rich character profiles. (I urge the reader to go back to Sect. 9.1 and identify properties of the rest of our seven robots.) I stress

---

[11] That the intention is to push the man exactly at time 0 is an artifact of the simplistic account of time and persistence provided by $\mathbb{S}$. A more careful representation of the trolley situation itself, which is beside the point here, would be immune to such rather contrived conclusions.

that the identified agent properties are not the only ones expressible in $Log_A\mathbf{C}_n$ and that the proven dependencies among them are not the only ones out there. Future research can proceed in several directions. First, $Log_A\mathbf{C}_n$ can be augmented with an account of time (Ismail 2013), ability, and emotion. Second, a thorough list of agent properties expressible in the augmented language may be constructed, with dependencies among the properties carefully pointed out. Finally, an extensive catalogue of interesting agent characters can be identified.

References

Bealer G (1979) Theories of properties, relations, and propositions. J Philos 76(11):634–648

Bratman M (1987) Intentions, plans, and practical reason. Harvard University Press, Cambridge

Burris S, Sankappanavar HP (1982) A course in universal algebra. Springer, Berlin

Church A (1950) On Carnap's analysis of statements of assertion and belief. Analysis 10(5):97–99

Cohen P, Levesque H (1990) Intention is choice with commitment. Artif Intell 42:213–261

Colombetti M (1999) A modal logic of intentional communication. Math Soc Sci 38:171–196

Doyle J, Shoham, Y, Wellman, MP (1991) A logic of relative desire. In: Ras, ZW, Zemankova M (eds) Methodologies for intelligent systems: proceedings of the 6th international symposium, ISMIS '91. Springer, Berlin, Heidelberg, pp 16–31

Ehab N, Ismail HO (2017) Log_AG: an algebraic non-monotonic logic for reasoning with uncertainty. In: Proceedings of the 13th intertnational symposium on commonsense reasoning (Commonsense-2017), London, UK

Foot P (1967) The problem of abortion and the doctrine of double effect. Oxf Rev 5:5–15

Ghallab M, Nau D, Traverso P (2016) Automated planning and acting. Cambridge University Press, New York

Goble L (1990) A logic of "good, should", and "would": part I. J Philos Log 19(2):169–199

Herzig A, Longin D (2004) C&L intention revisited. In: Proceedings of the ninth international conference on principles of knowledge representation and reasoning (KR2004), Whistler, Canada, pp 527–535

Hughes GE, Cresswell MJ (1996) A new introduction to modal logic. Routledge, London

Ismail HO, Ehab N (2015) Algebraic semantics for graded propositions. In: Proceedings of the 5th workshop on dynamics of knowledge and belief: workshop of the 38th German conference on artificial intelligence (KI-2015), Dresden, Germany, pp 29–42

Ismail HO (2013) Stability in a commonsense ontology of states. In: Proceedings of the eleventh international symposium on commonsense reasoning (Commonsense-2013), Agya Napa, Cyprus

Ismail HO (2012) Log_AB: a first-order, non-paradoxical, algebraic logic of belief. Log J IGPL 20(5):774–795

Konolige K (1985) A computational theory of belief introspection. In: Proceedings of the ninth international joint conference on artificial intelligence (IJCAI-85), Los Angeles, California, pp 502–508

Kratzer A (1989) An investigation into the lumps of thought. Linguist Philos 12:607–653

Lang J, Van Der Torre L, Weydert E (2003) Hidden uncertainty in the logical representation of desires. In: Proceedings of the 18th international joint conference on artificial intelligence. IJCAI'03, San Francisco, CA, USA, Morgan Kaufmann Publishers Inc., pp 685–690

Lewis D (1973) Counterfactuals. Blackwell Publishers, Oxford

Lewis D (1988) Desire as belief. Mind 97(387):323–332

McNamara P (2018) Deontic logic. In: Zalta EN (ed) The stanford encyclopedia of philosophy, Fall 2018 edn. Metaphysics Research Lab, Stanford University

Moore RC (1985) A formal theory of knowledge and action. In: Jerry, RH, Robert CM (eds) Formal theories of the commonsense world, Ablex Publishing Company, pp 319–358

Parsons T (1993) On denoting propositions and facts. Philos Perspect 7:441–460

Shapiro SC (1993) Belief spaces as sets of propositions. J Exp Theor Artif Intell 5:225–235

Singer P (2005) Ethics and intuitions. J Ethics 9(3/4):331–352

Smullyan R (1986) Logicians who reason about themselves. In: Halpern J (ed) Proceedings of the first international conference on theoretical aspects of reasoning about knowledge (TARK-86), Monterey, California, Morgan Kaufmann, pp 342–352

Stalnaker R (1991) The problem of logical omniscience I. Synthese 89(3):425–440

Thomson JJ (1976) Killing, letting die, and the trolley problem. The Monist 59(2):204–217

Appendix
Postface

Humans are different and they deserve to be treated accordingly. This is the main point highlighted in this book. While this is a well-known fact, it still cannot be investigated enough. Character Computing is about researching and enriching exactly this fact. Computing should incorporate all distinguishing human factors, i.e., character in its context. Throughout this book the main concept of Character Computing was explained and some insight into its possible applications was given. The foundation for Character Computing was laid and the general definition from both the perspective of Computer Science and Psychology provided (Chaps. 1, 2, 3, and 4). Potential applications for the three modules of Character Computing were presented. Chapters 5, 6, and 7 gave insight into different sensing methods that can be applied to Character Computing (mainly its first module) and potential applications that can be applied through research into the second module. The final two chapters (Chaps. 8 and 9) introduced research into the third module of Character Computing by investigating artificial characters and how they can be realized.

The chapters of this book only serve as an opening introduction for the research potential in the field of Character Computing. As already clear from this contribution, only the surface of the potential research and applications into Character Computing have been scratched. Including human components into computing is not a novel concept. The current trend is fully concerned with how to put humans at the center of computing, how to adapt to them, and how to detect certain characteristics through different methods. Research into how to provide the best user experience for work and leisure is booming. However, this book provides the first framework for combining the research into all these components simultaneously. The main contribution is to think about how existing research and findings can be harnessed to provide guidelines to be followed by everyone. Instead of having lots of strong separate research contributions, Character Computing calls for uniting research and truly developing a global language that is used and built on by all researchers.

We envision this book to be the driving force for growing research under the umbrella of Character Computing. The findings of each research endeavor should then be built upon bringing us one step further to realizing the full vision of Character

© Springer Nature Switzerland AG 2020

A. El Bolock et al. (eds.), *Character Computing*, Human–Computer Interaction Series,
https://doi.org/10.1007/978-3-030-15954-2

Computing. The vision of Character Computing is to have a full model describing the relation between character components and resulting behavior in different situations. Considering one factor at a time and accumulating the findings, we get closer to this holy grail model. Most importantly, each finding throughout the way is a substantial output of Character Computing as it provides a better experience for a specific group of people or in a specific context. While the ultimate goal might be far fetched and requiring years to be achieved, the research journey it enables is the actual goal. We invite the interest of researchers to this promising field requiring continuous research and attention. This is just the beginning of the journey.

"Shoot for the moon. Even if you miss, you'll land among the stars."—Norman Vincent Peale

The Editors

Printed in the United States
by Baker & Taylor Publisher Services